W9-CKW-413

PSYCHOLOGY:

THE COMIC BOOK INTRODUCTION

PSYCHOLOGY:

THE COMIC BOOK INTRODUCTION

BY GRADY KLEIN AND
DANNY OPPENHEIMER, Ph.D.

W. W. NORTON & COMPANY
INDEPENDENT PUBLISHERS SINCE 1923
NEW YORK | LONDON

PRINTED IN THE UNITED STATES OF AMERICA
FIRST EDITION

FOR INFORMATION ABOUT PERMISSION TO REPRODUCE SELECTIONS FROM THIS BOOK, WRITE TO PERMISSIONS, W. W. NORTON & COMPANY, INC., 500 FIFTH AVENUE, NEW YORK, NY 10110

FOR INFORMATION ABOUT SPECIAL DISCOUNTS FOR BULK PURCHASES, PLEASE CONTACT W. W. NORTON SPECIAL SALES AT SPECIALSALES@WWNORTON.COM OR 800-233-4830

MANUFACTURING BY VERSA PRESS

ISBN 978-0-393-35195-8 (PBK.)

W. W. NORTON & COMPANY, INC.
500 FIFTH AVENUE, NEW YORK, N.Y. 10110
WWW.WWNORTON.COM

W. W. NORTON & COMPANY LTD.
15 CARLISLE STREET, LONDON W1D 3BS

1 2 3 4 5 6 7 8 9 0

FOR ANNE AND LIAM AND BENJAMIN
—GK

FOR MY STUDENTS, WHO TAUGHT ME HOW TO TEACH PSYCHOLOGY.
—DO

CONTENTS

INTRODUCTION

WHAT THE *@$&?

LIFE IS **CRAZY.**
IT'S **CONFUSING...**
...CONFOUNDING...
WHAT JUST HAPPENED?
WHY DID IT HAPPEN?
...MISLEADING...
...UNPREDICTABLE...
DID THAT **ACTUALLY HAPPEN?**
IS IT GONNA **HAPPEN AGAIN?**
...AND ABOVE ALL, **AMBIGUOUS.**
MAYBE YOU WERE A VICTIM OF **HAPPENSTANCE.**

YET SOMEHOW WE MANAGE TO **MAKE SENSE OF THE WORLD...**

LOOK OUT!

...AND **OURSELVES...**

...AND **EACH OTHER.**

WHEW, I WAS **FREAKED** THERE!

I COULD **TELL.**

THIS BOOK IS ABOUT **HOW WE DO THAT.**

WE **MAKE ORDER OUT OF CHAOS!**

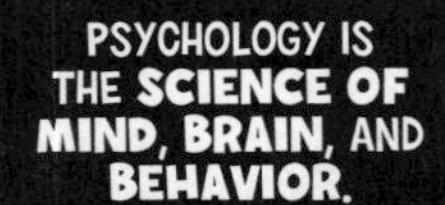
PSYCHOLOGY IS THE **SCIENCE OF MIND, BRAIN,** AND **BEHAVIOR.**

WHAT ARE WE **THINKING?**
HOW ARE WE THINKING?
WHAT ARE WE **DOING?**

MANY PEOPLE THINK PSYCHOLOGY IS ABOUT **PARANOID DELUSIONS...**

...AND **CHILDHOOD TRAUMAS...**

THE CIA IS **SPYING ON MY THOUGHTS!**
TELL ME ABOUT YOUR **MOTHER.**

...AND **DRUGS...**

...AND **COURT HEARINGS...**

...AND **LAB RATS.**

HAVE YOU CONSIDERED **BLOLOFT®?**

YOUR HONOR, THIS DEFENDANT HAS THE **MENTAL ABILITY OF A PUPPY.**

WHEN YOU HEAR THE **BELL,** DO THE **HOKEY POKEY.**

ALL OF THESE ARE **PARTS** OF PSYCHOLOGY, BUT ONLY **SMALL PARTS.**

AS WE'LL LEARN, PSYCHOLOGY IS REALLY ABOUT **ALL OF HUMAN EXPERIENCE:**
IT'S ABOUT **LOVE...**
...**SPORTS...**
...**MUSIC...**
...**STATUS...**
...**GROWTH...**
...**TRAGEDY...**
...**HUMOR...**
...**ME...**
...**YOU...**
...AND **EVERYTHING** IN BETWEEN.
FROM **FAITH** TO **SKEPTICISM.**
FROM **HUNGER** TO **GLUTTONY.**
FROM **RACISM** TO **TOLERANCE.**
FROM **HOPE** TO **DESPAIR.**

BECAUSE WE **ALL LEARN FROM OUR EXPERIENCES...**
...WE'RE ALL **AMATEUR PSYCHOLOGISTS.**

I **BELIEVED** HIM WHEN HE **SAID HE LOVED ME**, BUT IT TURNED OUT HE WAS JUST **USING ME.**
THAT'S BECAUSE HE'S A **PSYCHOPATH.**
AS SUCH, WE'RE ALWAYS **JUDGING OURSELVES...**
...AND **OTHERS...**
...AND **MAKING UP EXPLANATIONS FOR EVERYTHING.**

HE DOESN'T LOVE ME BECAUSE OF MY **WEIGHT.**
NO, HE DOESN'T LOVE YOU BECAUSE HE'S A **JERK!**
YOU'RE **WET** AND **UNHAPPY** BECAUSE YOU HAVE A **BROKEN HEART.**

THE DIFFERENCE, HOWEVER, BETWEEN **OUR OWN EXPLANATIONS...**
...AND **WHAT'S IN THIS BOOK...**
I UNDERSTAND **WHAT MAKES PEOPLE TICK!**
ER, SORRY, JUST BECAUSE YOU'RE **CONFIDENT**, DOESN'T MEAN YOU'RE **COMPETENT.**
SEE **PAGE 85** FOR MORE ON THAT.
...IS THAT THE PRINCIPLES IN THIS BOOK ARE ALL BASED ON **RIGOROUS EXPERIMENTAL STUDIES.**
WE DON'T JUST **TRUST** OUR INTUITIONS, WE **TEST** THEM!
SUBJECT APPEARS **UNHAPPY.**
NO CHANGE IN THE **CONTROL SUBJECT.**

DOING SCIENCE IS **COMPLICATED:**

NO MATTER **WHAT WE'RE STUDYING...**

WHAT HAPPENS WHEN WE **ZAP THINGS** WITH **ELECTRICITY?**
DO THEY **EXPLODE?**
DO THEY **STINK?**

...WE HAVE TO **KEEP OUR EXPERIMENTS UNDER CONTROL...**

WE BETTER MAKE SURE THE **LABORATORY IS CLEAN.**

...AND WE HAVE TO MAKE SURE NOBODY'S **EXPECTATIONS** ARE **MESSING UP THE RESULTS...**

I **REALLY WANT** MY EXPERIMENT TO **WORK!**
I REALLY WANT **HER** EXPERIMENT TO WORK.
WE BETTER **BLINDFOLD EVERYBODY.**

...AND MAKE SURE WE'RE **NOT DOING HARM.**

IF WE **FLOOD THE ATMOSPHERE WITH CO^2,** WHAT WILL **HAPPEN TO THE CLIMATE?**
CAN WE **NOT DO THAT EXPERIMENT?**

BUT IN PSYCHOLOGY, BECAUSE OUR **SUBJECTS ARE PEOPLE...**

WHAT HAPPENS WHEN WE ZAP **PEOPLE** WITH ELECTRICITY?
DO THEY **STOP SIGNING UP FOR EXPERIMENTS?**

...WE HAVE TO DEAL WITH **ANOTHER LEVEL OF COMPLEXITY.**

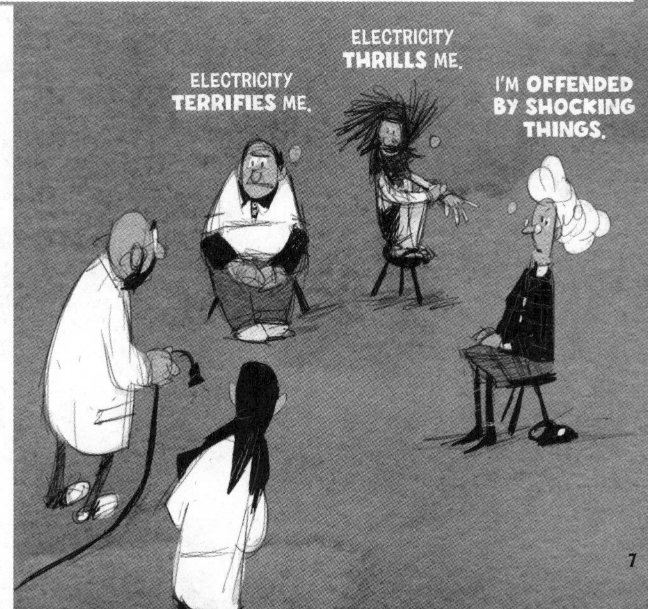
ELECTRICITY **TERRIFIES** ME.
ELECTRICITY **THRILLS** ME.
I'M **OFFENDED BY SHOCKING THINGS.**

THE **BIG CHALLENGE** IN DOING SCIENTIFIC EXPERIMENTS **ON PEOPLE** HAS TO DO WITH HOW **FANTASTICALLY COMPLICATED** WE ARE.
WHO YOU **LOOKING AT?**
LOOK AT **ME**, LOOK AT **ME**.
LOOK CLOSER AND I'LL SHOW YOU THINGS **YOU NEVER IMAGINED.**
WE DO SCIENTIFIC EXPERIMENTS TO **TEST RULES**...
...BUT WITH PEOPLE, THERE ARE NUMEROUS **INDIVIDUAL EXCEPTIONS** TO NEARLY EVERY RULE...
FOR EXAMPLE, DOES **POKING PEOPLE** MAKE THEM **ANGRY?**
EVERYTHING MAKES ME ANGRY!
I **LIKE** TO BE **POKED.**
...AND THOSE INDIVIDUAL EXCEPTIONS CAN **RUIN OUR STUDIES.**
IF THERE'S LOTS OF **NATURAL VARIATION** IN THE **POPULATION**...
...HOW DO WE KNOW IF WE **CAUSED** ANGER WITH POKING...
...OR JUST HAPPENED UPON A GROUP OF PEOPLE WHO WERE **GONNA GET ANGRY ANYWAY?**
WE GET AROUND THIS PROBLEM WITH **SEVERAL STEPS.**

FIRST, WE GATHER A RANDOM SAMPLE FROM THE OVERALL POPULATION WE WANT TO KNOW ABOUT.

WE'RE STUDYING **ANGER** IN **ALL PEOPLE**...
...SO WE SHOULDN'T ONLY TEST PEOPLE IN **BIKER BARS**...
...OR **MEDITATION STUDIOS**.
INSTEAD, WE GRAB **SOME OF EVERYBODY**.

SECOND, WE **ALWAYS** SET ASIDE A RANDOM SAMPLE FROM THAT RANDOM SAMPLE...

...AND **DO NOTHING TO THEM.**

YOU'RE THE **CONTROL GROUP**...
...**IDENTICAL** TO THE REST OF THE GROUP IN EVERY WAY.

THEN, BY COMPARING RESULTS FROM THE GROUP **WE TEST**...

...AND THE **GROUP WE DO NOTHING TO**...

HOW ANGRY ARE YOU **NOW?**

...WE CAN ENSURE THAT ANY INDIVIDUAL EXCEPTIONS WILL **CANCEL THEMSELVES OUT.**

I'M ALWAYS **ANGRY!**
POKE ME, BABY.
THERE WILL PROBABLY BE **JUST AS MANY INDIVIDUAL EXCEPTIONS IN BOTH GROUPS.**
I **LOVE** POKING.
I **DARE YOU TO POKE ME!**

THESE STEPS ADD SEVERAL LAYERS OF **COMPLEXITY** TO OUR EXPERIMENTS...

BECAUSE OF **RANDOM ASSIGNMENTS** AND **CONTROL CONDITIONS**, WE CAN USE **STATISTICS!**

OH **GOODY**.

...BUT WITHOUT THEM, PSYCHOLOGICAL STUDIES WOULD BASICALLY BE **IMPOSSIBLE.**

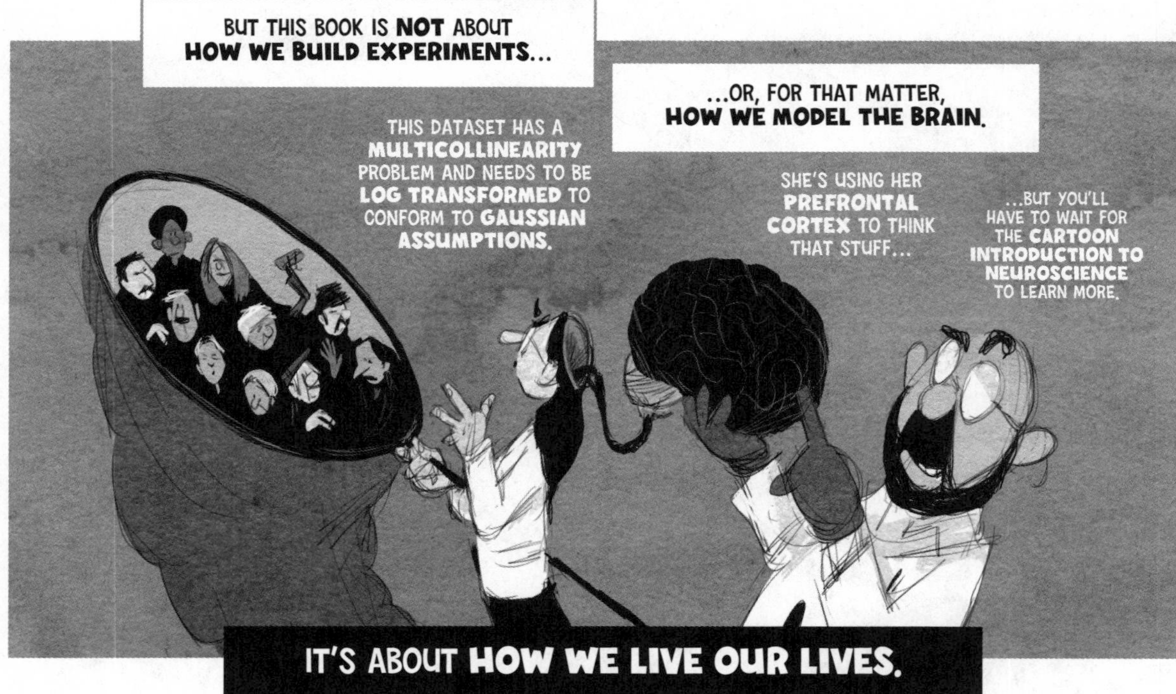
BUT THIS BOOK IS **NOT** ABOUT **HOW WE BUILD EXPERIMENTS...**
THIS DATASET HAS A **MULTICOLLINEARITY** PROBLEM AND NEEDS TO BE **LOG TRANSFORMED** TO CONFORM TO **GAUSSIAN ASSUMPTIONS.**
...OR, FOR THAT MATTER, **HOW WE MODEL THE BRAIN.**
SHE'S USING HER **PREFRONTAL CORTEX** TO THINK THAT STUFF...
...BUT YOU'LL HAVE TO WAIT FOR THE **CARTOON INTRODUCTION TO NEUROSCIENCE** TO LEARN MORE.
IT'S ABOUT **HOW WE LIVE OUR LIVES.**

THIS BOOK IS FOR **ANYBODY WHO IS A PERSON...**

...OR WILL EVER HAVE TO **INTERACT WITH ONE.**

SO LET'S GET ON WITH IT, AND HAVE A **LOOK AROUND.**

PART ONE

MAKING SENSE OF THE WORLD

CHAPTER 1
PERCEPTION AND ATTENTION

WHY ARE WE **SEEING SPOTS?**

WHY ARE WE **NOT SEEING SPOTS?**

OBVIOUSLY, WE GET INFORMATION FROM THE WORLD **THROUGH OUR SENSES.**

HOWEVER, WHILE OUR SENSES MOST OFTEN **FEEL TRUSTWORTHY...**

...THEY'RE **NOT ALWAYS RELIABLE.**

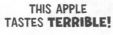

THIS APPLE TASTES TERRIBLE!

IT'S AN ONION.

THAT'S BECAUSE WHAT WE **THINK** WE PERCEIVE...

...IS **NEVER** WHAT'S **REALLY THERE.**

MIRAGE!

INSTEAD, IT'S THE RESULT OF **LOTS OF MENTAL PROCESSING.**

NOTHING GETS INTO YOUR BRAIN EXCEPT ELECTRICAL SIGNALS...
...AND WHAT YOU'RE AWARE OF IS HOW YOU INTERPRET THEM.

FOR EXAMPLE, WHEN **LIGHT HITS OUR EYES** IT CREATES LOTS OF **ELECTRICAL SIGNALS IN OUR BRAINS**...

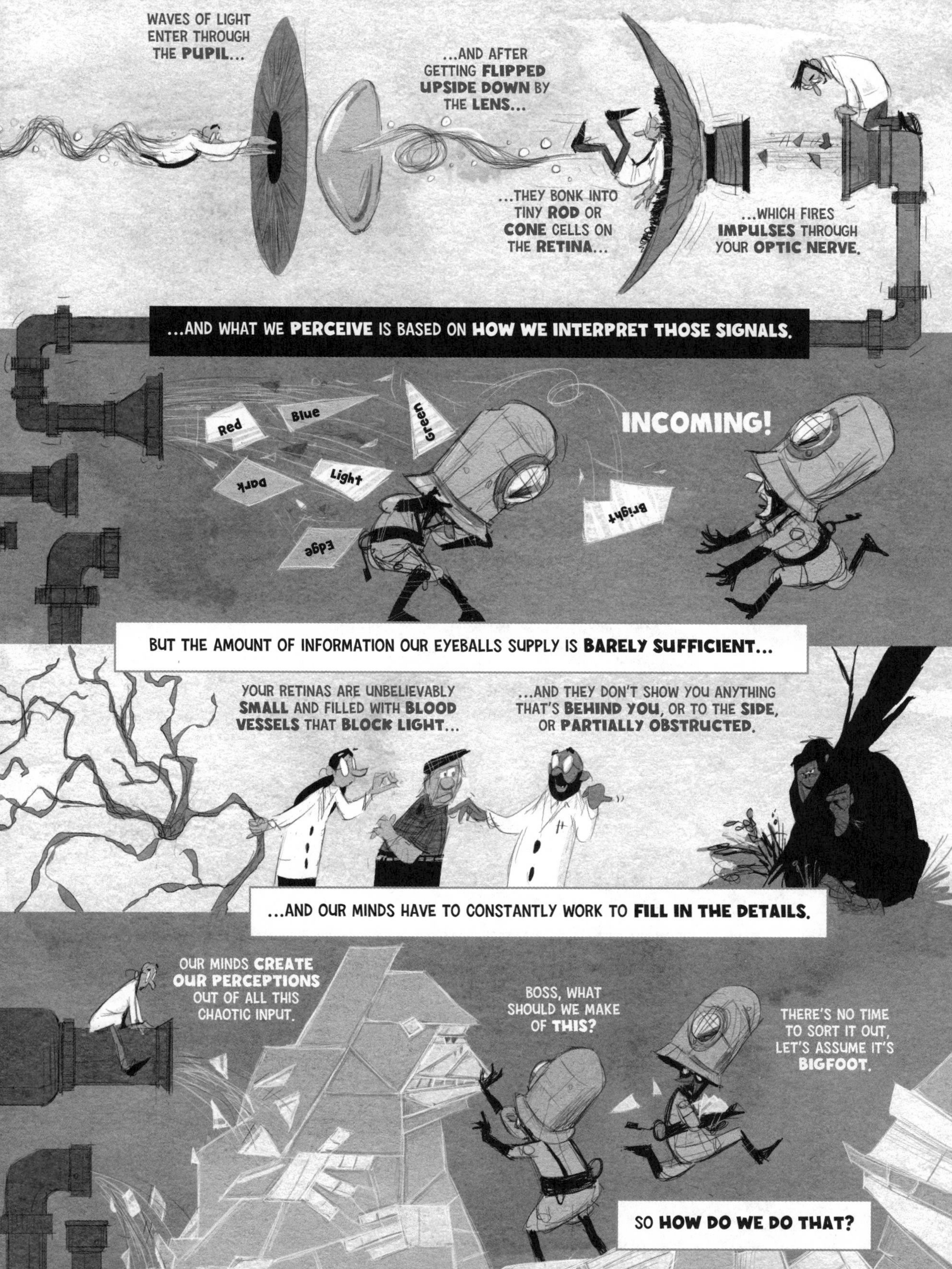

WAVES OF LIGHT ENTER THROUGH THE **PUPIL**...
...AND AFTER GETTING **FLIPPED UPSIDE DOWN** BY THE **LENS**...
...THEY BONK INTO TINY **ROD** OR **CONE** CELLS ON THE **RETINA**...
...WHICH FIRES **IMPULSES** THROUGH YOUR **OPTIC NERVE**.
...AND WHAT WE **PERCEIVE** IS BASED ON **HOW WE INTERPRET THOSE SIGNALS**.
Red
Blue
Green
Dark
Light
Edge
Bright
INCOMING!
BUT THE AMOUNT OF INFORMATION OUR EYEBALLS SUPPLY IS **BARELY SUFFICIENT**...
YOUR RETINAS ARE UNBELIEVABLY **SMALL** AND FILLED WITH **BLOOD VESSELS** THAT **BLOCK LIGHT**...
...AND THEY DON'T SHOW YOU ANYTHING THAT'S **BEHIND YOU**, OR TO THE **SIDE**, OR **PARTIALLY OBSTRUCTED**.
...AND OUR MINDS HAVE TO CONSTANTLY WORK TO **FILL IN THE DETAILS**.
OUR MINDS **CREATE OUR PERCEPTIONS** OUT OF ALL THIS CHAOTIC INPUT.
BOSS, WHAT SHOULD WE MAKE OF **THIS?**
THERE'S NO TIME TO SORT IT OUT, LET'S ASSUME IT'S **BIGFOOT**.
SO **HOW DO WE DO THAT?**

THE WAY OUR MINDS BUILD OUR PERCEPTIONS IS LARGELY **BASED ON CONTEXT.**

WHAT DOES **THIS** MEAN?
DEPENDS ON **WHERE YOU FOUND IT.**

FOR EXAMPLE, IF **NOT MUCH LIGHT** IS HITTING OUR EYE...

...WE MIGHT BE IN A **DARK PLACE**...

...**OR** WE MIGHT BE LOOKING AT A **DARK THING.**

BUT SINCE WE DON'T GET **ENOUGH INFORMATION** TO KNOW FOR CERTAIN WHICH IS TRUE...

SO WHICH IS IT, A **DIM BULB** OR A **DARK DRESS?**
MAYBE IT'S A DIM BULB **IN** A DARK DRESS.

...WE CAN ONLY **MAKE A GUESS** BASED ON WHAT ELSE IS AROUND.

MORE PRECISELY, TO DETERMINE HOW **BRIGHT** SOMETHING IS, WE **COMPARE IT WITH ITS BACKGROUND.**

IF IT'S **DARKER** THAN ITS SURROUNDINGS WE'LL ASSUME IT'S A **DARK THING.**

IF IT'S **LIGHTER** THAN ITS SURROUNDINGS, WE'LL ASSUME IT'S A **LIGHT THING.**

THAT'S WHY THESE TWO IDENTICAL DRESSES LOOK SO DIFFERENT.

YOUR MIND IS DOING **STATISTICS.**

IT'S **INFERRING BRIGHTNESS** BASED ON CONTEXT.

IN FACT, THIS IS THE SAME WAY THAT OUR BRAINS PROCESS **ALL OUR INPUT**:

WE DON'T GET ENOUGH DATA TO BE CERTAIN...
...SO WE USE CONTEXT TO GUIDE OUR GUESSES.

EVERYTHING FROM **SMELLS** AND **TASTES...**

...TO **OTHER PHYSICAL SENSATIONS.**

SMELLS LIKE **HOTDOG** BUT TASTES LIKE **CHICKEN...**

...SO I'M ASSUMING IT'S SAFE TO EAT.

I'M ALL JITTERY BUT SHE'S PRETTY, SO I MUST BE IN LOVE.
FIND OUT MORE ABOUT THAT IN CHAPTER 6.

SO LET'S LOOK AT A **FEW MORE EXAMPLES.**

WE DO THE SAME SORT OF THING TO PERCEIVE **WHERE AN OBJECT IS IN SPACE...**

...AND **WHAT SIZE IT IS.**

YOU'RE REALLY **FAR AWAY!**
NOPE, I'M JUST **SMALL.**

ONCE AGAIN, OUR EYES GIVE US **SOME INFORMATION...**

...BUT **NEVER ENOUGH TO BE CERTAIN.**

WE'VE GOT **LITTLE DATA!**
IS IT **SMALL** OR **FAR AWAY** OR **BOTH?**
WE JUST GOTTA **GUESS.**

SO WE FILL IN DETAILS USING NUMEROUS OTHER **CONTEXTUAL CUES,** LIKE **WHERE SHADOWS FALL...**

I'M **FLOATING!**

I'M **NOT.**

...AND HOW **LINES RELATE TO ONE ANOTHER.**

THESE TWO SHAPES ARE THE **SAME SIZE!**
BUT SINCE **RECEDING LINES** MAKE US PERCEIVE **DEPTH,** THIS ONE LOOKS **LONGER.**

THOUGH OUR MINDS CRANK AWAY AT THESE CONTEXTUAL CUES **ALL THE TIME...**

YOU'RE GROWING SO **FAST!**

ACTUALLY I'M JUST **WALKING TOWARD YOU**, GRAMMA.

...WE'RE ONLY AWARE OF IT WHEN THEY CLASH AND CREATE **OPTICAL ILLUSIONS.**

TRY TO FOLLOW THE **PARALLEL LINES.**

AND CRUCIALLY, BECAUSE **ALL OUR PERCEPTIONS WORK THIS WAY...**

ALL DAY LONG, WE TAKE IN **LIMITED SENSORY DATA...**
...FROM THE **HANDS,** THE **NOSE,** THE **TONGUE,** YOU NAME IT.
THEN WE **FILL IN THE GAPS.**

...THERE EXIST PLENTY OF SENSORY ILLUSIONS **IN OUR OTHER PERCEPTUAL SYSTEMS...**

...WE JUST **CAN'T DEPICT THEM HERE.**

THIS **CHEESE** IS SO **RIPE** I'M **SALIVATING.**
ACTUALLY, THAT SMELL IS YOUR **FEET.**

UNFORTUNATELY, OUR PUBLISHER WON'T PAY FOR **SCRATCH AND SNIFF** EXAMPLES.

OF COURSE, IN ORDER TO **COMPARE OBJECTS...**

...WE FIRST HAVE TO BE ABLE TO **DISTINGUISH THEM FROM THEIR SURROUNDINGS.**

WHICH OF THOSE APES IS BIGGER?
ARE THOSE EVEN APES...
...OR JUST LUMPY PARTS OF THAT TREE?

IN THE **EARLY 1900'S**, GERMAN PSYCHOLOGISTS THEORIZED ABOUT HOW WE **DIFFERENTIATE FOREGROUND FROM BACKGROUND.**

IT'S THE GESTALT MOVEMENT!
NOPE! IT'S A VASE!

THEY NOTED THAT WE TEND TO MAKE USE OF **PARTICULAR VISUAL QUALITIES** SUCH AS **SIMILARITY...**

...SYMMETRY...

THE LUMPS HAVE HAIR BUT THE TREE DOESN'T, SO THEY MUST BE APES.

THE TREE IS PRETTY SYMMETRICAL BUT THE LUMPS DON'T FIT...
...SO I AGREE!

...PROXIMITY...

...AND **CLOSURE.**

THE LUMPS ARE SO **CLOSE TO THE TRUNK**, THEY MUST BE **PARTS OF THAT TREE!**

PLUS, THEY LOOK CONTAINED WITHIN THE REST OF THE TREE...
...SO I AGREE!

AND MORE RECENT RESEARCH HAS ADDED **ANOTHER LAYER** TO THIS UNDERSTANDING.

IN INDIA, **PROJECT PRAKASH** GIVES **SIGHT TO CHILDREN WHO HAVE BEEN BLIND SINCE BIRTH.**

MANY FORMS OF BLINDESS CAN BE EASILY **CURED WITH SURGERY.**

AND WHILE OBSERVING THESE CHILDREN AS THEY **LEARNED TO VISUALLY DISTINGUISH OBJECTS FOR THE FIRST TIME...**

EVERYTHING IS **FUZZY.**

...SCIENTISTS DISCOVERED THAT **MOTION** PLAYS A BIG ROLE.

THAT **MUST** BE DIFFERENT...
...FROM **THAT.**

OTHER STUDIES ARE PUSHING THE BOUNDARIES OF OUR UNDERSTANDING WITH **NEW TECHNOLOGY.**

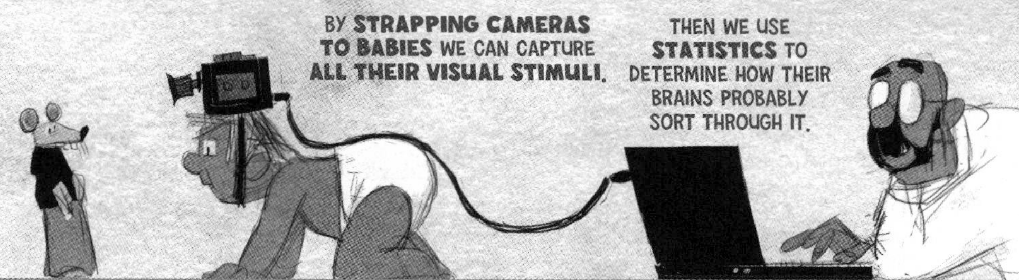
BY **STRAPPING CAMERAS TO BABIES** WE CAN CAPTURE **ALL THEIR VISUAL STIMULI.**
THEN WE USE **STATISTICS** TO DETERMINE HOW THEIR BRAINS PROBABLY SORT THROUGH IT.

OF COURSE, ONCE WE'VE LEARNED THAT A THING IS A THING, IT BECOMES **EASIER TO RECOGNIZE...**

I KNOW THAT **THIS BUTT** IS ATTACHED TO **THAT HEAD** BECAUSE THEY **MOVE TOGETHER...**

...AND BECAUSE HE'S MY DOG.

...WHICH BRINGS US TO ANOTHER **ESSENTIAL POINT.**

GIVEN THAT OUR PERCEPTION OF THE WORLD INVOLVES A CONTINUOUS STREAM OF **BEST GUESSES...**
FEELS LIKE AN ELEPHANT...
...WHERE DO WE GET THE INFORMATION WE USE TO **MAKE THOSE GUESSES?**
SMELLS LIKE AN ELEPHANT...
SOUNDS LIKE AN ELEPHANT...
...BUT HOW DO WE EVEN **KNOW WHAT AN ELEPHANT IS?**
IT TURNS OUT, IT COMES FROM **TWO SOURCES:**
BOTTOM UP...
...AND **TOP DOWN.**
THAT'S DATA WE GET **DIRECTLY FROM OUR SENSES.**
THAT'S DATA WE GET FROM OUR **PRIOR KNOWLEDGE.**
AND OUR IMMEDIATE EXPERIENCE OF THE WORLD **DEPENDS ON BOTH.**
LIGHT WAVES HIT YOUR **RETINA.**
SOUNDWAVES HIT YOUR **EARDRUMS.**
MOLECULES HIT YOUR **TONGUE** AND **NOSTRILS.**
YOU RETRIEVE **MEMORIES, IDEAS, HABITS,** AND **REACTIONS** FROM **STORAGE.**
AND YOU PROCESS ALL OF THAT TO DETERMINE **WHAT'S HAPPENING.**

ONE FUN WAY TO **TEST** THE DIFFERENCE BETWEEN **BOTTOM UP** AND **TOP DOWN PROCESSING** INVOLVES **VODKA...**

...WHICH, IT TURNS OUT, IS **ESSENTIALLY TASTELESS.**

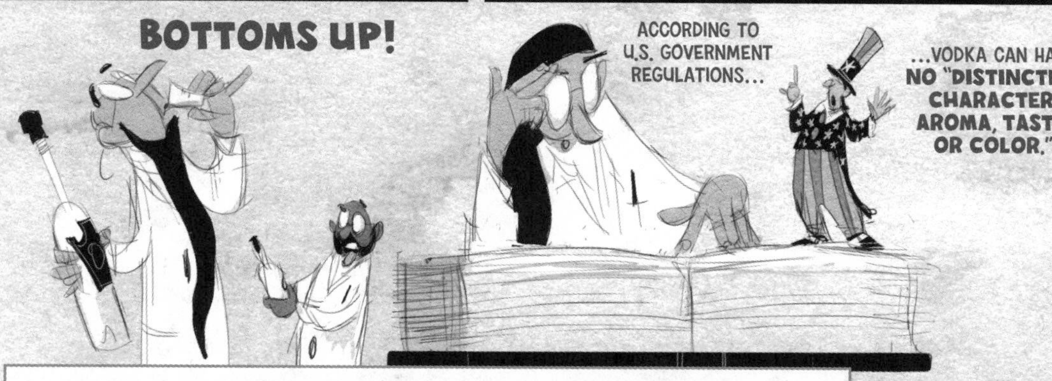
BOTTOMS UP!
ACCORDING TO U.S. GOVERNMENT REGULATIONS...
...VODKA CAN HAVE NO "DISTINCTIVE CHARACTER, AROMA, TASTE, OR COLOR."

AS A RESULT, **BOTTOM UP**, ALL VODKA BRANDS **TASTE THE SAME...**

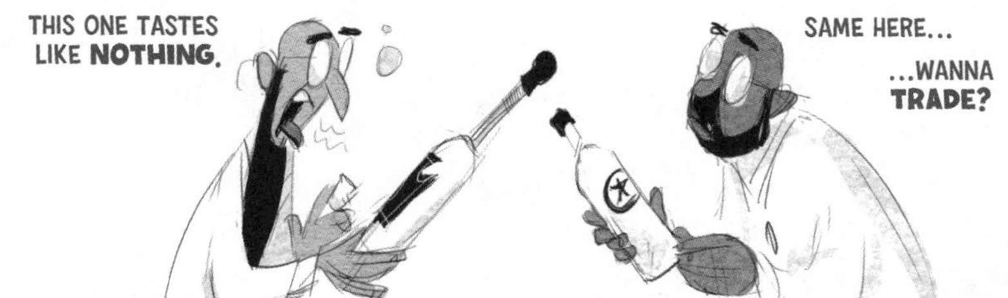
THIS ONE TASTES LIKE NOTHING.
SAME HERE...
...WANNA TRADE?

...AND THE **ONLY WAY** WE CAN COMPARE THEM IS BY USING **TOP DOWN INTERPRETATION...**

YOUR TASTEBUDS TELL YOU NOTHING...
...SO YOU BUILD YOUR PREFERENCES ON SOCIAL AND NARRATIVE FEATURES.
THIS VODKA MUST BE BETTER!
IT'S GOT A GOLD LABEL, AND COST $100, AND IT'S HAND DISTILLED BY A COMMUNIST WEARING A FUZZY HAT!

...A FACT THAT MARKETERS **LOVE TO EXPLOIT.**

ON OUR LABEL, THE FUZZY HAT IS WORN BY A BUXOM WOMAN!
OOOH.

BUT IN LIFE, WE'RE RARELY FACED WITH **TOO LITTLE** INFORMATION...

...BECAUSE MOST OF THE TIME WE GET **FAR TOO MUCH.**

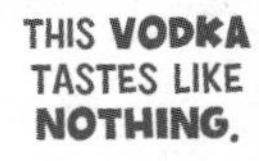

THIS **VODKA** TASTES LIKE **NOTHING.**

THIS **WINE** TASTES LIKE **GOOSEBERRIES, JUNIPER, BANDAGES, RAINDROPS, RODENT DROPPINGS, DANDRUFF, HALITOSIS...**

ESPECIALLY WHEN YOU CONSIDER ALL THE INFORMATION CONSTANTLY FLOWING THROUGH **ALL OUR DIFFERENT PERCEPTUAL SYSTEMS.**

Eyes
Ears
Mouth
Nose
Other Sensitive Parts
Red
Blue
Screechy
Loud
Sweet
Savory
Rank
Stinky
Soft
Slippery
HELP!

AND BECAUSE THE WORLD IS **FAR TOO COMPLEX** FOR US TO NOTICE IT ALL...

...WE **DON'T.**

INSTEAD, WE **PAY ATTENTION TO SOME OF IT...**

...AND **MAKE ASSUMPTIONS ABOUT THE REST.**

I WISH THAT DUDE WOULD STOP **TAILGAITING** ME.
PEOPLE ARE SO **AGGRESSIVE.**

THERE ARE SEVERAL **FAMOUS EXPERIMENTS** THAT SHOW THE **LIMITS OF OUR ATTENTION.**

IN ONE, RESEARCHERS **ASKED RANDOM PEOPLE FOR DIRECTIONS...**

WHERE'S THE **NEAREST HOT DOG STORE?**

...BUT WHEN **ONE RESEARCHER** WAS QUICKLY **SWAPPED OUT FOR ANOTHER...**

UM, GO DOWN **5TH**, TAKE A **LEFT ON 7TH**, THEN WALK **THREE BLOCKS** TO THE CORNER WITH THE **BURGER PALACE** AND...

...MANY PEOPLE **FAILED TO NOTICE.**

THANKS!

YOU'RE **WELCOME!**

IN ANOTHER, RESEARCHERS ASKED RANDOM PEOPLE **TO CLOSELY OBSERVE A TEAM PRACTICING...**

COUNT THE **NUMBER OF PASSES.**

...AND MANY PEOPLE, FOCUSED ON THE PLAYERS, FAILED TO NOTICE A **GORILLA DANCING THROUGH THE SCENE.**

OF COURSE, THESE RESULTS WOULD HAVE BEEN DIFFERENT IF THE PARTICIPANTS **KNEW WHAT TO EXPECT...**

COUNT THE **GORILLAS.**

...BUT THE POINT IS, **IF WE DON'T EXPECT IT, WE OFTEN DON'T NOTICE IT.**

GORILLA?! WHAT GORILLA?

IN FACT, THERE'S SO MUCH STUFF ALWAYS GOING ON AROUND US, IT WOULD BE **IMPOSSIBLE TO TAKE IT ALL IN AT ONCE.**
THAT'D BE **OVERWHELMING!**
SO PARTS OF OUR PERCEPTUAL SYSTEMS BECOME **AUTOMATIC.**

THIS HAPPENS AS WE LEARN TO **RIDE A BIKE...**
...OR **PLAY AN INSTRUMENT...**
...OR **READ.**
I USED TO HAVE TO **THINK** TO DECODE THESE SYMBOLS!
ONE OUTCOME OF THIS IS THE **STROOP EFFECT.**

IF YOU ASK PEOPLE TO **COUNT THE NUMBER OF TIMES A WORD IS PRINTED...**

dog
dog
dog
dog
FOUR!
cat
cat
TWO!
skunk
skunk
skunk
skunk
skunk
FIVE!
...THEY'LL TAKE **SLIGHTLY LONGER** IF IT'S A **NUMBER WORD...**
six
six
six
six
UM...FOUR
one
one
OK...TWO.
seven
seven
seven
seven
seven
MERCY.

...BECAUSE THEIR MINDS **AUTOMATICALLY ASSOCIATE THE NAME WITH THE MEANING** AND IT TAKES EXTRA EFFORT TO **UNTANGLE THEM.**

THE SAME THING HAPPENS WITH **COLOR WORDS.**
THAT'S WHITE... NO, IT'S **BLACK!**
THAT'S BLACK... NO, IT'S **WHITE!**
WHITE
BLACK

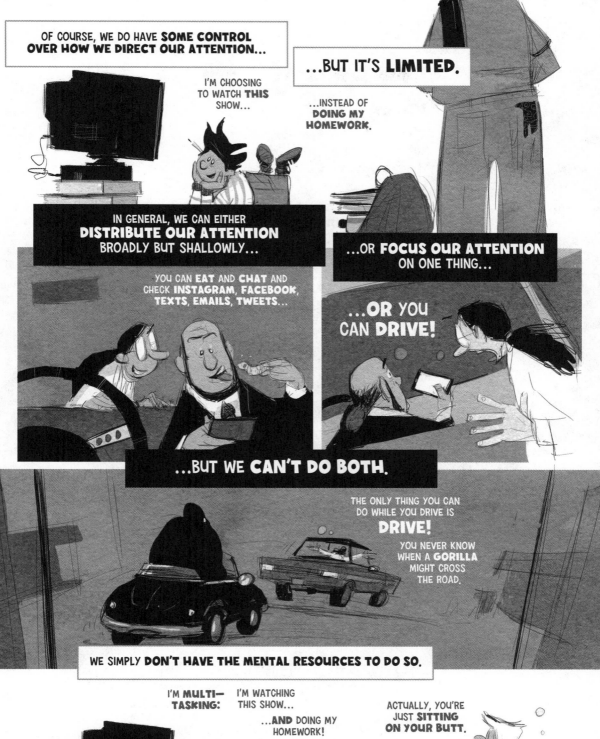

OF COURSE, WE DO HAVE **SOME CONTROL OVER HOW WE DIRECT OUR ATTENTION...**

...BUT IT'S **LIMITED.**

I'M CHOOSING TO WATCH **THIS** SHOW...

...INSTEAD OF **DOING MY HOMEWORK.**

IN GENERAL, WE CAN EITHER **DISTRIBUTE OUR ATTENTION** BROADLY BUT SHALLOWLY...

...OR **FOCUS OUR ATTENTION** ON ONE THING...

YOU CAN **EAT** AND **CHAT** AND CHECK **INSTAGRAM, FACEBOOK, TEXTS, EMAILS, TWEETS...**

...OR YOU CAN **DRIVE!**

...BUT WE **CAN'T DO BOTH.**

THE ONLY THING YOU CAN DO WHILE YOU DRIVE IS **DRIVE!**

YOU NEVER KNOW WHEN A **GORILLA** MIGHT CROSS THE ROAD.

WE SIMPLY **DON'T HAVE THE MENTAL RESOURCES TO DO SO.**

I'M **MULTI-TASKING:**
I'M WATCHING THIS SHOW...
...AND DOING MY HOMEWORK!
ACTUALLY, YOU'RE JUST **SITTING ON YOUR BUTT.**

IN SUM, THIS CRAZY WORLD IS FILLED WITH **AN OVERABUNDANCE OF STIMULI**...
...BUT WHAT OUR SENSES TAKE IN IS OFTEN **DISTORTED** OR **AMBIGUOUS**...
WHAT ON EARTH IS **GOING ON OUT THERE?**
...SO OUR MINDS ARE CONSTANTLY WORKING TO **CREATE ORDER FROM CHAOS.**
BOTTOM UP!
TOP DOWN!
AND EVEN THOUGH WHAT WE PERCEIVE **ISN'T WHAT'S ACTUALLY OUT THERE**...

INSIDE, IT'S ALL **MENTAL IMAGES** ASSEMBLED FROM **ELECTRICAL SIGNALS IN YOUR BRAIN.**
OUTSIDE, IT'S ALL VAST **SWIRLS OF ATOMS AND ENERGY.**

...THE PROCESS **WORKS REMARKABLY WELL TO GET US BY.**

GOOD THING MY **REACTIONS** WERE SO FAST.
IT FELT LIKE I HIT THE BRAKES **BEFORE I SAW HIM.**

CHAPTER 2
LEARNING

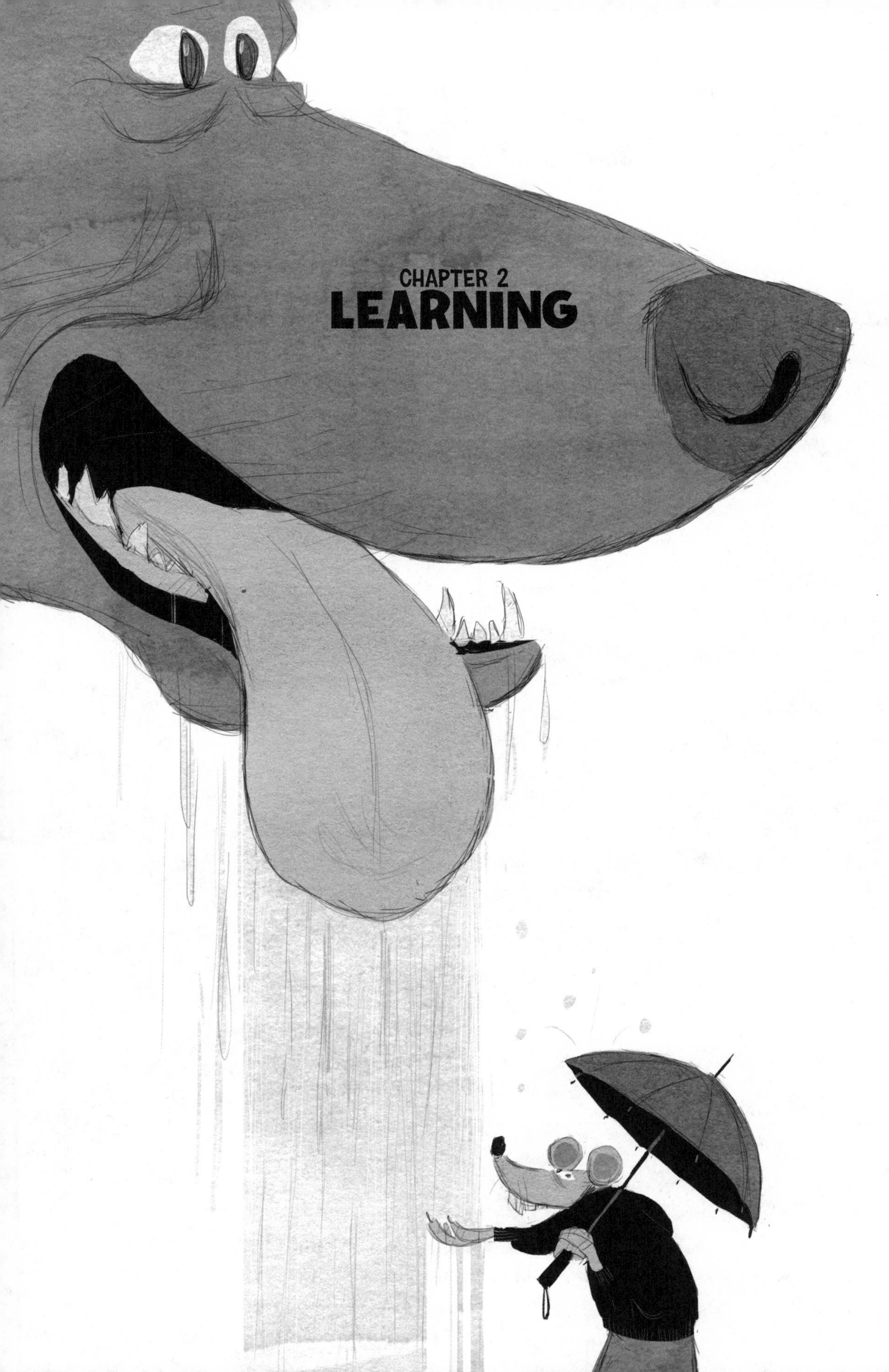

IN THE PREVIOUS CHAPTER, WE LEARNED THAT THE INFORMATION WE GET THROUGH OUR SENSES IS **INHERENTLY AMBIGUOUS.**

WYAIERARRAE

WHAT'S THAT **AWFUL** SOUND?

A **CHILD** BEING **TORTURED...**

...OR **CATS MAKING WHOOPIE?**

SO, TO BETTER UNDERSTAND THE WORLD, WE USE **TOP DOWN PROCESSING...**

The Neighbor Feeds Stray Cats
This Happens Every Night
No Babies Live Nearby

...INCORPORATING OUR **PRIOR KNOWLEDGE** TO MAKE SENSE OF THINGS.

MUST BE TIME TO GET A **DOG.**

THE WAY WE GET THAT PRIOR KNOWLEDGE IS THROUGH **LEARNING.**

WE'RE **CONSTANTLY LEARNING THINGS,** NOT JUST WHEN WE'RE **FORCED TO...**

LISTEN TO YOUR TEACHER OR YOU WON'T LEARN ANYTHING.

LISTEN TO YOUR BOSS OR YOU WON'T GET PAID.

...BUT ALSO WHEN WE'RE **SIMPLY LIVING OUR LIVES.**

LISTEN AT THE DOOR OR MOM WILL CATCH US.

SO IN THIS CHAPTER WE'RE GOING TO EXPLORE **HOW WE LEARN STUFF...**

RIPE BANANAS ARE YELLOW!

EVERY TIME I STEP ON A RIPE BANANA...
...I SLIP.

YOU SHOULDN'T STEP ON RIPE BANANAS.

...BY EXAMINING **THREE TYPES OF LEARNING IN CLOSER DETAIL:**

WE LEARN THROUGH **ASSOCIATIONS...**

yellow
Ripe

1. CLASSICAL CONDITIONING

...THROUGH **REWARD AND PUNISHMENT...**

2. OPERANT CONDITIONING

...AND **FROM OTHERS.**

3. SOCIAL LEARNING

1. CLASSICAL CONDITIONING

LOTS OF THINGS **HAPPEN AT THE SAME TIME...**

...AND TO HELP OURSELVES NAVIGATE THE WORLD, WE **MAKE ASSOCIATIONS BETWEEN THEM.**

Rain!
Cloudy Skies

Nobody's Talking
Mom and Dad are Grumpy

Gramma
Peculiar Smells

SO HOW DO WE **LEARN** THOSE ASSOCIATIONS?

Thing a

Thing b

ONE OF THE FIRST PEOPLE TO EXPLORE **ASSOCIATIVE LEARNING** WAS THE RUSSIAN PHYSIOLOGIST, **IVAN PAVLOV,** IN THE 1920'S.

WHAT CAN I SAY? I HAVE **GOOD GUT INSTINCTS**

PAVLOV WAS STUDYING **HOW DOGS SLOBBER WHEN THEY EAT...**

HERE'S SOME **MEAT POWDER,** REX!
LET'S SEE **HOW MUCH DROOL** YOU PRODUCE.

...WHEN HE NOTICED THAT HIS DOGS HAD LEARNED TO SLOBBER **BEFORE** THEY ATE.

DING DING!
TIME FOR DINNER, REX!

HIS REAL STROKE OF GENIUS CAME WHEN HE REALIZED HE COULD **TRICK THEM INTO SALIVATING...**

...USING ALL SORTS OF **UNRELATED STIMULI.**

IF I DO THIS LITTLE **DANCE EVERY TIME I FEED THEM...**
...THEN AFTER A WHILE THEY START **SALIVATING WHEN I DANCE.**

THEY CAN LEARN TO ASSOCIATE **ANY OLD CRAZY THING...**
...WITH MEAT POWDER!

PAVLOV'S EXPERIMENTS WORKED BECAUSE **CERTAIN STIMULI** IN THE WORLD **PROVOKE AN AUTOMATIC PHYSIOLOGICAL REACTION** WITHIN US.

WHEN I'M COLD...
...I SHIVER.

WHEN THE CAT SITS ON MY LAP...
...I SNEEZE.

WHEN I SMELL GARBAGE...
...I FEEL NAUSEATED.

BUT IF **OTHER UNRELATED STIMULI...**

...CO-OCCUR REPEATEDLY WITH THOSE **SPECIFIC PHYSIOLOGICAL REACTIONS...**

WHENEVER I SIT IN THIS PARTICULAR CHAIR...

...THE COLD NIGHT AIR MAKES ME SHIVER.

WHENEVER I CHEW CINNAMON GUM...
...THE CAT SITS ON MY LAP AND I SNEEZE.

WHENEVER I PLAY COUNTRY MUSIC...

...I'M NEAR THE GARBAGE AND I FEEL NAUSEATED.

...WE LEARN TO **ASSOCIATE** THE NEW STIMULI WITH THOSE REACTIONS...

WHENEVER I SIT IN THIS CHAIR, CHEWING CINNAMON GUM, AND PLAYING COUNTRY MUSIC...
...I SHIVER, SNEEZE, AND FEEL NAUSEATED.

...EVEN WHEN WE'RE **NOT AWARE** IT'S HAPPENING.

IN PSYCHOLOGY JARGON, ONCE AN ASSOCIATION HAS BEEN MADE, WE SAY IT'S BEEN **CONDITIONED.**

THE **CONDITIONED STIMULUS** IS THE **CAUSE.**
WHEN I SMELL **THIS PERFUME...**
...I **MISS MY GRANDMA.**
THE **CONDITIONED RESPONSE** IS THE **EFFECT.**

IN REAL LIFE, THOUGH WE'RE **OFTEN UNAWARE** OF IT, WE LEARN TO MAKE ASSOCIATIONS LIKE THIS **ALL THE TIME...**

...MOSTLY BECAUSE IT'S **HELPFUL.**

WHEN I HEAR A **GRINDING SOUND...**
...I **JUMP UP** BECAUSE I ASSOCIATE THAT SOUND WITH **COFFEE.**

I **GET TO WORK FASTER!**

HOWEVER, IT DOES HAVE **DOWNSIDES...**

WHEN I SEE THIS **CUTE WOMAN IN THE FURRY HAT...**
...I FEEL ATTRACTED TO **THIS BRAND OF VODKA.**

...SOME OF WHICH ARE **MORE SERIOUS THAN OTHERS.**

IN MY EXPERIENCE, **GRAY PEOPLE** ARE **CRIMINALS.**
WE'LL TALK MORE ABOUT **STEREOTYPING** IN CHAPTER **12.**

SOON AFTER PAVLOV, SOME PSYCHOLOGISTS DECIDED TO TEST HIS TECHNIQUES **ON A BABY.**

IT WORKS GREAT ON **FIDO**...
...LET'S SEE HOW IT WORKS ON **LI'L ALBERT!**

GOOD IDEA!

IN PARTICULAR, THEY WONDERED HOW CONDITIONED ASSOCIATIONS BECOME **GENERALIZED.**

IF WE MAKE LI'L ALBERT **SCARED OF RATS**...
...**WHAT ELSE** WILL HE BECOME AFRAID OF?
GOOD QUESTION!

SO THEY GAVE HIM A **CUTE FURRY RAT** TO PLAY WITH, THEN ASSAULTED HIM WITH **TERRIFYING NOISES.**

THE CUTE FURRY RAT IS HIS **CONDITIONED STIMULUS!**
KLANG!!
CRYING IS HIS **CONDITIONED RESPONSE.**

UNFORTUNATELY, HE NOT ONLY LEARNED TO **FEAR THE RAT...**

...HE **ALSO** BECAME TERRIFIED OF **ALL OTHER CUTE FURRY THINGS...**

WAAAAAAA!
AWESOME!

WAAAAAAA!
FANTASTIC!

...AND THAT SUCCESS MADE THE EXPERIMENT **INFAMOUS.**

WAAAA!
HOW DO WE MAKE HIM **STOP?**

WHEREAS **CLASSICAL CONDITIONING** INFLUENCES **HOW WE LEARN TO ASSOCIATE EVENTS IN THE WORLD...**
WHEN I SEE ANYTHING **CUTE** AND **FURRY...**
...IT REMINDS **ME** OF **TERRIBLE NOISES...**
...AND **ME** OF **VODKA.**

...ANOTHER TYPE OF LEARNING MORE DIRECTLY **SHAPES OUR ACTIONS.**

Push Me!

IN PARTICULAR, **OPERANT CONDITIONING** DESCRIBES HOW WE LEARN WHEN OUR BEHAVIOR...

...IS **REWARDED...**

YOU GET A **CHOCOLATE BAR!**

...OR **PUNISHED.**

YOU GET **BROCCOLI!**

2. OPERANT CONDITIONING

THE SIMPLEST PRINCIPLE IN OPERANT CONDITIONING IS **THE LAW OF EFFECT.**

IF A BEHAVIOR LEADS TO A **POSITIVE OUTCOME...**

...WE'RE **LIKELY TO DO IT AGAIN.**

IF A BEHAVIOR LEADS TO A **NEGATIVE OUTCOME...**

...WE'RE **UNLIKELY TO DO IT AGAIN.**

THAT MIGHT SEEM TOTALLY **OBVIOUS...**

...BUT IN PRACTICE IT CAN GET **VERY COMPLICATED.**

IF AN ORGANISM DOES WHAT'S **BAD** FOR IT, IT'LL **GO EXTINCT.**

THEN HOW DO YOU EXPLAIN **SMOKING**, AND **DRINKING**, AND **DRUGS**, AND **SKYDIVING**, AND **HOMEWORK**, AND...

...AND ALL OF THE ABOVE WHILE **TEXTING?**

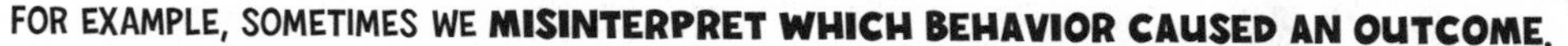
FOR EXAMPLE, SOMETIMES WE MISINTERPRET WHICH BEHAVIOR CAUSED AN OUTCOME.

LAST WEEK, HE FORGOT TO WASH HIS SOCKS...
...THEN HE HIT A HOME RUN.
HE HASN'T WASHED HIS SOCKS SINCE.

OTHER TIMES WE **REPEAT ACTIVITIES** THAT HAVE **SHORT TERM REWARDS**, BUT **LONG TERM NEGATIVE OUTCOMES**...

-POKE-
-POKE-
-POKE-
-POKE-
-POKE-

...OR GET **BAMBOOZLED BY CONFOUNDING PRECONDITIONS.**

YOU GET 30 BONUS MINUTES EVERY OTHER THURSDAY BETWEEN 2PM AND 4PM PROVIDED YOU ALREADY USED ALL YOUR FREE DATA AND YOU'VE CALLED YOUR MOTHER IN THE PAST WEEK AND HAVEN'T MADE ANY INTERNATIONAL CALLS DURING NON-PEAK HOURS OR...
YEAH, WHATEVER, JUST SIGN ME UP.

TO STUDY THESE COMPLEXITIES, IN THE 1930'S THE BEHAVIORAL PSYCHOLOGIST **B.F. SKINNER** INVENTED A **SPECIAL KIND OF BOX.**

HOP IN, I'LL GIVE YOU A COOKIE.

IT'S GOT A BUTTON, A MINI FRIDGE, DISCO LIGHTS, SPEAKERS, AND A DANCE FLOOR.
WHAT MORE COULD YOU ASK FOR?!

SKINNER BOXES ARE TINY LABORATORIES DESIGNED TO STUDY **HOW CRITTERS LEARN TO DO THINGS...**

WHEN THE MUSIC STARTS, **PRESS THAT BUTTON.**

...AND, IN PARTICULAR, HOW DIFFERENT **REWARDS...**

...AND **PUNISHMENTS...**

GOOD JOB, HERE'S A **COOKIE!**

SINCE YOU DID GOOD, WE TURNED **OFF** THE **ELECTRIFIED FLOOR!**

HEY! WHEN I PRESSED IT THEY **LOCKED THE FRIDGE!**

ZZZZZZAP!

...**INFLUENCE THAT PROCESS.**

THE MUSIC STARTED, **WANNA PRESS IT AGAIN?**

YES, PLEASE.
ZZZZZT

NAH. THEY MIGHT TAKE SOMETHING **ELSE** AWAY.

NO!

BECAUSE THESE REWARDS AND PUNISHMENTS CAN BE DOLED OUT FOR **PARTIAL ACTIONS** OR EVEN **RANDOM MOVEMENTS...**

...THEY'VE BEEN USED TO TEACH ANIMALS ALL SORTS OF **SILLY TRICKS...**

PUT YOUR LEFT FOOT IN AND I'LL GIVE YOU A COOKIE!
SHAKE IT ALL ABOUT, OR I'LL TURN THE FLOOR UP TO **11!**
...NOW DO THE **HOKEY POKEY...**

...ALONG WITH SOME **VERY USEFUL SKILLS.**

PIGEONS HAVE ACUTE **COLOR VISION**, AND IF WE REWARD THEM FOR **PECKING TOWARD CERTAIN COLORS** THEY CAN HELP US **FIND PEOPLE LOST AT SEA.**

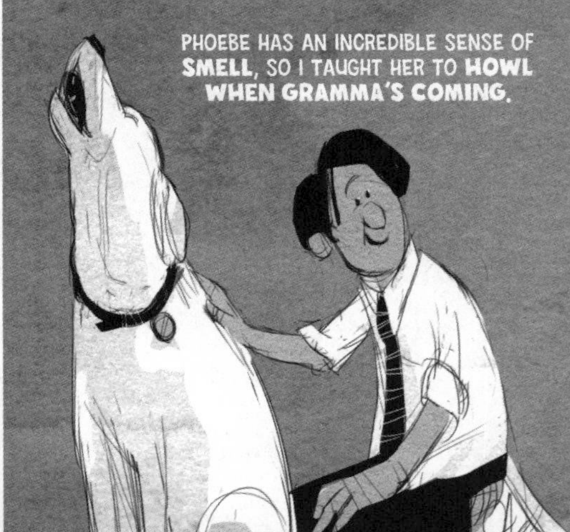
PHOEBE HAS AN INCREDIBLE SENSE OF **SMELL**, SO I TAUGHT HER TO **HOWL WHEN GRAMMA'S COMING.**

AGAINST SKINNER'S OWN INCLINATIONS, THESE EXPERIMENTS HAVE BEEN MOSTLY **LIMITED TO ANIMALS...**

...BUT THE INSIGHTS GAINED FROM OPERANT CONDITIONING **CLEARLY APPLY TO PEOPLE TOO.**

WE SHOULD PUT A BABY IN THERE WITH THE RAT!
GOOD IDEA!
I'M SICK OF THE RAT RACE.
TELL ME ABOUT IT.

FOR EXAMPLE, AS WE LEARN MORE DETAILS ABOUT **HOW OUR OWN REWARD SYSTEMS FUNCTION...**

DOPAMINE IS FLOODING YOUR **NUCLEUS ACCUMBENS.**

...WE DEEPEN OUR UNDERSTANDING ABOUT **ECONOMIC INCENTIVES...**

...AND ABOUT OUR OWN **RELATIONSHIPS...**

FOR ONLY **49 CENTS** EVERYONE WANTS TO GET **SUPERSIZED!**

WHAT WOULD HAPPEN IF THEY CHARGED A **DOLLAR?**

SHE'LL PUT HER UNDERWEAR IN THE **LAUNDRY** INSTEAD OF ON THE **FLOOR...**

...BUT ONLY IF I **COOK DINNER ONCE A WEEK.**

...AND ABOUT WHY **SOCIAL PROBLEMS INVOLVING ADDICTION** ARE SO WIDESPREAD.

WHICH BRINGS US TO OUR **NEXT TOPIC.**

3. SOCIAL LEARNING

LAST BUT NOT LEAST, WE **LEARN FROM OTHERS.**

WHAT ARE WE **LINING UP** FOR?
I DONNO, BUT IT MUST BE **IMPORTANT.**

MORE SPECIFICALLY, WE CAN LEARN FROM OTHER PEOPLE'S BEHAVIOR, EVEN WHEN WE **DON'T OBSERVE ANY CONSEQUENCES.**

SHE KEEPS **PRESSING THAT BUTTON.**
SHE MUST BE **GETTING SOMETHING OUT OF IT.**

ONE OF THE BEST STUDIES OF THIS PHENOMENON IS **ALBERT BANDURA'S** CLASSIC **BOBO DOLL** STUDY...

...WHEREIN KIDS WHO **DID** SEE AN ADULT BEHAVING **AGGRESSIVELY**...

...WHEN COMPARED WITH KIDS WHO **DIDN'T**...

TAKE **THAT**, BOBO!

...WERE **MORE AGGRESSIVE** AFTER THE ADULT LEFT THE ROOM.

ANYONE UP FOR **CHESS?**

THIS SORT OF **MIMICRY** IS **NOT LIMITED TO HUMAN BEINGS...**
LOOK, THE APES ARE **APING EACH OTHER!**
...AND THERE'S SOME EVIDENCE THAT CERTAIN ANIMALS SHARE **CULTURE** LIKE PEOPLE DO.
FIRST, ALL THE **BULLIES** IN OUR **FOREST TROOP** ATE POISONED MEAT AND **DIED.**
THEN THE **PEACEFUL BABOONS** TOOK OVER.
AND AFTER THAT, NEWLY ARRIVING BABOONS **ASSIMILATED!**
YO, WHO DO I HAVE TO **BEAT UP** TO GET WITH THIS TROOP?
SORRY BRO, THAT'S **NOT** HOW WE DO THINGS HERE.

BUT BECAUSE **HUMAN SOCIAL LEARNING** IS SO **UNIQUELY COMPLEX...**

TO BE PART OF **OUR TROOP** YOU HAVE TO LEARN TO **HOKEY POKEY BLINDFOLDED** AND **BACKWARDS.**

...AND, AT TIMES, **CONFOUNDING** AND **CONTRADICTORY...**

OF COURSE I **LEARN FROM HIS BEHAVIOR.**

HE'S MY **DAD!**

I ALWAYS **DO THE OPPOSITE OF WHAT HE DOES.**

...WE'LL BE EXPLORING IT MORE RIGOROUSLY IN **PART 3.**

BECAUSE MANY PSYCHOLOGICAL STUDIES **SEEM SIMPLE**...

WHY DO I CARE ABOUT **PUSHING BUTTONS?**

...AND INVOLVE **ANIMALS** INSTEAD OF PEOPLE...

WHAT DOES **DOG SALIVA** SAY ABOUT **ME?**

...IT CAN BE **HARD TO TAKE THEM SERIOUSLY.**

WHAT DOES IT **MATTER** WHETHER I LEARN THE **HOKEY POKEY?**

SO TO END THIS CHAPTER, LET'S CONSIDER THE CHILLING CASE OF **LEARNED HELPLESSNESS,** DISCOVERED BY THE PSYCHOLOGIST **MARTIN SELIGMAN.**

I CAN TEACH PHOEBE TO **DO TRICKS!**

I CAN TEACH HER TO **DO NOTHING.**

HE FOUND THAT IF YOU **RANDOMLY SHOCK DOGS IN A SKINNER BOX...**

ZZZZZT

ZZZZZT

...AND GIVE **SOME** OF THEM A WAY **TO LEARN TO AVOID THE SHOCK...**

...BUT **WITHOLD THAT CONTROL** FROM OTHERS...

IF YOU PRESS THE BUTTON, IT'LL **END.**

SORRY, THERE'S **NOTHING** YOU CAN DO ABOUT IT.
ZZZZZT

...THEN PUT EACH DOG IN A DIFFERENT BOX, WHERE THEY CAN AVOID SHOCKS BY **JUMPING AWAY FROM THEM...**

...THOSE DOGS WHO EARLIER HAD NO CONTROL, **WON'T BOTHER...**

ZZZZZT

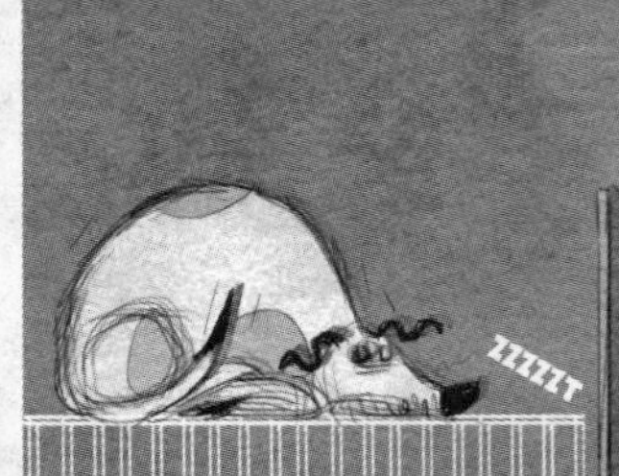
ZZZZZT

...BECAUSE THEY'VE **LEARNED TO BE HELPLESS.**

SELIGMAN'S DISCOVERY SPARKED THE REALIZATION THAT THIS IS SOMETHING **PEOPLE LEARN TOO...**

JUST AS WE CAN LEARN TO DO THINGS TO **GET REWARDS...**

...WE CAN ALSO LEARN THAT OUR BEHAVIOR **HAS NO EFFECT.**

...WITH **PROFOUND SOCIAL CONSEQUENCES.**

PEOPLE TOLERATE **ABUSE AND MISTREATMENT...**

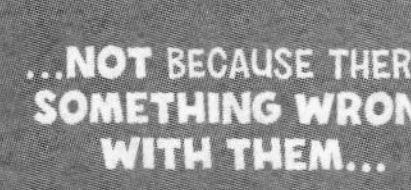

...**NOT** BECAUSE THERE'S **SOMETHING WRONG WITH THEM...**

...BUT BECAUSE THEY'VE LEARNED, REPEATEDLY, THAT THEY **HAVE NO CONTROL OVER IT.**

Violence
Corruption
Injustice
Why Bother?

FORTUNATELY, SELIGMAN'S WORK **ALSO** POINTS TOWARD SOMETHING **HOPEFUL...**

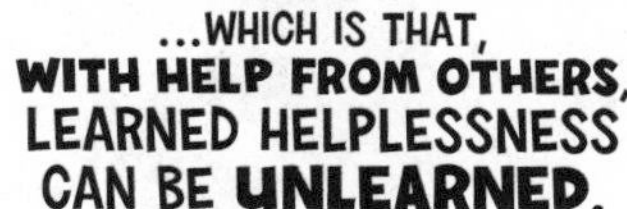

...WHICH IS THAT, **WITH HELP FROM OTHERS,** LEARNED HELPLESSNESS CAN BE **UNLEARNED.**

WHO KNEW AN **OLD DOG** COULD TEACH US **NEW TRICKS.**

We Can
Fix it
Together

OUTSIDE THE LABORATORY, THE WAY WE LEARN IS AS **MESSY** AND **CHAOTIC** AND FULL OF **AMBIGUITY** AS EVERYTHING ELSE.

I MISS MY JOB **AT THE LAB.**

BUT ONCE WE'VE LEARNED SOMETHING, WHETHER IT'S **SIMPLE**...

I CAN RECITE THE **ALPHABET!**

...OR **COMPLICATED**...

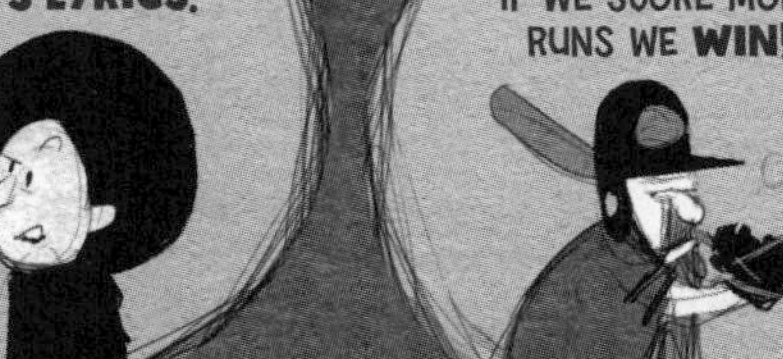

I CAN RECITE **SNOOP DOGG'S LYRICS.**

...**TRUE**...

IF WE SCORE MORE RUNS WE **WIN!**

...OR **FALSE**...

IF I WASH MY SOCKS, **WE'LL LOSE!**

...WE USE IT TO **ORGANIZE OUR EXPERIENCES.**

ONCE YOU KNOW THE **ALPHABET** YOU'LL **NEVER SEE THE WORLD THE SAME WAY AGAIN.**
THE SAME IS TRUE OF **SNOOP DOGG.**

IT'S **TOP DOWN PROCESSING!**

AS WE'LL SEE NEXT, WHAT WE LEARN NOT ONLY ALLOWS US TO **MAKE SENSE OF OUR SENSES**...

WHAT'S THAT **FUNK?**
THAT'S THE SMELL OF **VICTORY!**

...IT ALSO **SHAPES OUR MEMORIES.**

I'VE **ALWAYS** BEEN A BETTER HITTER WHEN MY SOCKS ARE DIRTY.

CHAPTER 3
MEMORY

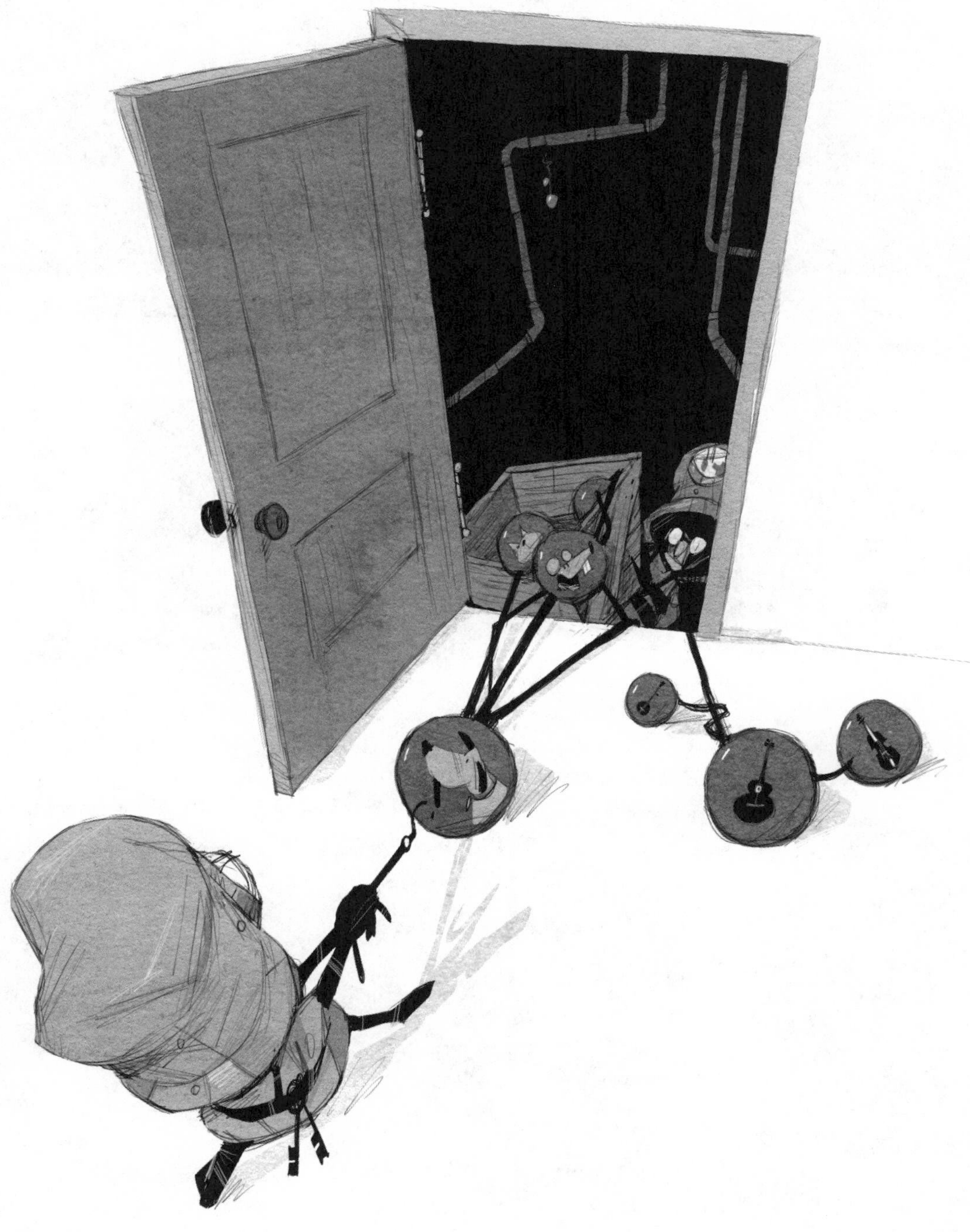

IN THIS CHAPTER WE'RE GOING TO LEARN ABOUT **TWO BASIC TYPES OF MEMORY...**
Working Memory
Long Term Memory

...AND **HOW THOUGHTS AND IDEAS PASS BETWEEN THEM.**

THERE ARE **OTHER TYPES** OF MEMORY...
...BUT WE'RE GOING TO FOCUS ON THE **BASICS.**
Procedural Memory
Implicit Memory
Iconic Memory
LET'S **FORGET ABOUT THOSE** FOR NOW.

WORKING MEMORY
[ALSO KNOWN AS SHORT TERM MEMORY]
CONTAINS **WHATEVER YOU'RE THINKING ABOUT RIGHT NOW.**

LONG TERM STORAGE
CONTAINS **ALL THE STUFF YOU KNOW,** BUT THAT YOU'RE **NOT** THINKING ABOUT RIGHT NOW.

I got 674 Likes
I Should Be Studying
My Hair Looks Hot

The Capital of Russia is Moscow
My Sister Hates Bananas
I have Algebra at 2pm on Mondays

AS WE'LL SEE, WE'RE CONSTANTLY SHUFFLING **INFORMATION** BETWEEN THE TWO...

STORAGE!

RETRIEVAL!

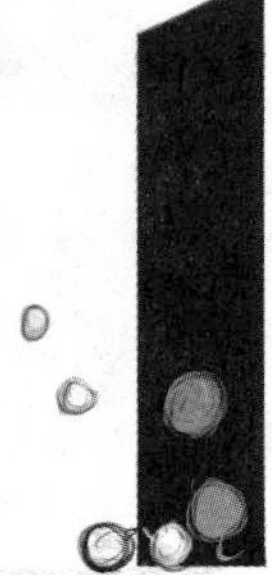

...AND MUCH OF IT GETS **LOST OR DISTORTED ALONG THE WAY.**

Said will Drive Me Home Tuesday
Born in 1950
Brown Eyes
Hates Mayo
Green Eyes
Facts About Mom
Facts About Dad
Stern
Born in 1947
Hates Eggs
Wants Socks For Christmas

OUR WORKING MEMORY IS LIMITED...
...AND HAS TO BE ACTIVELY MAINTAINED.
KEEP JUGGLING OR YOU'LL FORGET THEM.
IN FACT, WE CAN ONLY PROCESS ABOUT 7 MEANINGFUL UNITS OF INFORMATION AT ONCE.
I Want Some Root Beer
My Breath Stinks
My Jacket's Too Hot
CATCH!
Hi, My Name is Jenny
That Girl is Pretty
Mom Doesn't Know Where I Am
Cookie
I'LL HAVE TO DROP SOMETHING!
The Time is 3:15

THERE ARE WAYS TO **CHUNK INFORMATION** TO MAKE IT EASIER TO JUGGLE...

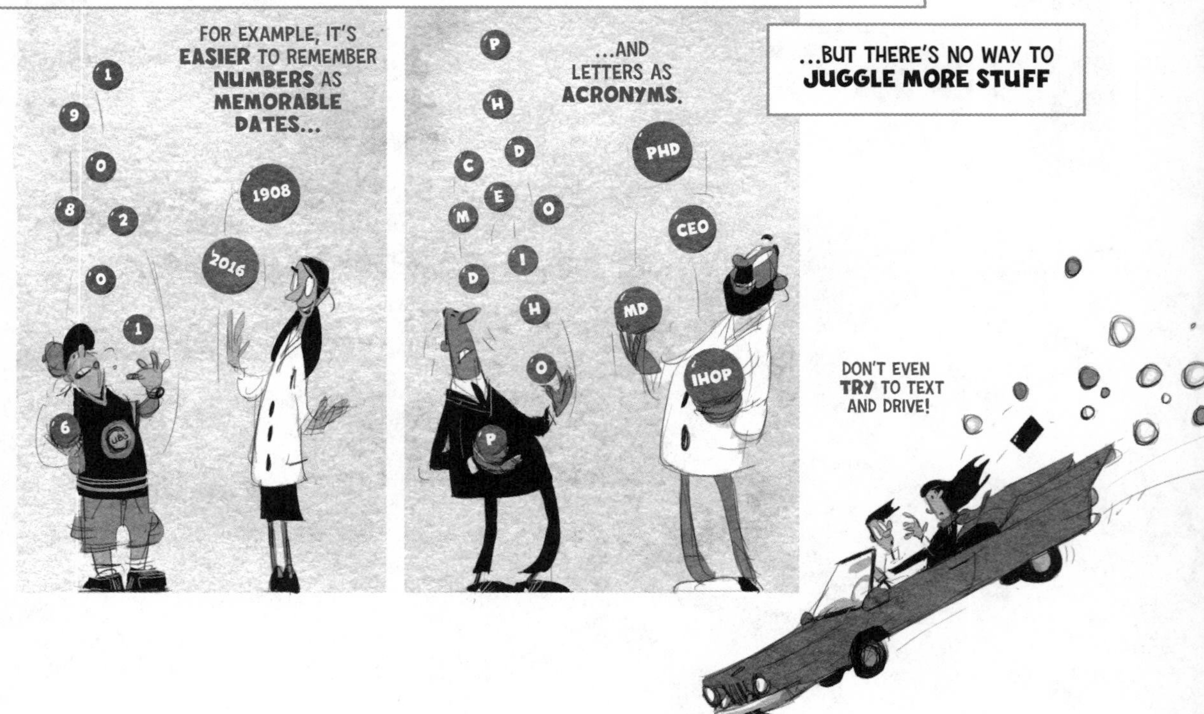
FOR EXAMPLE, IT'S EASIER TO REMEMBER NUMBERS AS MEMORABLE DATES...
1908
2016
...AND LETTERS AS ACRONYMS.
PHD
CEO
MD
IHOP
...BUT THERE'S NO WAY TO JUGGLE MORE STUFF
DON'T EVEN TRY TO TEXT AND DRIVE!

THE PSYCHOLOGIST **ALAN BADDELEY** THEORIZED THAT WE JUGGLE **VERBAL INFORMATION...**

...SEPARATELY FROM **VISUAL INFORMATION.**

WE HAVE AN INNER VOICE...
...FOR PROCESSING SOUNDS.
Her Name is "Jenny"
She's From "Dubuque"
Her cell is "86753" Something
IT'S THE AUDITORY LOOP!
AND WE HAVE AN INNER CHALKBOARD...
...FOR PROCESSING VISIONS AND PLACES.
BAR
IT'S THE VISUO-SPATIAL SKETCHPAD!

THIS THEORY HELPS EXPLAIN PARTICULAR **QUIRKS** ABOUT HOW OUR WORKING MEMORY HANDLES **NUMBERS** ...

...AND **LETTERS...**

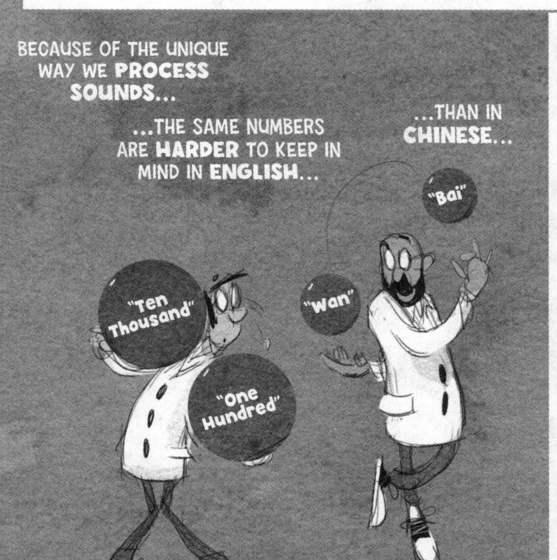

BECAUSE OF THE UNIQUE WAY WE PROCESS SOUNDS...
...THE SAME NUMBERS ARE HARDER TO KEEP IN MIND IN ENGLISH...
...THAN IN CHINESE...
"Bai"
"Ten Thousand"
"Wan"
"One Hundred"

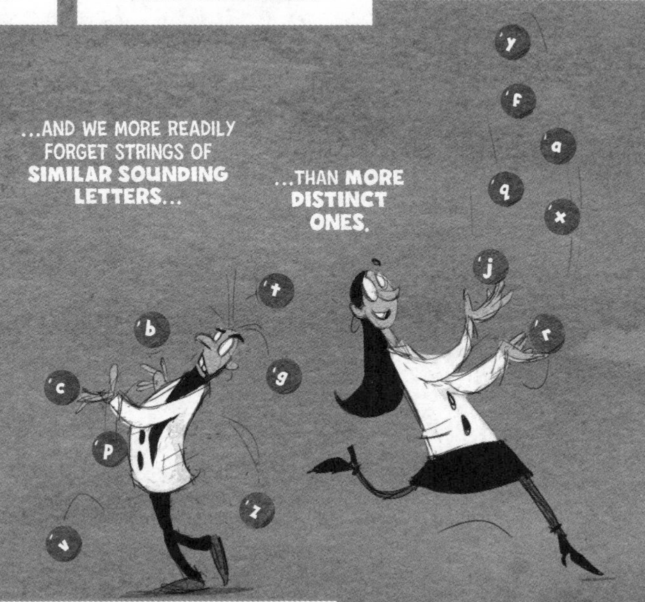

...AND WE MORE READILY FORGET STRINGS OF SIMILAR SOUNDING LETTERS...
...THAN MORE DISTINCT ONES.
y
f
a
q
x
j
t
b
g
c
r
p
z
v

...AS WELL AS CERTAIN OTHER **COGNITIVE LIMITATIONS.**

IT'S PRETTY EASY TO LISTEN TO SOMEONE TALK AND DRAW PICTURES.
GOT IT.

BUT IT'S MUCH HARDER TO LISTEN AND WRITE WORDS.
HI, MY NAME IS BOOMCHIGGER McFUSTHAUSEN AND I'LL GIVE YOU A MILLION DOLLARS IF YOU SHAKE MY HAND.

WHEN WE THINK SOMETHING WILL BE **USEFUL LATER**, WE MOVE IT FROM WORKING MEMORY...

...AND **ENCODE IT IN LONG TERM MEMORY.**

867
5309
"Dubuque"
Long
Term
Memory

FOR BETTER OR WORSE, THIS PROCESS IS **INCOMPLETE...**

LOTS OF WHAT WE EXPERIENCE **NEVER GETS ENCODED.**

"Dubuque"

HOW EXACTLY WERE YOU **WEARING YOUR HAIR** BACK THEN?

...SLOPPY...

WHAT DOES GET ENCODED IS OFTEN **MISSING DETAILS.**

I REMEMBER BEING **DAZZLED BY YOUR LIPSTICK**, BUT I CAN'T REMEMBER **WHAT COLOR IT WAS.**

...AND **CHAOTIC.**

EVEN IF A MEMORY IS SUCCESSFULLY ENCODED, IT'S OFTEN **DIFFICULT TO FIND LATER...**

...BECAUSE OTHER INFORMATION **GETS IN THE WAY.**

WHAT WAS THE **NAME OF THE PLACE WE MET?**
IT'S GOTTA BE **IN THERE SOMEWHERE.**

NEVERTHELESS, THE PROCESS IS **SURPRISINGLY EFFECTIVE...**
WHEN'S OUR **ANNIVERSARY?**
DIG AROUND. I'M SURE YOU CAN **FIND IT.**
...AND THERE ARE WAYS TO **IMPROVE IT.**
IN GENERAL, THE **HARDER YOU WORK** TO **LINK AN IDEA TO OTHER MENTAL ASSOCIATIONS...**
IF YOU WANT TO REMEMBER MY NAME IS **MIKE...**
...PICTURE ME RIDING A **BIKE...**
...RAPPING INTO A **MIC...**
...WHILE BOXING **MIKE TYSON.**
IT'S **DEPTH OF PROCESSING!**
...THE EASIER IT WILL BE TO **FIND LATER.**
NOW YOU HAVE **CUES TO GUIDE YOUR SEARCH.**
"Bike"
"Mic"
"Mike"
"Mike Tyson"
MEMORY ATHLETES USE THAT FACT TO **INCREASE THEIR ABILITIES.**
I CONSTRUCT AN IMAGINARY **PALACE IN MY MIND...**
...AND I **PLACE ASSOCIATED CONCEPTS** IN **SPECIFIC ROOMS INSIDE.**
THEN, WHEN I WANT TO REMEMBER THOSE IDEAS, I FOLLOW A MENTAL PATH **BACK INTO THOSE ROOMS.**
My anniversary is Flag day, June 14th...
...my wife looks like Betsy Ross ...
...a June Bug nibbles her noggin.

AS THEY ARE ENCODED, OUR LONG TERM MEMORIES FORM **WEBS OF ASSOCIATIONS...**

WHENEVER I RECALL MY OLD DOG **SAM**...

...I THINK ABOUT BUYING **SLURPEES**...

...WHICH REMINDS ME OF THE COLOR **RED**...

...WHICH MAKES ME THINK OF **VAMPIRES**.

...WHICH PSYCHOLOGISTS REFER TO AS **NEURAL NETWORKS**.

THE CONCEPTS IN OUR MINDS ARE **INTERCONNECTED**.

Sweet
Bright Red
Blood
Lick
Joy
Sam
Slurpee
Vampires
Sneeze
Dogs
Cats
My best friends
Bite
Scratch
Ed
Claw
Pain
Ed's cat

CRUCIALLY, ACTIVATING **ONE PART** OF A NETWORK...

...STIMULATES THE **CONNECTED PARTS** OF THE NETWORK...

...AND MAKES THEM **EASIER TO RECALL**.

WHEN I **SNEEZE**...

...IT SENDS ACTIVATION TO **CATS** AND **CLAWS** AND **PAIN**...

...WHICH REMINDS ME OF **ED**.

Sneeze
Claw
Cats
Pain
Ed's cat

THIS EFFECT IS KNOWN AS **PRIMING...**

THINKING **CERTAIN THINGS...**
...PRIMES US TO REMEMBER **OTHER THINGS...**

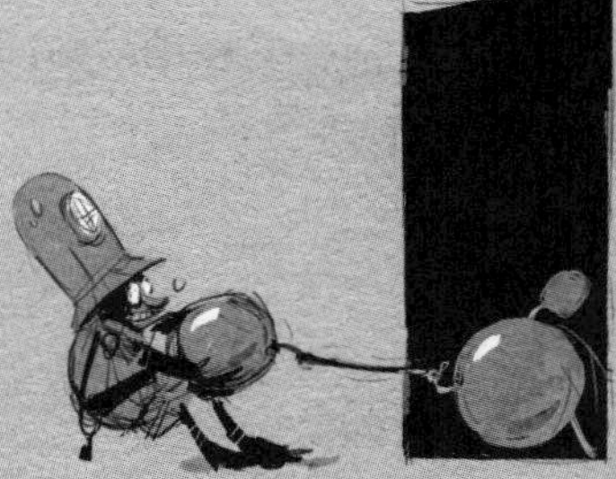
...BECAUSE THE TWO ARE **ASSOCIATED IN OUR MINDS.**

...AND IT INFLUENCES **ALL ASPECTS OF OUR COGNITIVE EXPERIENCE,** INCLUDING HOW WE PROCESS **SIGHTS, SOUNDS, SMELLS...**

PLEASE DON'T WEAR **THAT** PERFUME!
your hot legs
Roses
That perfume
Grandma
wigs
dentures

...INCLUDING OUR **IMMEDIATE REACTIONS TO EVENTS.**

TOP-DOWN PROCESSING FROM CHAPTER 1 OFTEN WORKS LIKE THIS.

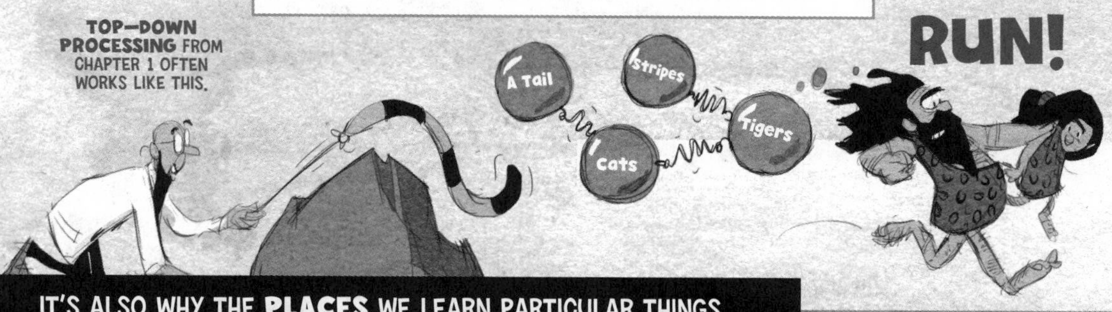
A Tail
Stripes
Cats
Tigers
RUN!

IT'S ALSO WHY THE **PLACES** WE LEARN PARTICULAR THINGS...

Go get Billy
Desk
at Bugger King

Pressure Tables
Safety Facts
Under-water

...CAN **DRAMATICALLY INFLUENCE HOW WELL WE RECALL THEM.**

WHEN I WAS **AT MY DESK,** BILLY TOLD ME WHERE TO PICK HIM UP...
...BUT NOW THAT I'M **IN MY CAR** I CAN'T REMEMBER WHERE I'M SUPPOSED TO GET HIM!

I MEMORIZED SOME IMPORTANT STUFF **UNDERWATER...**
...BUT NOW THAT I'M **ON LAND** I CAN'T REMEMBER IT!
IT'S **STATE-DEPENDENT MEMORY!**

OVER TIME, OUR NEURAL NETWORKS CAN BECOME **EXTREMELY COMPLEX.**

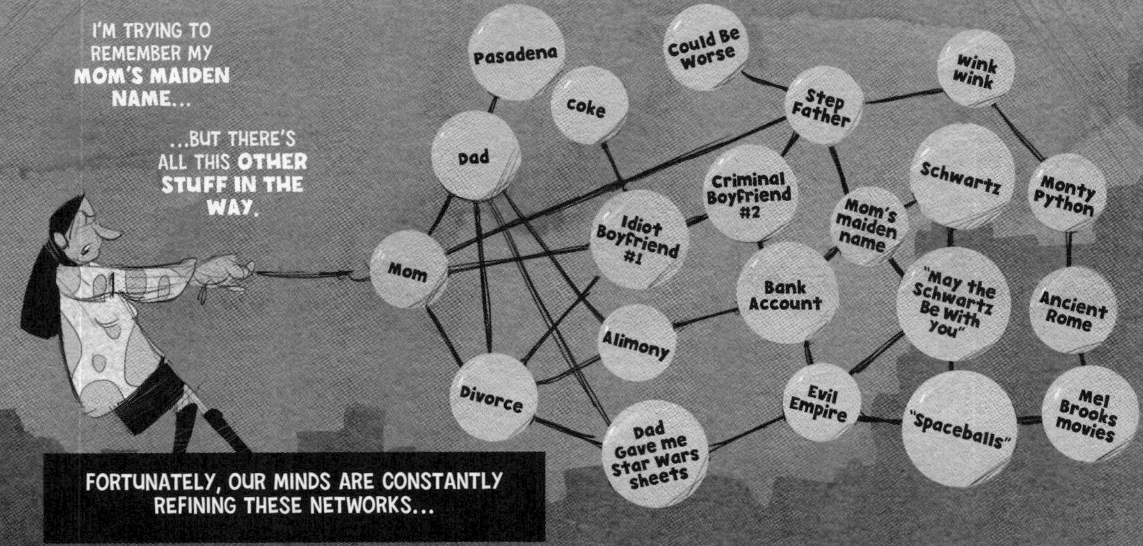

I'M TRYING TO REMEMBER MY **MOM'S MAIDEN NAME...**
...BUT THERE'S ALL THIS **OTHER STUFF IN THE WAY.**
Pasadena
Could Be Worse
Wink Wink
Coke
Step Father
Dad
Criminal Boyfriend #2
Schwartz
Monty Python
Idiot Boyfriend #1
Mom's maiden name
Mom
Bank Account
"May the Schwartz Be With You"
Ancient Rome
Alimony
Divorce
Evil Empire
"Spaceballs"
Mel Brooks movies
Dad Gave me Star Wars sheets

FORTUNATELY, OUR MINDS ARE CONSTANTLY REFINING THESE NETWORKS...

...BY **STRENGTHENING THE LINKS WE MOST OFTEN USE.**

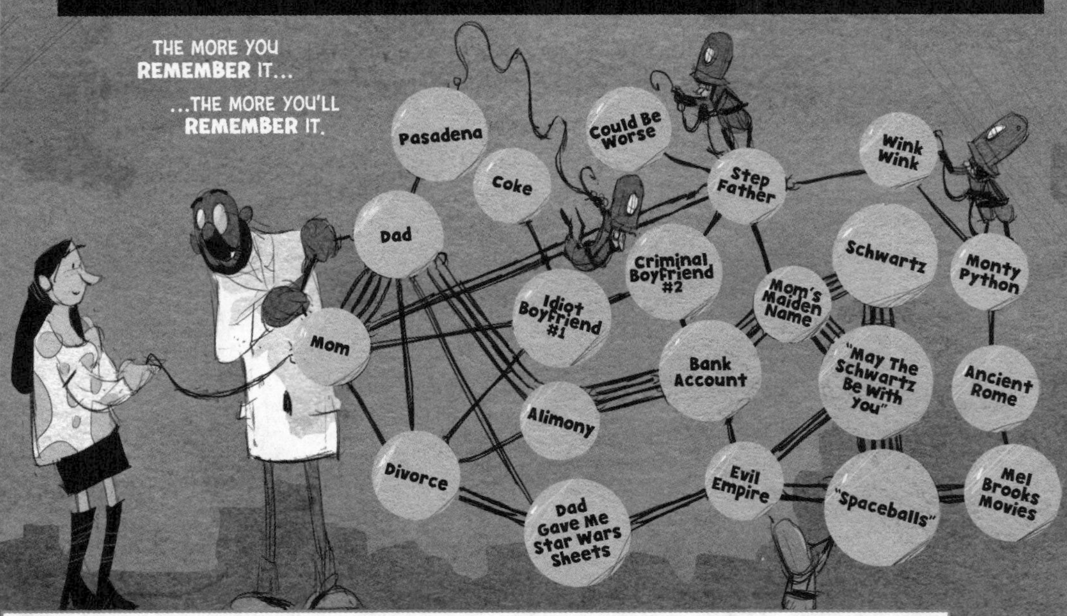

THE MORE YOU **REMEMBER** IT...
...THE MORE YOU'LL **REMEMBER** IT.
Pasadena
Could Be Worse
Wink Wink
Coke
Step Father
Dad
Criminal Boyfriend #2
Schwartz
Monty Python
Idiot Boyfriend #1
Mom's Maiden Name
Mom
Bank Account
"May The Schwartz Be With You"
Ancient Rome
Alimony
Divorce
Evil Empire
"Spaceballs"
Mel Brooks Movies
Dad Gave Me Star Wars Sheets

AND OF COURSE WE CAN STRENGTHEN THEM FURTHER BY **WORKING HARD AT IT.**

IF YOU WANT TO REMEMBER HER MAIDEN NAME, THINK OF HER LIKE **THIS.**

MAY THE **SCHWARTZ** BE WITH YOU.

IN FACT, IT TURNS OUT THAT THE **HARDER WE WORK** TO RETRIEVE PARTICULAR MEMORIES...

...THE **EASIER IT GETS TO RETRIEVE THEM.**

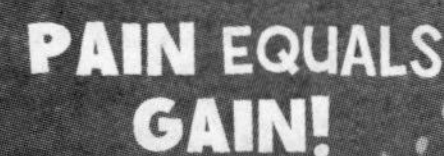

PAIN EQUALS **GAIN!**

THAT MAY BE WHY **TAKING A TEST** CAN BUILD MORE LASTING MEMORIES THAN EXTRA STUDYING.

AFTER MEMORIZING A **SET OF FACTS...**

...HALF A GROUP OF STUDENTS WERE **GIVEN PRACTICE TESTS...**

...AND HALF WERE INSTEAD GIVEN **MORE TIME TO STUDY.**

Van Gogh
=Starry Night
Degas
=Ballerinas
Magritte
=Apple Face
Leonardo
=Mona Lisa

TIME'S UP!
RETRIEVE YOUR MEMORIES **NOW!!**
OUCH!
THIS IS A **PIECE OF CAKE.**

AND WHILE THE EXTRA STUDY TIME **HELPED A BIT IN THE SHORT TERM...**

...IN THE LONG TERM IT HAD THE **OPPOSITE EFFECT!**

YOU LEARNED **A BIT MORE NOW!**
Proportion Remembered **5 minutes later**
0.8
0.7
0.6
0.5
0.4
0.3
0.2
0.1
Study, Study
Study, Test

YOU **FORGOT LOTS MORE LATER!**

Proportion Remembered **1 week later**

0.8
0.7
0.6
0.5
0.4
0.3
0.2
0.1

Study, Study

Study, Test

UNFORTUNATELY, **NOBODY SEEMED TO LEARN THE LESSON.**

WANNA TAKE ANOTHER **TEST?**
NO!

WE'LL COME BACK TO THIS IN **CHAPTER 5**, ON **METACOGNITION.**

ON THE FLIP SIDE, WHENEVER WE **STRENGTHEN CERTAIN LINKS...**

...WE **WEAKEN OTHERS.**

WHEN YOU ACTIVATE **THESE CUES...**
Roses
Tingly Feeling
Strong
Tough
Princess Leia
Pretty
Jenny
Hair
Good at Math
Good at Speeling
Smart
...IT MAKES **NEARBY CUES LESS EFFECTIVE.**

TECHNICALLY, THIS IS CALLED **RETRIEVAL INDUCED FORGETTING.**

IF WE MEMORIZE A **SET OF WORD ASSOCIATIONS...**

...THEN PRACTICE RETRIEVING **ONLY SOME OF THEM...**

Apple
Kiwi
Fruit
Pear
Orange
OK, WHAT FRUIT STARTS WITH **"AP"?**
APPLE!
WHAT FRUIT STARTS WITH **"PE"?**
PEAR!

...IT **DECREASES OUR ABILITY** TO **RETRIEVE THE WORDS WE DIDN'T PRACTICE!**

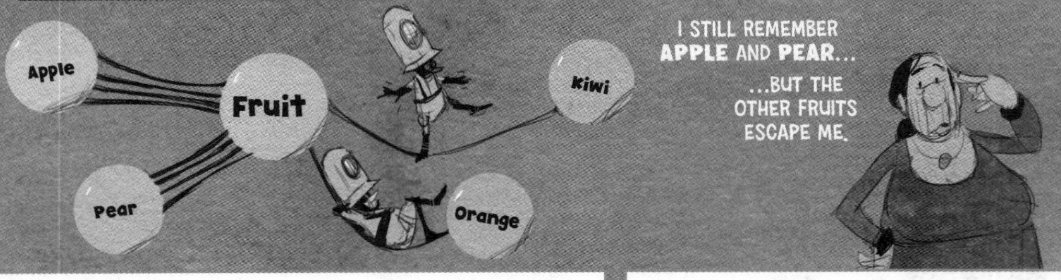
Apple
Fruit
Kiwi
Pear
Orange
I STILL REMEMBER **APPLE** AND **PEAR...**
...BUT THE OTHER FRUITS ESCAPE ME.

WHILE THIS SORT OF THING IS USUALLY PRETTY **HELPFUL...**

...IT CAN CREATE PROBLEMS WHEN WE ACTUALLY **NEED OLD INFORMATION.**

D4
B6
G2
E7
I DON'T CARE WHERE I PARKED **THE LAST THREE TIMES** I WAS HERE.
I NEED TO REMEMBER WHERE MY CAR IS **TODAY!**
April Fools
Wife's Birthday
Tax Day
Dates in April
Easter
*&$#!

MORE GENERALLY, **FORGETTING** IS A **NECESSARY RESULT OF THE WAY OUR MEMORY WORKS.**

IF ONLY I WERE **SMARTER,** I'D **REMEMBER CALCULUS** FROM WHEN I WAS IN SCHOOL.

IT'S OK DAD, YOU'VE GOT **MORE USEFUL THINGS TO THINK ABOUT.**

LIKE **WHAT TO COOK US FOR DINNER.**

WHEN WE **FORGET THINGS,** IT DOESN'T MEAN THEY'VE **WITHERED AWAY...**

...BUT RATHER THAT THEY'VE BECOME **HARDER TO FIND** BECAUSE **OTHER MEMORIES ARE CHOKING UP THE WORKS.**

I CAN'T REMEMBER **WHAT YOU USED TO LOOK LIKE.**

Your Now Face
Smell of Your Breath
My Granny
Your Teeth
Jay Z's Teeth
Where I put my teeth
Favorite Mug
Mint Tea
Favorite Chair
Grand Kids
Dickens
Dig Dug
Donkey Kong
Nintendo
Super Mario Bros.
Bach
Bad Jokes
"Bark"
My First Dog
Your Then Face
Gorilla
Jungle
Parrots

THAT'S WHY, WHEN PEOPLE ARE **CONVINCED THEY'VE TOTALLY FORGOTTEN SOMETHING...**

...CERTAIN CUES CAN MAKE IT **ALL COME FLOODING BACK.**

I CAN'T REMEMBER ANYTHING ABOUT MY CHILDHOOD!

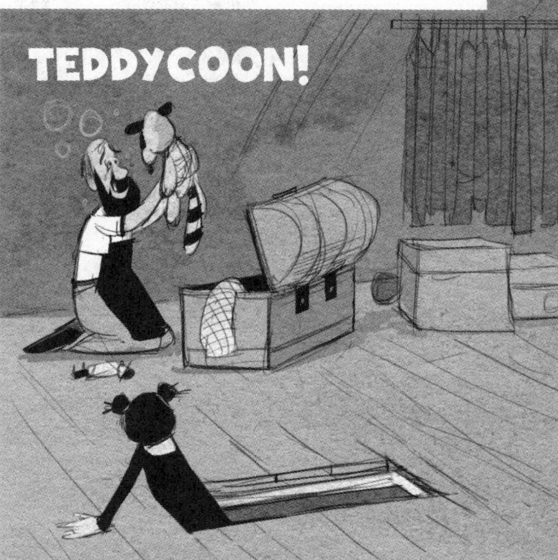
TEDDYCOON!

SO HOW MUCH SHOULD WE TRUST OUR MEMORIES?

WE HONEYMOONED IN VEGAS.
NOPE! IT WAS PARIS!

FOR BETTER OR WORSE, WHEN WE **ENCODE** MEMORIES WE **TEND TO LOSE DETAILS...**

THIS HONEYMOON IS SO ROMANTIC.

...THEN LATER, WHEN WE RETRIEVE THEM, WE TEND TO **FILL IN THE BLANKS** WITH **WHATEVER'S CLOSE AT HAND.**

WHERE WAS YOUR HONEYMOON?
QUICK, WE NEED A PLACE ASSOCIATED WITH A ROMANTIC MEMORY!
THIS WILL HAVE TO DO.
Romantic
Candles
Wine
Eiffel Tower
Paris
Vegas

AS A RESULT, OUR MEMORIES ARE OFTEN **BIASED BY OUR CURRENT ASSOCIATIONS...**

I'VE **ALWAYS** BEEN VERY WELL PUT TOGETHER.

ACTUALLY, **IN COLLEGE YOU DIDN'T SHAVE YOUR LEGS!**

HOT DOGS HAVE ALWAYS MADE ME NAUSEOUS.
ACTUALLY, YOU USED TO GOBBLE THEM BEFORE YOU ATE TOO MANY AND GOT SICK.

...AND WHAT WE THINK ACTUALLY HAPPENED IS OFTEN A MASHUP OF **NEW STUFF MIXED IN WITH THE OLD.**

WE'VE ALWAYS HATED EACH OTHER.
ACTUALLY, WE WERE IN LOVE BEFORE WE GOT MARRIED.

OH LOOK, IT WAS NEWARK.
I'M SURE IT FELT ROMANTIC AT THE TIME.

THIS CAN HAVE **DISTURBING** CONSEQUENCES.

OUR MEMORIES CAN BE **MANIPULATED.**

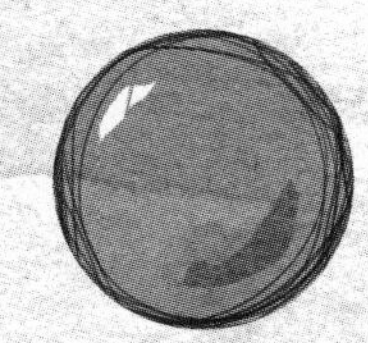

FOR EXAMPLE, IN SEVERAL STUDIES WHERE PEOPLE WATCHED **CAR CRASH VIDEOS...**

AAAAIIIIIEEEEE!!!

...THE PARTICULAR QUESTIONS THEY ANSWERED **IMMEDIATELY AFTER VIEWING...**

...LED THEM TO **REMEMBER DETAILS LATER** THAT **WEREN'T ACTUALLY THERE.**

HOW MANY PEOPLE WERE STANDING ON THE CORNER BY THE **YIELD SIGN?**
Volvo
Crash
Corner
4 People
4
Yield Sign

I REMEMBER **4 PEOPLE** NEAR THE YIELD SIGN.
THERE WAS **NO YIELD SIGN** IN THE VIDEO.

HOW FAST WAS THE CAR GOING WHEN IT **SMASHED** THE OTHER CAR?
Volvo
Corner
Crash
4 People
FAST
Smash

Fast
Broken Glass
Shatter
WHEN THEY **SMASHED**, BROKEN GLASS SHATTERED ALL OVER.
THERE WAS **NO BROKEN GLASS.**

IT SEEMS THAT AS WE ANSWER **LEADING QUESTIONS** LIKE THESE, WE ACTUALLY **INSERT DETAILS INTO OUR MEMORIES...**

SO HOW TALL WAS THIS **PERP** WHO **BATTERED YOU, ICED YOUR FRIEND** AND **STOLE YOUR DOUGH?**

Batter
Dough
Icing
Baker

...WHICH CAN CREATE **TERRIBLE PROBLEMS FOR CRIMINAL JUSTICE.**

IT MUST HAVE BEEN **HIM.**

IN SUM, MEMORY **IS LIKE A GAME OF TELEPHONE.**

A **HEDGEHOG** CRAWLED INTO THE **CAN.**
THE **FARTHER YOU GET FROM THE SOURCE...**
...THE **LESS RELIABLE IT IS.**
A **HOT DOG** FELL INTO THE **JAM?**

WHAT WE REMEMBER **ISN'T LIKE A SNAPSHOT.**

INSTEAD IT'S A **STORY** WE TELL OURSELVES ABOUT WHAT HAPPENED.

IT WAS A **FIGHTER,** SO **STRONG** I COULD **BARELY REEL IT IN.**
AND IT WAS **SO BIG,** IT **FLOPPED OVER THE EDGE OF THE BOAT.**

AND BECAUSE WE **ALTER OUR NEURAL NETWORKS** WHENEVER WE **ACTIVATE THEM...**

...TELLING THE STORY LITERALLY CHANGES OUR MEMORY OF IT.

Ugly
Fighter
My Arms Ached
I Was 6
I Was Scrawny
My First Fish
My Canoe Was Tiny
Mean
Strong
It Was Big
IT WAS AS **STRONG AS ME,** AND **MEAN** AND **UGLY ...**
...AND **SO BIG** IT **WOULDN'T FIT IN THE BOAT.**

I ONCE CAUGHT A FISH **THAT BIG.**
REALLY, I **DID!**

CHAPTER 4
THINKING

THUS FAR, WE'VE LEARNED ABOUT HOW WE MAKE SENSE OF THINGS WE'VE **DIRECTLY EXPERIENCED.**

BUT THE WORLD IS FULL OF **THINGS WE'VE NEVER PREVIOUSLY ENCOUNTERED...**

...AND WE NEED TO **MAKE SENSE OF THOSE TOO.**

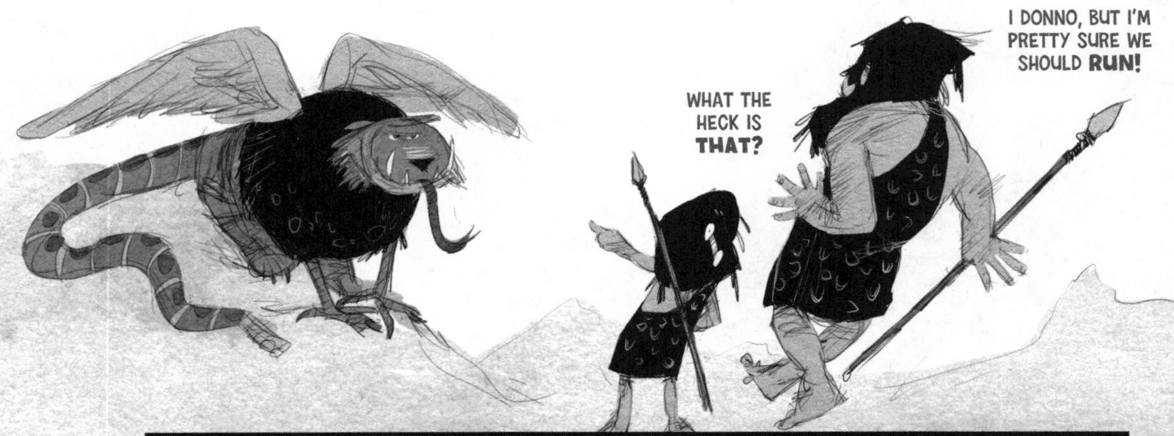
WHAT THE HECK IS THAT?
I DONNO, BUT I'M PRETTY SURE WE SHOULD RUN!

SO IN THIS CHAPTER WE'LL EXPLORE **HOW WE THINK ABOUT THINGS WE'VE NEVER EXPERIENCED.**

HOW DO WE KNOW IT'S **NOT FRIENDLY?**

CATEGORIES!

HEURISTICS!

HYPOTHESIS TESTING!

PROSPECT THEORY!

AS WE'LL SEE, IT'S A **MESSY PROCESS** THAT'S GOVERNED BY **ONE URGENT FACT.**

OUR MENTAL POWER IS **LIMITED.**

RECALL FROM CHAPTER 3 THAT OUR **WORKING MEMORY...**
...IS LIMITED TO **ABOUT 7 ITEMS!**

SO TO GET THE **BIGGEST BANG FOR OUR MENTAL BUCK**, WE'RE ALWAYS TRYING TO **CONSERVE OUR MENTAL RESOURCES.**

WE SAVE ENERGY BY **GROUPING IDEAS EFFECTIVELY...**
...AND **USING COGNITIVE SHORTCUTS...**
...AND SWITCHING FROM INCANDESCENT TO **L.E.D.**

AND THAT PROCESS INFLUENCES **ALL OUR THINKING...**

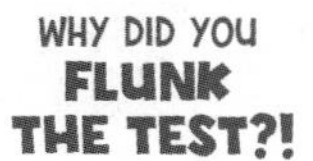
WHY DID YOU **FLUNK THE TEST?!**

...NO MATTER WHAT WE'RE THINKING **ABOUT.**

BECAUSE I'M GOOD AT **CONSERVING MY MENTAL RESOURCES.**

WITH THAT IN MIND, LET'S LEARN ABOUT HOW WE PROCESS **CATEGORIES.**

MANY OF THE THINGS WE ENCOUNTER IN THE WORLD CAN BE **GROUPED TOGETHER** BY THEIR **COMMON FEATURES.**
THINGS THAT LOOK LIKE **THAT...**
...AND **MOO...**
...AND CAN BE **MILKED...**
...ARE **COWS.**
THINGS THAT LOOK LIKE **THAT...**
...AND **GROWL...**
...AND **POUNCE...**
...ARE **SCARY JUNGLE CATS.**
THE RESULTING **MENTAL CATEGORIES** HELP US **PREDICT OTHER FEATURES.**
Milk
Moo
SO, WHEN YOU SEE ONE OF **THOSE**, DON'T TRY TO **MILK IT!**
Growl
Pounce
OF COURSE THERE'S NO GUARANTEE THAT OUR MENTAL CATEGORIES WILL **ALWAYS BE ACCURATE...**
I THOUGHT **CUTE** AND **SOFT** ALSO MEANT **CUDDLY...**
...BUT IT TURNS OUT THOSE THINGS ALSO **BITE.**
...BUT THEY'RE SO **USEFUL**, WE'RE CONSTANTLY **BUILDING AND REFINING THEM.**
Soft
Cute
Mean
Cuddly
SO WHAT MAKES A **GOOD CATEGORY?**

IN GENERAL, CATEGORIES THAT ARE TOO BROAD...
...ARE USELESS.
THAT'S A THING.
OH, AND THAT'S ALSO A THING.
YOU CAN'T SEE THE THINGS FOR THE THING THAT CONTAINS THE THINGS.
AND CATEGORIES THAT ARE TOO NARROW...
...TAKE TOO MUCH EFFORT TO REMEMBER.
THAT'S AN 11-BRANCH, WEST-LEANING, 27,489-LEAF ELONGATED PERENNIAL.
AND THAT'S A 13-BRANCH, EAST-LEANING, 43,843-LEAF GRAFFITI'D WOODY ORGANISM.
YOU CAN'T SEE THE FOREST FOR THE 13-BRANCH, EAST-LEANING, 43,843-LEAF GRAFFITI'D WOODY ORGANISM!
THAT'S WHY, WHEN YOU ASK PEOPLE TO IDENTIFY WHAT'S AROUND THEM...
CAR!
ROCK!
DOG!
NO, RAT!
NO...
...DOG!
...THEY TEND TO CHOOSE DESIGNATIONS THAT FIT THE SWEET SPOT BETWEEN THESE TWO EXTREMES.
TOO BROAD
JUST RIGHT
TOO NARROW
Animal
Dog
Terrier
Vehicle
Car
Ford Speculum
Food
Pasta
Fusilli
Plant
Tree
Hickory
BUT HOW DO OUR MINDS FIGURE THAT OUT?

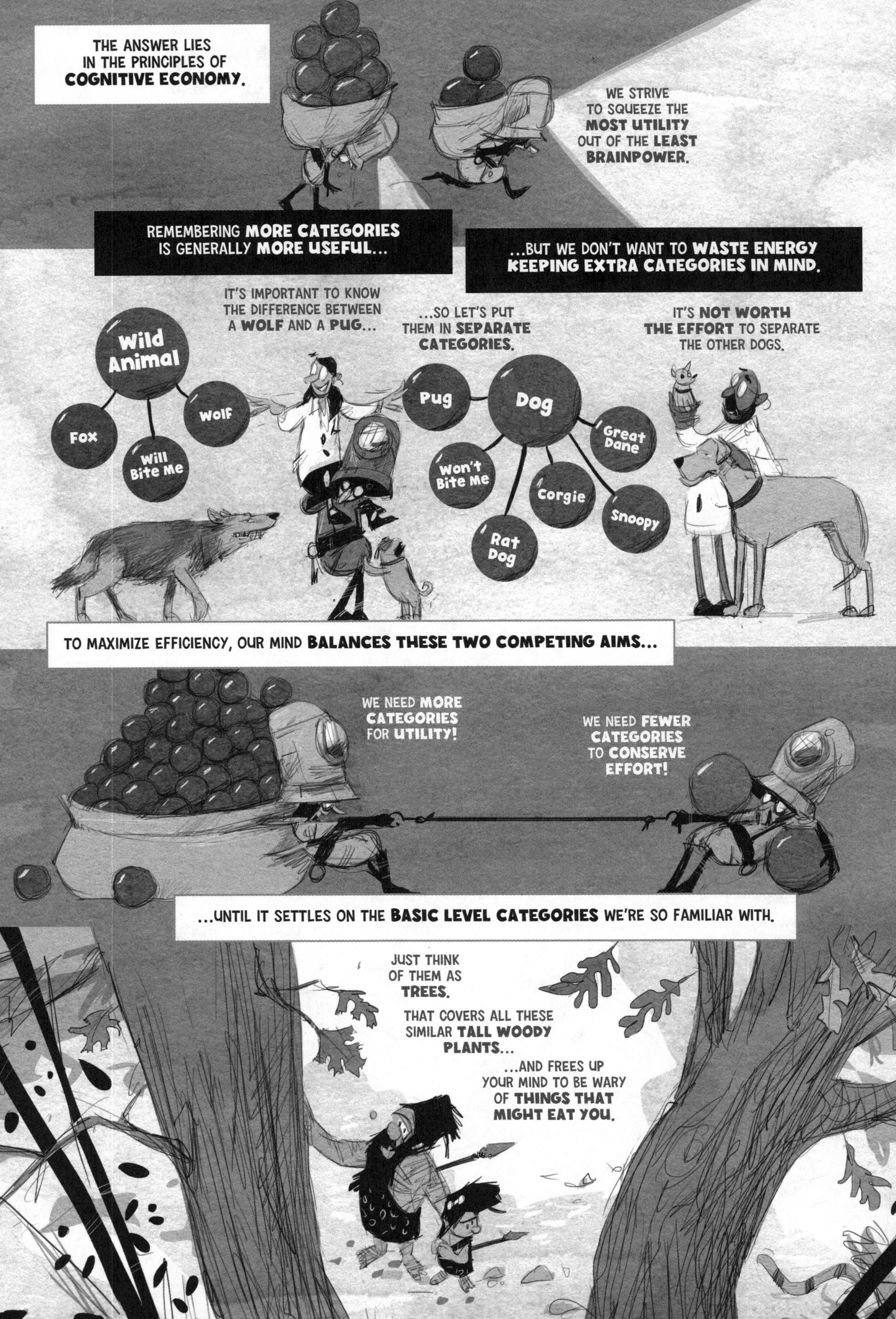
THE ANSWER LIES IN THE PRINCIPLES OF COGNITIVE ECONOMY.
WE STRIVE TO SQUEEZE THE MOST UTILITY OUT OF THE LEAST BRAINPOWER.
REMEMBERING MORE CATEGORIES IS GENERALLY MORE USEFUL...
...BUT WE DON'T WANT TO WASTE ENERGY KEEPING EXTRA CATEGORIES IN MIND.
IT'S IMPORTANT TO KNOW THE DIFFERENCE BETWEEN A WOLF AND A PUG...
...SO LET'S PUT THEM IN SEPARATE CATEGORIES.
IT'S NOT WORTH THE EFFORT TO SEPARATE THE OTHER DOGS.
Wild Animal
Fox
Will Bite Me
Wolf
Pug
Dog
Great Dane
Won't Bite Me
Corgie
Snoopy
Rat Dog
TO MAXIMIZE EFFICIENCY, OUR MIND BALANCES THESE TWO COMPETING AIMS...
WE NEED MORE CATEGORIES FOR UTILITY!
WE NEED FEWER CATEGORIES TO CONSERVE EFFORT!
...UNTIL IT SETTLES ON THE BASIC LEVEL CATEGORIES WE'RE SO FAMILIAR WITH.
JUST THINK OF THEM AS TREES.
THAT COVERS ALL THESE SIMILAR TALL WOODY PLANTS...
...AND FREES UP YOUR MIND TO BE WARY OF THINGS THAT MIGHT EAT YOU.

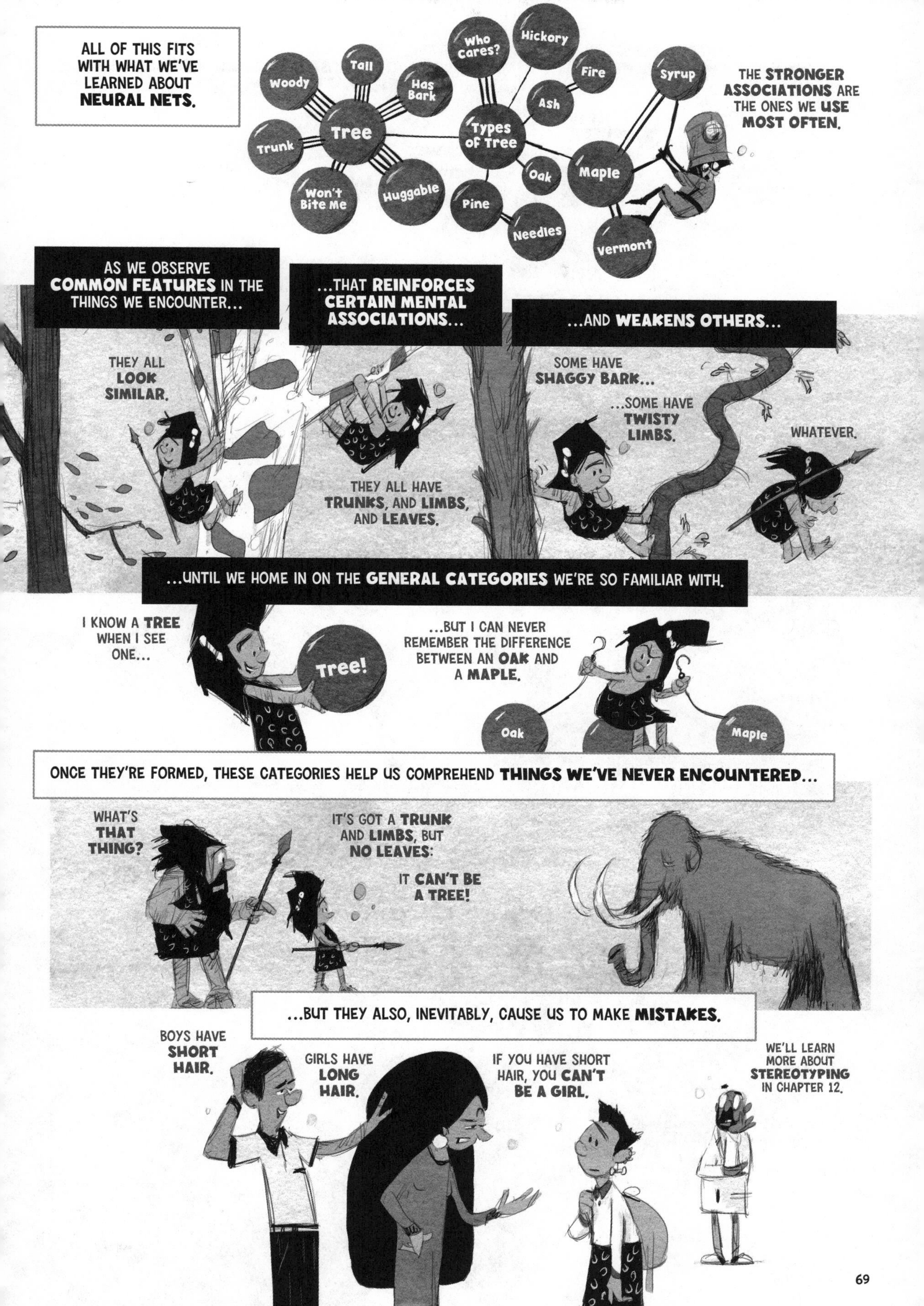

ALL OF THIS FITS WITH WHAT WE'VE LEARNED ABOUT **NEURAL NETS.**

Woody
Tall
Has Bark
Tree
Trunk
Won't Bite Me
Huggable
Who cares?
Hickory
Fire
Ash
Types of Tree
Oak
Pine
Needles
Syrup
Maple
Vermont

THE **STRONGER ASSOCIATIONS** ARE THE ONES WE **USE MOST OFTEN.**

AS WE OBSERVE **COMMON FEATURES** IN THE THINGS WE ENCOUNTER...

THEY ALL LOOK SIMILAR.

...THAT **REINFORCES CERTAIN MENTAL ASSOCIATIONS...**

THEY ALL HAVE TRUNKS, AND LIMBS, AND LEAVES.

...AND **WEAKENS OTHERS...**

SOME HAVE SHAGGY BARK...
...SOME HAVE TWISTY LIMBS.
WHATEVER.

...UNTIL WE HOME IN ON THE **GENERAL CATEGORIES** WE'RE SO FAMILIAR WITH.

I KNOW A TREE WHEN I SEE ONE...
Tree!
...BUT I CAN NEVER REMEMBER THE DIFFERENCE BETWEEN AN OAK AND A MAPLE.
Oak
Maple

ONCE THEY'RE FORMED, THESE CATEGORIES HELP US COMPREHEND **THINGS WE'VE NEVER ENCOUNTERED...**

WHAT'S THAT THING?
IT'S GOT A TRUNK AND LIMBS, BUT NO LEAVES:
IT CAN'T BE A TREE!

...BUT THEY ALSO, INEVITABLY, CAUSE US TO MAKE **MISTAKES.**

BOYS HAVE SHORT HAIR.
GIRLS HAVE LONG HAIR.
IF YOU HAVE SHORT HAIR, YOU CAN'T BE A GIRL.
WE'LL LEARN MORE ABOUT STEREOTYPING IN CHAPTER 12.

AS WE MAKE SENSE OF THE WORLD, WE OFTEN **TAKE WHAT WE KNOW**...

...AND USE IT TO MAKE **ESTIMATES AND PREDICTIONS ABOUT WHAT WE DON'T KNOW.**

I LIKE CHEESE...
...AND I LIKE MACARONI.
BUT WILL I LIKE MACARONI AND CHEESE?

IDEALLY, WE'D DO THIS LIKE A **SUPER COMPUTER**...

...PROCESSING **ALL** THE **AVAILABLE INFORMATION** TO MAKE **OPTIMAL DECISIONS.**

I AM **RATIONAL MAN!**

IF I MULTIPLY THE **PRICE** BY THE **INVERSE SQUARE OF THE YELP REVIEW** PLUS THE **LOG OF THE UMAMI INDEX** AND GET A VALUE **GREATER THAN 47**...

...IT'S THE **RIGHT DECISION.**

BUT IN REALITY, WE OFTEN HAVE TO DEAL WITH **MORE INFORMATION THAN WE CAN PROCESS**...

...AND WE RESPOND BY USING IMPERFECT **MENTAL SHORTCUTS**...

THIS **MENU IS OVERWHELMING!**

YOU CAN **REDUCE THE AMOUNT OF INFORMATION** YOU CONSIDER...

...OR **REDUCE THE AMOUNT OF THINKING** YOU DO ABOUT IT.

...CALLED **HEURISTICS.**

CRUCIALLY, WHILE THESE HEURISTICS **SAVE US MENTAL ENERGY...**

...THEY CAN ALSO **BIAS OUR JUDGMENT.**

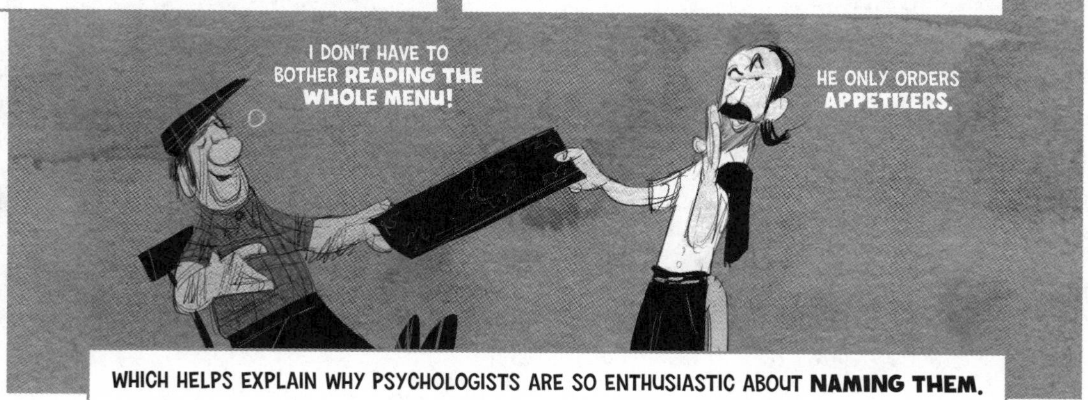
I DON'T HAVE TO BOTHER READING THE WHOLE MENU!
HE ONLY ORDERS APPETIZERS.

WHICH HELPS EXPLAIN WHY PSYCHOLOGISTS ARE SO ENTHUSIASTIC ABOUT **NAMING THEM.**

AUDIENCE RESPONSE HEURISTIC, BRAND NAME HEURISTIC, CONSENSUS HEURISTIC, COUNTRY OF ORIGIN HEURISTIC, DISTINCTIVENESS HEURISTIC, DOMRAN HEURISTIC, DO NO HARM HEURISTIC, EFFORT HEURISTIC, ENDORSEMENT HEURISTIC, EQUAL WEIGHTING HEURISTIC, EXPERTISE HEURISTIC, LEXICOGRAPHIC HEURISTIC, LIKEABILITY HEURISTIC, MINIMALIST HEURISTIC, OUTRAGE HEURISTIC, PEAK END HEURISTIC, PRICE HEURISTIC, PRIORITY HEURISTIC, QUICK-EST HEURISTIC, SCARCITY HEURISTIC, TAKE THE BEST HEURISTIC, WARM GLOW HEURISTIC, WEIGHTED PROS HEURISTIC...

LET'S CALL IT THE **NAMING HEURISTICS HEURISTIC!**

ONE OF THE MOST PROMINENT IS **THE AVAILABILITY HEURISTIC:**

WE TEND TO THINK PARTICULAR EVENTS ARE **MORE LIKELY...**

OF COURSE I WON'T **GO IN THE OCEAN!**

...JUST BECAUSE THEY'RE EASY TO CALL TO MIND.

HAVEN'T YOU SEEN **JAWS?**

OR **SHARKNADO?**

AS A RESULT, WE TEND TO MAKE OUR DECISIONS **BASED ON SUBOPTIMAL INFORMATION.**

ACTUALLY, EACH YEAR VENDING MACHINES KILL MORE PEOPLE THAN SHARKS.
WOAH!
I GUESS THEY SHOULD MAKE ONE CALLED SNACKNADO.

ANOTHER MENTAL SHORTCUT IS **THE ANCHORING HEURISTIC:**

HOW LONG WILL WE BE STUCK IN THIS PORT, CAPTAIN?

I DONNO, **99 DAYS?**

Anchor Sale: $99.99

WHEN WE NEED TO **ESTIMATE A VALUE...**

...WE TEND TO **ANCHOR THAT ESTIMATE** NEAR WHATEVER **OTHER NUMBERS WE'VE JUST HEARD ABOUT...**

HOW MUCH WOULD YOU PAY FOR THIS CAR?
I DONNO, **$30,000?**
THE SALESMAN SAID **$33,000**, AND HE COULDN'T HAVE BEEN FAR OFF.

...EVEN WHEN THOSE NUMBERS ARE **TOTALLY IRRELEVANT** TO THE JUDGMENT WE'RE MAKING.

I WEIGH **98 POUNDS.** HOW **OLD** DO YOU THINK I AM?
I DONNO, **SEVENTY?**

I WEIGH **7 STONES.** HOW **OLD** DO YOU THINK I AM?
I DONNO, **TWENTY-FIVE?**

AGAIN, THIS **SAVES MENTAL ENERGY...**

...BUT CREATES PROBLEMS WHEN WE USE ANCHORS THAT ARE **WRONG.**

WHAT SHOULD WE **PAY** FOR THIS WINE.
HMMM, IT'S A **VINTAGE CABERNET FROM BORDEAUX...**
...LET'S JUST SAY **$99.**
99

THAT WINE IS **CHEAP!**
I'M **THIRTY-SEVEN!**
AND YOU CAN GET ONE OF THESE FOR ONLY **$20,000!**

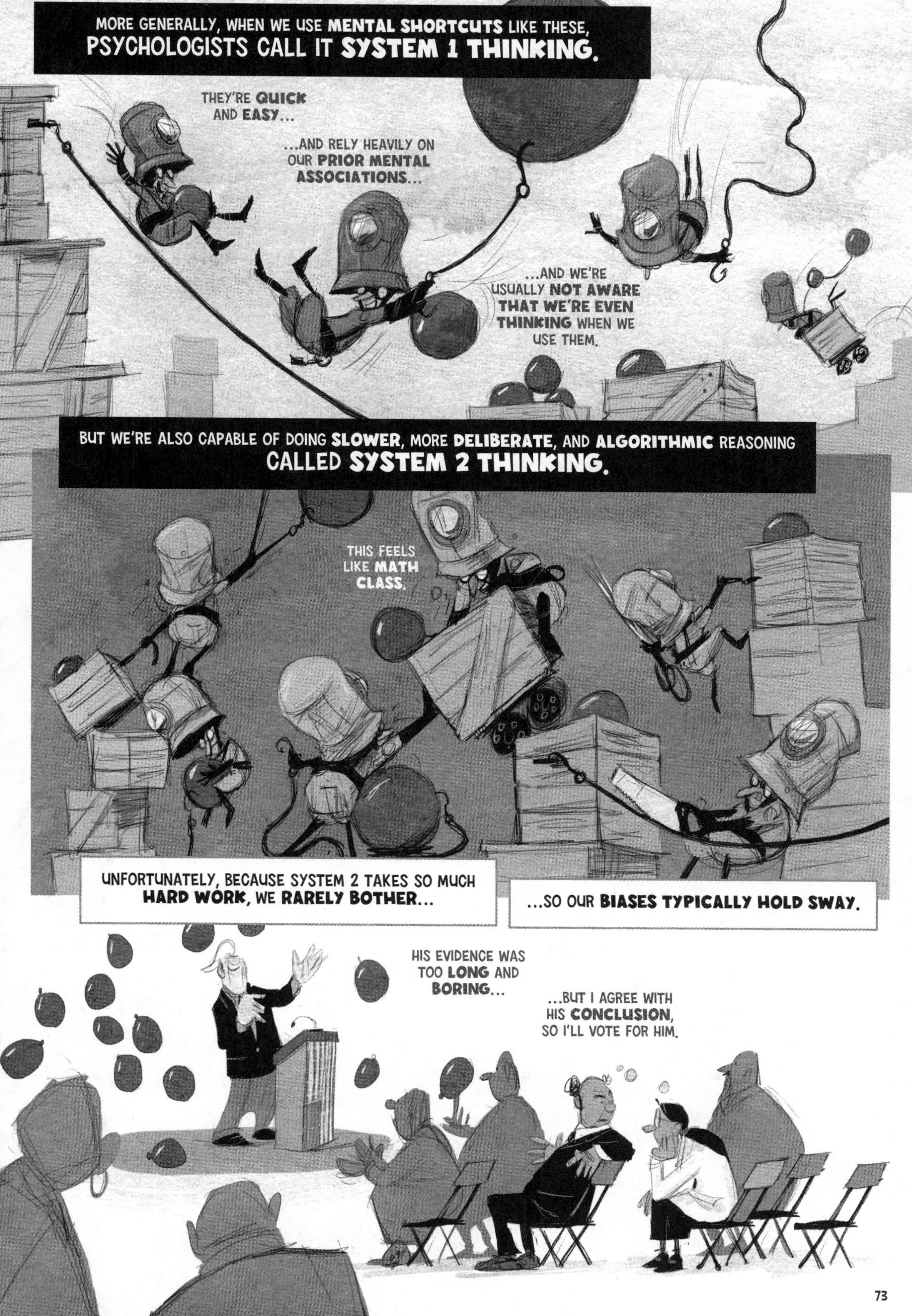
MORE GENERALLY, WHEN WE USE MENTAL SHORTCUTS LIKE THESE, PSYCHOLOGISTS CALL IT SYSTEM 1 THINKING.
THEY'RE QUICK AND EASY...
...AND RELY HEAVILY ON OUR PRIOR MENTAL ASSOCIATIONS...
...AND WE'RE USUALLY NOT AWARE THAT WE'RE EVEN THINKING WHEN WE USE THEM.
BUT WE'RE ALSO CAPABLE OF DOING SLOWER, MORE DELIBERATE, AND ALGORITHMIC REASONING CALLED SYSTEM 2 THINKING.
THIS FEELS LIKE MATH CLASS.
UNFORTUNATELY, BECAUSE SYSTEM 2 TAKES SO MUCH HARD WORK, WE RARELY BOTHER...
...SO OUR BIASES TYPICALLY HOLD SWAY.
HIS EVIDENCE WAS TOO LONG AND BORING...
...BUT I AGREE WITH HIS CONCLUSION, SO I'LL VOTE FOR HIM.

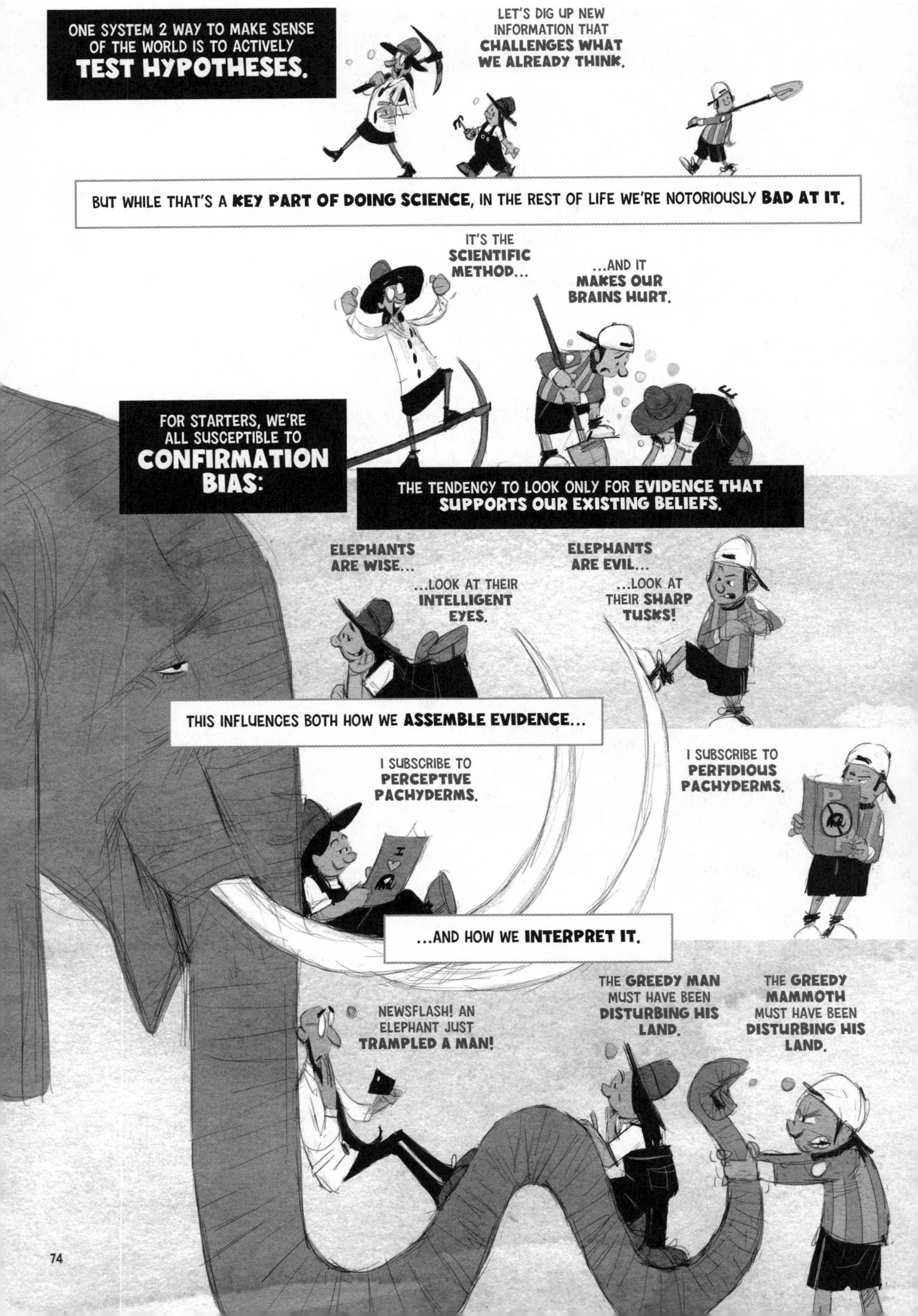

ONE SYSTEM 2 WAY TO MAKE SENSE OF THE WORLD IS TO ACTIVELY **TEST HYPOTHESES.**

LET'S DIG UP NEW INFORMATION THAT **CHALLENGES WHAT WE ALREADY THINK.**

BUT WHILE THAT'S A **KEY PART OF DOING SCIENCE**, IN THE REST OF LIFE WE'RE NOTORIOUSLY **BAD AT IT.**

IT'S THE **SCIENTIFIC METHOD...**

...AND IT **MAKES OUR BRAINS HURT.**

FOR STARTERS, WE'RE ALL SUSCEPTIBLE TO **CONFIRMATION BIAS:**

THE TENDENCY TO LOOK ONLY FOR **EVIDENCE THAT SUPPORTS OUR EXISTING BELIEFS.**

ELEPHANTS ARE WISE...

...LOOK AT THEIR **INTELLIGENT EYES.**

ELEPHANTS ARE EVIL...

...LOOK AT THEIR **SHARP TUSKS!**

THIS INFLUENCES BOTH HOW WE **ASSEMBLE EVIDENCE...**

I SUBSCRIBE TO **PERCEPTIVE PACHYDERMS.**

I SUBSCRIBE TO **PERFIDIOUS PACHYDERMS.**

...AND HOW WE **INTERPRET IT.**

NEWSFLASH! AN ELEPHANT JUST **TRAMPLED A MAN!**

THE **GREEDY MAN** MUST HAVE BEEN **DISTURBING HIS LAND.**

THE **GREEDY MAMMOTH** MUST HAVE BEEN **DISTURBING HIS LAND.**

WE CAN SEE THIS IN STUDIES SHOWING HOW **THE WAY WE RECALL SPORTING EVENTS...**

IT'S THE **TIGERS** VS **THE BIG GREEN.**

...AND **POLITICAL DEBATES...**

IT'S THE **ELEPHANTS** VS **THE DONKEYS.**

...DEPENDS ON **WHICH SIDE WE WERE ROOTING FOR.**

THEY CHEATED!

WE WON!

IN OTHER WORDS, BECAUSE OUR **CONVICTIONS** TEND TO **FIT WITH OUR EXPERIENCE...**

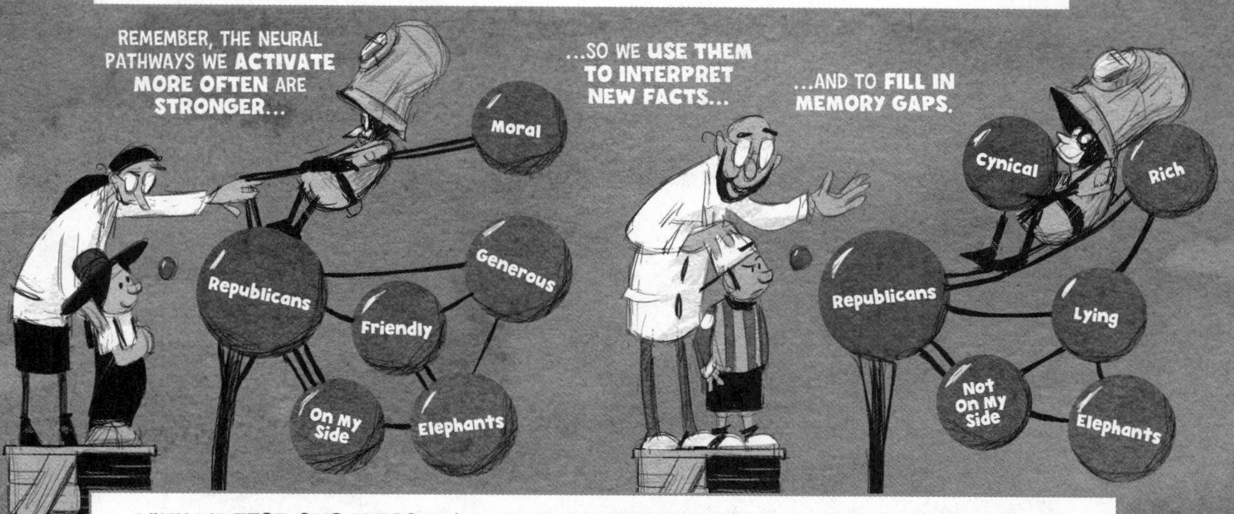
REMEMBER, THE NEURAL PATHWAYS WE **ACTIVATE MORE OFTEN** ARE **STRONGER...**
Moral
Republicans
Generous
Friendly
On My Side
Elephants
...SO WE **USE THEM TO INTERPRET NEW FACTS...**
...AND TO **FILL IN MEMORY GAPS.**
Cynical
Rich
Republicans
Lying
Not On My Side
Elephants

...WHEN WE **TEST OUR IDEAS** WE'RE OFTEN JUST **CONFIRMING WHAT WE ALREADY BELIEVE.**

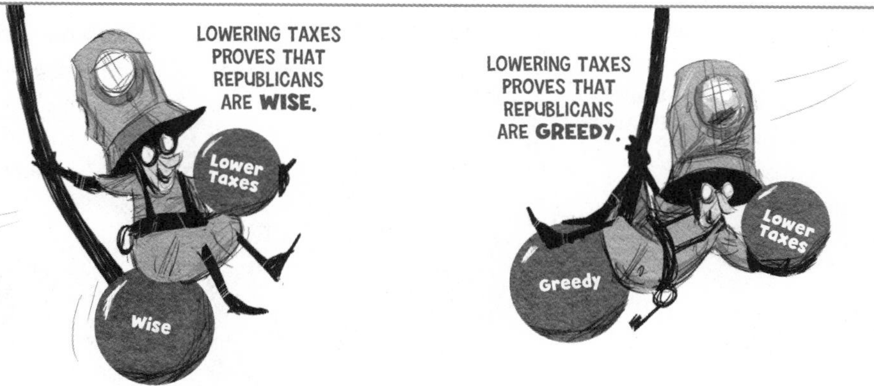
LOWERING TAXES PROVES THAT REPUBLICANS ARE **WISE.**
Lower Taxes
Wise
LOWERING TAXES PROVES THAT REPUBLICANS ARE **GREEDY.**
Greedy
Lower Taxes

FINALLY, OTHER BIASES INFLUENCE US WHEN WE **EVALUATE RISK.**

IT'S **PROSPECT THEORY...**

...BECAUSE IT'S ABOUT HOW WE EVALUATE OUR **PROSPECTS.**

FOR STARTERS, WE TEND TO BE **POOR JUDGES OF PROBABILITY:**

SHE'S A **SURE THING!**
EXCEPT IF YOU **CALCULATE THE ODDS.**

WE **OVERESTIMATE UNLIKELY EVENTS...**

THE CHANCES OF DEATH BY **SHARK** ARE ONLY **1 IN 250 MILLION.**
I'M **NOT** GETTING IN THE WATER!

...AND **UNDERESTIMATE LIKELY EVENTS.**

THERE'S A **98% CHANCE** OF **ANOTHER HURRICANE!**
I'LL **REBUILD HERE ANYWAY.**

BUT ON TOP OF THAT, THE WAY WE EVALUATE REWARDS AND LOSSES **SHIFTS DEPENDING ON THE CONTEXT...**

FINDING $100 **FEELS REALLY GOOD...**
LOSING $100 **FEELS REALLY BAD...**
...BUT WHO CARES ABOUT $100 **IF I JUST WON THE LOTTERY?**
...BUT WHO CARES ABOUT $100 **IF I JUST LOST MY SHIRT?**

...AND THIS IMPACTS OTHER ELEMENTS OF OUR **ECONOMIC DECISION MAKING.**

WE'RE MORE LIKELY TO **GO OUT OF OUR WAY...**
...TO SAVE **$20** ON A **$50 TOASTER...**
...THAN TO SAVE **$20** ON A **$20,000 CAR.**

EVEN THOUGH IN BOTH CASES YOU SAVE **$20.**

EVEN MORE STRIKING IS HOW MUCH WE **HATE LOSING.**

WHATEVER HAPPENS, I DON'T WANNA LOSE.

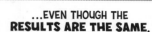

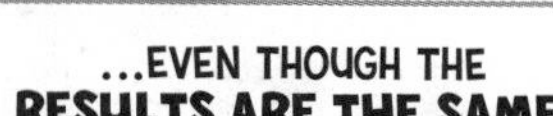
THAT'S LOSS AVERSION!

IT TURNS OUT THAT MOST OF US WOULD STRONGLY PREFER **THIS**...

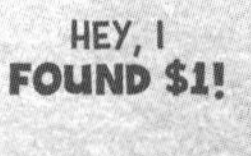
HEY, I FOUND $1!

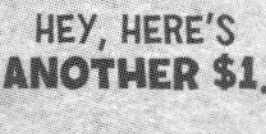
HEY, HERE'S ANOTHER $1.

...TO **THIS**...

HEY, I FOUND $3!

CRAP, I LOST $1.

...EVEN THOUGH THE **RESULTS ARE THE SAME.**

EITHER WAY YOU END UP WITH $2.

AND BECAUSE OUR **DESIRE TO AVOID LOSING IS SO STRONG**...

I WON $10 AT BLACKJACK...
...THEN I LOST A $10 BILL...
...AND I FEEL WORSE THAN BEFORE IT ALL STARTED.

...OUR DECISIONS ABOUT RISK ARE HEAVILY INFLUENCED BY **HOW THEY'RE FRAMED.**

WE'RE MORE LIKELY TO TAKE **A BET FRAMED BY LOSS**...

HERE'S $50.
DO YOU WANNA LOSE HALF OF IT, OR FLIP A COIN FOR ALL OR NOTHING?
I DON'T WANNA LOSE, I'LL TAKE THE BET.

...THAN **ONE FRAMED BY GAIN**...

HERE'S $50.
DO YOU WANNA KEEP HALF OF IT, OR FLIP A COIN FOR ALL OR NOTHING?
I WANNA BE SAFE, I'LL KEEP THE $25.

...EVEN THOUGH THE **ODDS ARE THE SAME.**

EITHER WAY YOU KEEP $25 OR FLIP A COIN FOR $50 OR NOTHING?

AND THIS **FRAMING EFFECT** HAS CONSEQUENCES **OUTSIDE OF CASINOS.**

THE REGION IS FLOODED WITH REFUGEES AND WE CAN PROBABLY SAVE SOME OF THEM.

HOW DO YOU WANT US TO FRAME OUR OPTIONS, MR. PRESIDENT?

IN SUM, NO MATTER WHAT WE'RE **THINKING** ABOUT, **WE'RE USUALLY USING MENTAL SHORTCUTS.**

AND WHILE THESE SHORTCUTS HELP US **CONSERVE MENTAL ENERGY**, THEY CAN ALSO **LEAD US ASTRAY.**

IT'S **EASIEST** TO **ALWAYS TURN RIGHT.**

BUT IF YOU DO THAT, YOU'LL **NEVER GET OUT OF HERE!**

AS WE'LL SEE NEXT, THIS DRIVE FOR COGNITIVE EFFICIENCY ALSO AFFECTS HOW WE THINK ABOUT **OURSELVES.**

YOU'RE A COGNITIVE MISER.
I KNOW YOU ARE, BUT WHAT AM I?

PART TWO

MAKING SENSE OF OURSELVES

CHAPTER 5
METACOGNITION

HOW DO YOU KNOW...
...YOU KNOW...
...WHAT YOU KNOW?
AND HOW DO YOU KNOW...
...WHAT YOU DON'T KNOW?

NOT ONLY DO WE **THINK.**

WE ALSO **THINK ABOUT THINKING.**

I JUST HAD A THOUGHT!

THAT'S METACOGNITION.

BUT **HOW GOOD ARE WE AT IT?**

WHAT DO I KNOW?
THAT'S METAKNOWLEDGE.

WHAT WILL I REMEMBER?
THAT'S METAMEMORY.

IN THIS CHAPTER WE'LL EXAMINE **OUR SELF ASSESSMENTS...**

...AND GAUGE **HOW RELIABLE THEY ARE.**

I THINK THEREFORE I AM.
BUT THAT DOESN'T MAKE YOU DEPENDABLE.

YOU'RE NOT TOO BAD AT REMEMBERING WHAT YOU USED TO KNOW.
BUT YOU'RE TERRIBLE AT REMEMBERING WHAT YOU USED TO NOT KNOW!

ALTHOUGH WE HAVE A **PRETTY ACCURATE GENERAL SENSE** OF WHAT WE KNOW...

THE CATEGORIES ARE **BOTANY**...
...**QUANTUM PHYSICS**...
...AND **BASEBALL**.
I'LL TAKE THE **LAST ONE**.

...WE HAVE SOME **SYSTEMATIC BIASES**, MANY OF WHICH HAVE TO DO WITH BEING **OVERCONFIDENT**.

I'VE TOTALLY **GOT THIS!**

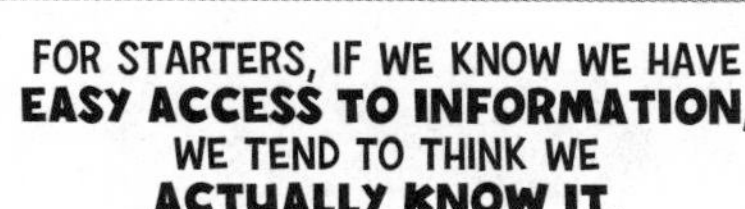

FOR STARTERS, IF WE KNOW WE HAVE **EASY ACCESS TO INFORMATION**, WE TEND TO THINK WE **ACTUALLY KNOW IT**.

HOW DID BASEBALL LEGEND **OIL CAN BOYD** GET HIS NAME?

I KNOW THAT!
JUST LEMME **GOOGLE THE ANSWER**.

WHICH MEANS WE MISTAKE THE FEELING OF **"I CAN GET IT NOW"**...

...FOR **"I HAVE IT IN MY BRAIN."**

I'M THE **SMARTEST KID IN SCHOOL**.

LET'S SEE HOW SMART YOU ARE **WITHOUT YOUR BOOKS**.

AND THERE'S **MORE...**

WE ALSO TEND TO **OVERESTIMATE HOW DEEPLY WE UNDERSTAND THINGS.**

IT'S THE **ILLUSION OF EXPLANATORY DEPTH!**

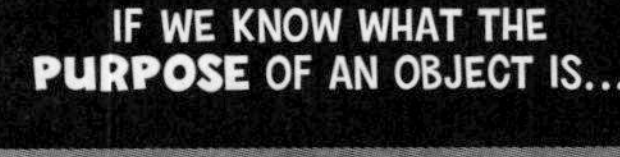

IF WE KNOW WHAT THE **PURPOSE** OF AN OBJECT IS...

IT **COOLS THE AIR, DUH!**

...AND WE KNOW WHAT THE **PARTS** ARE...

IT'S A **BOX** WITH **WIRES** AND A **FAN.**

...WE TEND TO THINK WE **UNDERSTAND IT...**

OF COURSE I UNDERSTAND HOW AN **AIR CONDITIONER WORKS!**

...AT LEAST UNTIL YOU ASK US TO **PROVE IT.**

CAN YOU **DRAW ONE FOR ME?**
YEAH, WHATEVER.

HERE'S WHERE THE AIR GOES IN. THEN IT GETS **COOLED DOWN SOMEHOW IN THERE,** AND...

...UM...

IN OTHER WORDS, IF WE HAVE **SURFACE KNOWLEDGE...**

...WE **ALSO** TEND TO THINK **WE HAVE A COMPLEX UNDERSTANDING...**

OF COURSE I UNDERSTAND **POLITICS...**
...I VOTE.

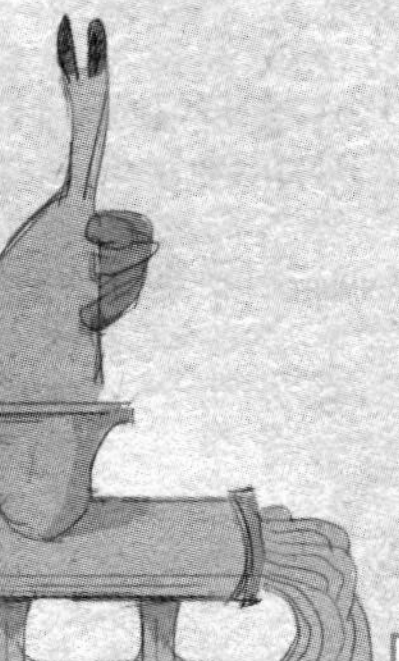

IT'S JUST LIKE **MAKING SAUSAGE.**

I NOMINATE **ME** FOR PRESIDENT!

...AND THAT RELATES TO AN EVEN **MORE STARTLING BIAS.**

WE TEND TO BE **SYSTEMATICALLY OVERCONFIDENT** ABOUT **OUR KNOWLEDGE.**

I'M SURE I GOT 9 OUT OF 10.
ACTUALLY YOU GOT 7 OUT OF 10.

THIS HAS BEEN BORNE OUT IN **STUDY AFTER STUDY**:

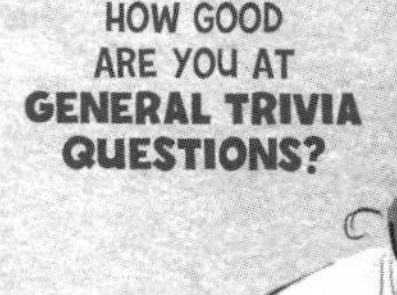

HOW GOOD ARE YOU AT GENERAL TRIVIA QUESTIONS?

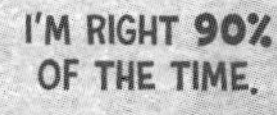

I'M RIGHT 90% OF THE TIME.

ACTUALLY, IT'S MORE LIKE 70%.
WHAT A COINCIDENCE, THAT'S HOW OFTEN I'M RIGHT!
ACTUALLY, YOU AVERAGE ABOUT 50%.

ASK US TO **RATE OUR KNOWLEDGE OF COMMON SUBJECTS...**

...AND OUR **CONFIDENCE USUALLY EXCEEDS OUR ACCURACY.**

HOW ABOUT SPELLING?
90% CORRECT!
80%
70% CORRECT?
60%

SIMILAR BIASES INFLUENCE ALL SORTS OF JUDGMENTS, **FROM HOW WE RATE OUR OWN INFLUENCE OVER EVENTS...**

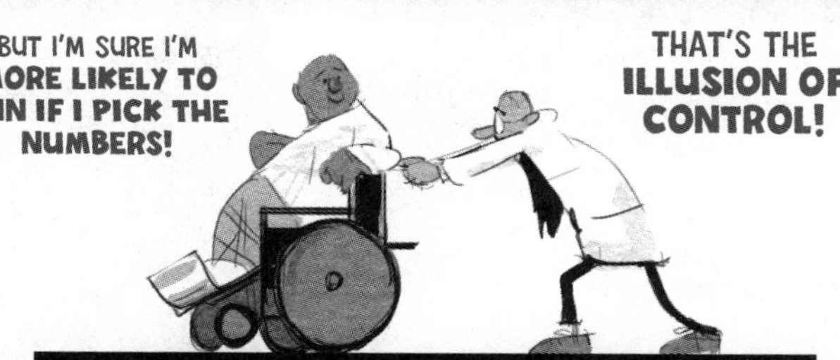

NOT THAT I'VE ACTUALLY EVER WON THE LOTTERY.
BUT I'M SURE I'M MORE LIKELY TO WIN IF I PICK THE NUMBERS!
THAT'S THE ILLUSION OF CONTROL!

...TO HOW **POORLY WE ALLOCATE OUR TIME.**

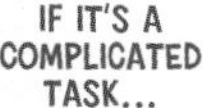

I'M SURE I CAN FINISH THIS IN AN HOUR.
NO CHANCE.
THAT'S THE PLANNING FALLACY!

IF IT'S A COMPLICATED TASK...

...WE ALL TEND TO **THINK** WE'RE GOING TO **FINISH IT SOONER THAN WE ACTUALLY DO.**

I WISH I HAD KNOWN THAT 4 HOURS AGO!

ON THE BOTTOM END OF THE SPECTRUM, **THE PEOPLE WHO KNOW THE LEAST** TEND TO BE THE **LEAST AWARE** OF HOW LITTLE THEY KNOW.

ACTUALLY YOU FAILED.

I'M SURE I GOT 'EM ALL RIGHT.

THIS COMBINATION HAS BEEN OBSERVED IN A **WIDE ARRAY OF STUDIES**...

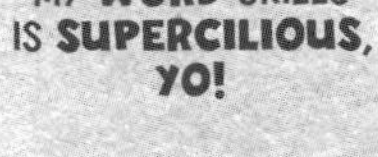

MY WORD SKILLS IS SUPERCILIOUS, YO!
I'M SO FUNNY I'M A PUN-DIT!

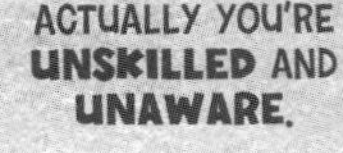

I'M SKILLED AND AWARE.
ACTUALLY YOU'RE UNSKILLED AND UNAWARE.
IT'S THE DUNNING-KRUGER EFFECT!

...THAT WERE INSPIRED BY A REAL WORLD EXAMPLE OF **STAGGERING INCOMPETENCE.**

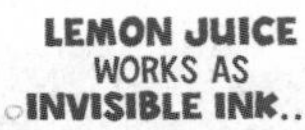

LEMON JUICE WORKS AS INVISIBLE INK...
...SO I RUBBED IT ON MY FACE WHILE I ROBBED TWO BANKS.

IN A WAY, IT'S A **MARRIAGE** THAT **MAKES PERFECT SENSE**...

IF YOU HAVE LOUSY METACOGNITION YOU DON'T REALIZE YOU NEED TO IMPROVE YOUR COGNITION.

...BUT IT SHOULD SERVE AS A WARNING FOR THOSE OF US WHO **AREN'T QUITE SO INEPT.**

THE FEELING THAT YOU KNOW SOMETHING...
...FEELS EXACTLY THE SAME WHETHER YOU'RE RIGHT OR WRONG.

ALMOST EVERYBODY RATES THEIR OWN ABILITIES AS **ABOVE AVERAGE...**

...WHICH MEANS SOME PORTION OF US **MUST BE WRONG.**

I'M BETTER THAN AVERAGE AT **POKER.**
YOUR **BANK ACCOUNT** DOESN'T AGREE WITH YOU.

IT SEEMS THAT WHEN ASKED TO EVALUATE OURSELVES IN **COMPARISON WITH OTHER PEOPLE...**

...WE **FORGET ABOUT THE OTHER PEOPLE.**

I'M **GOOD AT THIS!**
I'LL RANK MYSELF AS **HIGH.**

SO, IF A TASK **FEELS EASY**, WE TEND TO THINK WE'RE **ABOVE AVERAGE** AT IT...

I'M A **BETTER DRIVER** THAN MOST PEOPLE...
...ESPECIALLY WITH **POWER STEERING.**

...BUT IF A TASK **FEELS HARD**, WE TEND TO THINK WE'RE **BELOW AVERAGE** AT IT.

I'M A **WORSE JUGGLER** THAN MOST PEOPLE...

...ESPECIALLY WHILE **PLAYING CHESS.**

WHICH BRINGS US TO THE SUBJECT OF **FLUENCY.**

IT TURNS OUT THAT WHEN WE FIND INFORMATION **QUICK AND EASY TO PERCEIVE AND PROCESS...**

...WE TEND TO **TRUST IT MORE.**

THIS NEW BRIDGE IS **SHAPED LIKE A SWOOPING SWAN.**

WANNA **STEP ON IT?**

OK!

BUT IF IT TAKES **MORE COGNITIVE WORK...**

...WE TEND TO **FEEL MORE SUSPICIOUS ABOUT IT.**

THIS NEW **CANTILEVER** WAS **CAST** WITH A **CALIPER** TO **CALIBRATE** THE **COEFFICIENT** OF **CONTRACTION.**

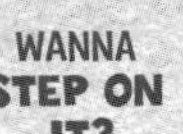
WANNA
STEP ON IT?

UM, I DONNO.

THIS BIAS TOWARD **COGNITIVE FLUENCY** IMPACTS A **HUGE NUMBER OF OUR DECISIONS...**

...ABOUT **POLITICS...**

THAT **LOUDMOUTH WON AGAIN!?**

HE'S **EASIER TO HEAR.**

...AND **FINANCE...**

A STOCK CALLED **POC** WILL START STRONGER THAN ONE CALLED **XKF.**

...AND **PHARMACEUTICALS...**

DON'T CALL IT **XGLYPHUNSCHIOX®...**

...CALL IT **EXPLODIUM.®**

...BUT IT MAY HAVE ORIGINALLY EVOLVED TO **HELP US SURVIVE.**

IF HE **FAMILIAR...**

...NO NEED WASTE ENERGY CHASING HIM OUT OF CAVE.

COGNITIVE FLUENCY CAN BE INCREASED BY SIMPLE **REPETITION.**

WHEN WE PROCESS ASSOCIATIONS **MORE OFTEN**...
...THEY BECOME **EASIER TO PROCESS.**
Idea #1
Idea #2
THAT'S WHY **ADVERTISERS REPEAT THEIR MESSAGES SO OFTEN.**
I USED TO HATE THIS JINGLE BUT **NOW I LOVE IT.**
MOUNTAIN SPRING MUD® IS SO **AWESOME**...
MOUNTAIN SPRING MUD® IS SO **GREAT**...
SMEAR IT ALL OVER YOUR BODY...
...AND **SMOOTH** ALL YOUR WRINKLES AWAY.
MOUNTAIN SPRING MUD®!

MORE INSIDIOUSLY, FLUENCY CAN EVEN BE INCREASED BY **REPEATED NEGATION.**
MY LOUDMOUTH OPPONENT IS **NOT** SMART...
...**NOT** INFORMED...
...**NOT** PATRIOTIC.
Smart
Loudmouth
Loud
Informed
Patriotic
HMMMM.
IN OTHER WORDS, HEARING OFTEN THAT SOMETHING IS **FALSE**...
...CAN MAKE YOU **FEEL THAT IT'S TRUE.**

STUDIES SHOW, MOUNTAIN SPRING MUD® **DOESN'T REDUCE WRINKLES!**
GIMME SUMMA THAT MOUNTAIN SPRING MUD®...
...I WANNA **REDUCE MY WRINKLES.**

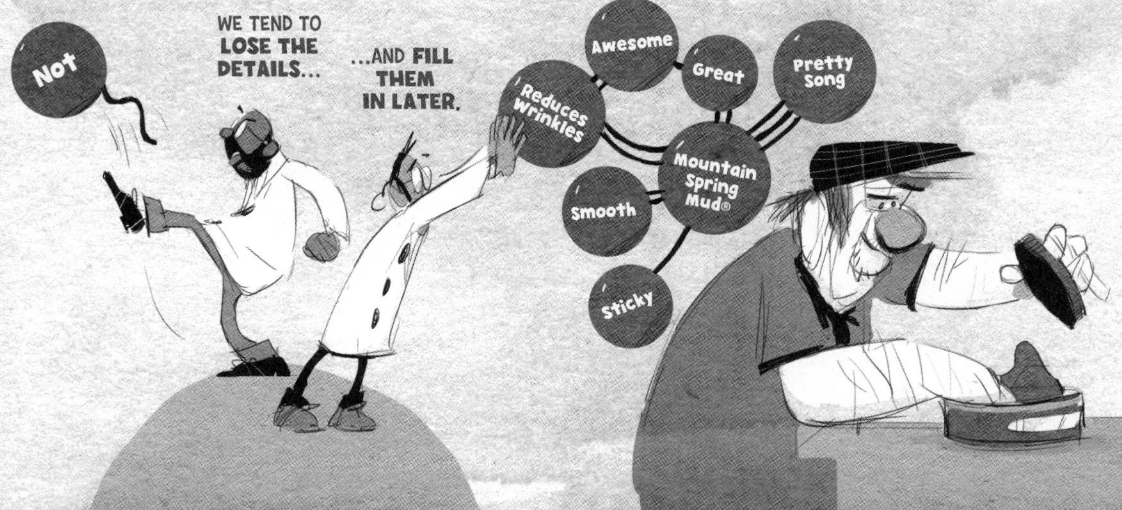
IT'S SHOCKING, BUT IT FITS WITH WHAT WE KNOW ABOUT OUR **NEURAL NETWORKS.**
Not
WE TEND TO **LOSE THE DETAILS**...
...AND **FILL THEM IN LATER.**
Awesome
Great
Pretty Song
Reduces Wrinkles
Mountain Spring Mud®
Smooth
Sticky

ONCE AGAIN, WE'VE SEEN HOW OUR **STRONGER MENTAL ASSOCIATIONS...**

...WHEN GIVEN A BIT OF **TIME...**

AAAHHH!

Dog
Bite
'Pain
DON'T FRET, KIDDO. NOT ALL DOGS BITE.

...CAN **CROWD OUT THE WEAKER ONES.**

NOT ALL DOGS BITE.
NOT ALL DOGS BITE.
NOT ALL DOGS BITE.
NOT ALL DOGS BITE.

RIGHT.

AAAHHH!

BUT HOW GOOD ARE WE AT **ANTICIPATING** THIS SORT OF THING?

HOW WILL **TIME** AFFECT MY MEMORY, GRAMPA?

IT AIN'T PRETTY, LITTLE GIRL.

IN THIS CASE, ALTHOUGH WE DO HAVE A DECENT **GENERAL SENSE** OF **WHAT WE'LL REMEMBER...**

I DON'T NEED TO WRITE DOWN YOUR ORDER.
OK, GIMME A HAMBURGER.

...WE'RE LIMITED BY THE FACT THAT WE'RE **NO GOOD AT TAKING UNPREDICTABLE EVENTS INTO ACCOUNT.**

WHY'D YOU BRING ME FISH SOUP?
SORRY, I FORGOT YOUR ORDER WHEN THE COOK CUT OFF HIS THUMB!

MORE SPECIFICALLY, WE TEND TO ASSUME THAT IF INFORMATION IS **EASY TO PROCESS NOW...**

...IT WILL BE **EASY TO RECALL LATER.**

BELOVED TOM,
YOU'RE **ALL I THINK ABOUT.**

WILL YOU REMEMBER ME **AFTER I RETURN FROM COLLEGE?**

OF COURSE!

BUT WE'RE **LOUSY AT ANTICIPATING** THE FACTORS THAT MIGHT **CHANGE HOW WE RECALL THINGS IN THE FUTURE:**

LIKE **HOW OFTEN WE MIGHT ENCOUNTER SIMILAR INFORMATION...**

Terry
Tom
Tim
Toby
Todd
Ted
Trey
I WAS SO SURE I'D REMEMBER HIS **NAME...**
...BUT THEN I DATED **TIM** AND **TED** AND **TODD** AND **TERRY** AND **TOBY** AND **TREY.**

...OR HOW **UNUSUAL EXPERIENCES MIGHT IMPACT OUR THINKING.**

MY NAME IS **GRIZZALDO**, I'M A **FISHERMAN**, MY DAD WAS A **FISHERMAN**, MY GRANDPA WAS A **FISHERMAN**, MY GREAT-GRANDPA WAS A...
YOU ARE SO **TOTALLY FORGETTABLE.**

AND THESE FACTORS LEAD TO **PREDICTABLE ERRORS IN METACOGNITION.**

YOU **FORGOT EVERYTHING ABOUT ME?**

SORRY TROY, I FORGOT **ALL** THE GUYS I DATED IN HIGH SCHOOL...

...ALL EXCEPT **GRIZZALDO!**

Grizzaldo

ALL OF WHICH **BEGS ANOTHER QUESTION.**

WE'VE SEEN HOW **COGNITIVE FLUENCY** IMPACTS OUR **JUDGMENTS**...

THINKING ABOUT HIM IS EASY FOR ME.
THAT'S WHY SHE LIKES HIM SO MUCH.

...BUT DOES IT IMPACT OUR **MEMORIES?**

THINKING ABOUT HIM IS EASY FOR ME.

WILL THAT HELP HER REMEMBER HIM?

ON THE ONE HAND, IF SOMETHING IS EASY TO THINK ABOUT, WE TEND TO ASSUME **WE'LL REMEMBER IT...**

I LOVE YOU FOREVER SAM FINKBEINER.
I ♡ SF

...EVEN THOUGH THERE ARE **NO GUARANTEES.**

SEE, I TOLD YOU I'VE ALWAYS BEEN A GIANTS FAN.
I ♡ SF

ON THE OTHER HAND, WHEN IT COMES TO ENCODING LONG TERM MEMORIES, **HARD WORK PAYS OFF...**

MEMORIZE!
HERE AT MNEMONICS CAMP, PAIN EQUALS GAIN!

...AND IF AN ASSOCIATION FEELS **UNCOMFORTABLE**, IT CAN INSPIRE US TO DO THAT EXTRA WORK.

NO NEED TO MEMORIZE COWS, THEY NEVER EAT YOU.
BUT THIS IS A MATTER OF LIFE AND DEATH.
Teeth
Claws
Scary Jungle Cat
Whiskers
Stripes
Spots

IN FACT, STUDIES SHOW THAT WHEN QUESTIONS ARE PUT TO US IN A **BLURRY FONT...**

HOW MANY OF EACH ANIMAL DID MOSES TAKE ON THE ARK?

...IT OFTEN PROMPTS US TO **THINK MORE DEEPLY.**

IT'S A **TRICK QUESTION!**

WAIT A MINUTE, **SOMETHING'S OFF HERE.**

IT WASN'T **MOSES!**
IT WAS **NOAH!**
HURRAH! YOU'RE USING **SYSTEM 2** FROM PAGE **73!**

AND OTHER EVIDENCE SUGGESTS THAT THIS **EXTRA EFFORT...**

e=mc²

MEMORIZE THAT!
OUCH.
I **HATE** THIS CAMP.

...ALSO HELPS US **REMEMBER THINGS BETTER IN THE LONG RUN.**

IT HURTS!

YOU'LL THANK ME WHEN YOU GET YOUR **TEST RESULTS BACK.**
IT'S **DEPTH OF PROCESSING** FROM PAGE **53!**

OF COURSE IF SOMETHING IS **TOO TAXING** WE WON'T BOTHER TO REMEMBER IT...

...BUT ADDING **MODERATE LEVELS OF DIFFICULTY** DOES SEEM TO INSPIRE **BETTER LEARNING.**

READING **JAMES JOYCE** IS NEAR IMPOSSIBLE...
...SO MAKING ***ULYSSES*** BLURRY ISN'T GOING TO HELP.

THE **NEW AND IMPROVED**

PSYCHOLOGY: THE COMIC BOOK INTRODUCTION...
...NOW INCLUDES **MILD ELECTRIC SHOCKS** TO **STIMULATE BETTER LEARNING!**

FINALLY, PERHAPS THE GREATEST **BLIND SPOT** WE FACE WHEN **THINKING ABOUT OUR THINKING...**

...IS THAT ONCE WE KNOW SOMETHING, IT'S HARD TO RECALL WHAT IT WAS LIKE **NOT TO KNOW IT**.

ONCE YOU KNOW HOW IT'S DONE, THE MAGIC IS **GONE.**

THAT'S BECAUSE ONCE AN IDEA HAS BEEN **INTEGRATED INTO OUR ASSOCIATIVE NETWORK...**

...WE CAN NO LONGER **SIMULATE HOW THAT NETWORK WOULD OPERATE WITHOUT IT.**

PALMER GOT INTO **PRINCETON...**

...WHICH MAKES ME THINK OF **PRINCE...**

...WHICH MAKES ME THINK OF **PURPLE.**

Palmer

Princeton

Prince

Purple

HOW WOULD I GET FROM **PALMER** TO **PURPLE** WITHOUT **PRINCETON?**

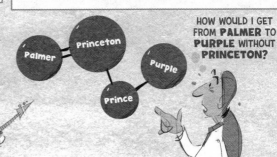

AS A RESULT, AFTER WE **LEARN NEW THINGS...**

...WE TEND TO **ASSUME WE ALWAYS KNEW THEM.**

DID YOU HEAR?
JENNY **STOLE** EMILY'S BOYFRIEND!

I **ALWAYS KNEW** SHE WAS A **BAD APPLE.**

THAT'S **HINDSIGHT BIAS!**

AND AFTER **THINGS HAPPEN...**

...WE TEND TO **FORGET THE UNCERTAINTY WE FACED** WHILE THEY WERE GOING ON.

MY HORSE **WON!**

I KNEW IT **ALL ALONG!**

THEN HOW COME YOU'VE **CHEWED YOUR FINGERNAILS OFF?**

EVEN WORSE, WE'RE NOT ONLY BAD AT **REMEMBERING OUR OWN IGNORANCE** AND **UNCERTAINTY**...

...WE'RE **ALSO BAD** AT **IMAGINING THESE QUALITIES IN OTHERS.**

I'VE ALWAYS BEEN GOOD AT RECOUNTING THE PAST...
...AND PREDICTING THE FUTURE.
YOU LOOK TRUSTWORTHY...
...DO YOU TAKE VISA?

THIS CAN LEAD TO ALL SORTS OF **UNFORTUNATE OUTCOMES** IN THE **CRIMINAL JUSTICE SYSTEM**...

BUT YOUR HONOR, ALL I DID WAS DRIVE HER TO THE BANK...
...I HAD NO WAY OF KNOWING SHE WAS GONNA ROB IT!
YOU SHOULD HAVE KNOWN BETTER!
30 YEARS!

...AS WELL AS MORE GENERAL PROBLEMS LIKE **THE CURSE OF KNOWLEDGE...**

I'M SHOCKED!
HOW COULD ANYONE NOT UNDERSTAND CALCULUS?
YOU MUST BE AN IDIOT!

...AND ITS EVIL TWIN, **THE IMPOSTOR EFFECT...**

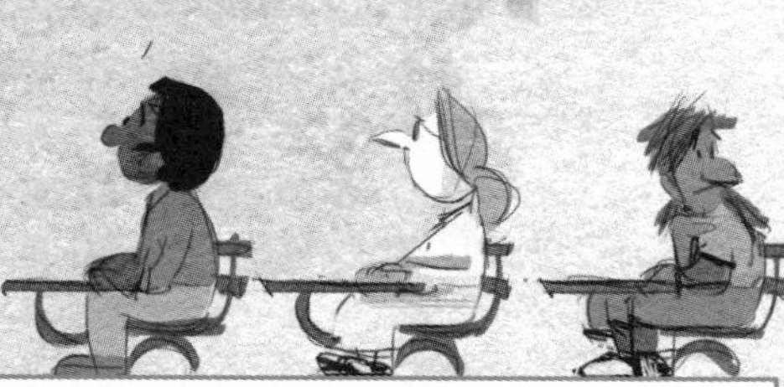

EVERYONE ELSE HERE MUST UNDERSTAND CALCULUS.
I MUST BE AN IDIOT.

...BOTH OF WHICH HAPPEN WHEN WE **DON'T ACCOUNT FOR THE GAPS IN OTHER PEOPLE'S KNOWLEDGE.**

IN SUM, THOUGH WE MIGHT **FEEL CONFIDENT** ABOUT **WHAT'S IN OUR MINDS...**

...WE'RE OFTEN **WRONG.**

I **KNOW** WHAT **I KNOW!**
BUT YOU **DON'T KNOW** WHAT YOU **DON'T KNOW...**
...OR WHAT YOU **DIDN'T KNOW IN THE PAST...**
... OR WHAT YOU **WON'T KNOW IN THE FUTURE.**

BECAUSE **ALL** OUR KNOWLEDGE IS **IMPERFECT.**

YOU **DON'T REALLY KNOW** WHAT'S ON THE **INSIDE.**

JUST LIKE YOU **DON'T REALLY KNOW** WHAT'S ON THE **OUTSIDE.**

TO COMPLICATE THINGS FURTHER, EVERYTHING IN OUR MINDS IS INFLUENCED BY **WHAT'S ALREADY IN THERE.**

WHAT YOU **THINK YOU KNOW...**
...DEPENDS ON WHAT YOU **ALREADY KNOW...**
...OR AT LEAST ON WHAT YOU **THINK YOU ALREADY KNOW.**

SO, TO MAKE SENSE OF OURSELVES AND THE WORLD, WE MAKE **INFERENCES**, WHICH ARE OFTEN **WRONG.**

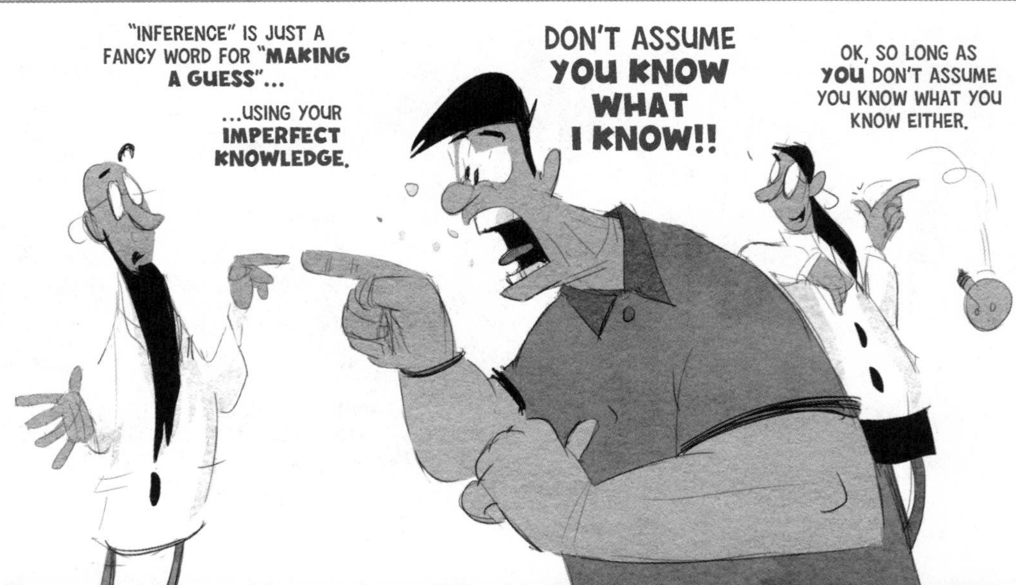

"INFERENCE" IS JUST A FANCY WORD FOR "**MAKING A GUESS**"...
...USING YOUR **IMPERFECT KNOWLEDGE.**
DON'T ASSUME **YOU KNOW WHAT I KNOW!!**
OK, SO LONG AS **YOU** DON'T ASSUME YOU KNOW WHAT YOU KNOW EITHER.

CHAPTER 6
EMOTION

WE ALL KNOW WHAT IT'S LIKE TO **FEEL EMOTIONS.**
IN THIS CHAPTER, WE'RE GOING TO LEARN **HOW TO THINK ABOUT THEM!**

SERIOUS THINKERS HAVE BEEN WRESTLING WITH EMOTIONS FOR **THOUSANDS OF YEARS.**

DAMN YOU, SOCRATES!
YOU MAKE ME SO ANGRY!
WHY?

AND IT'S **NO WONDER.**

NOT ONLY ARE EMOTIONS **FAST ACTING AND POWERFUL...**

...THEY CAN ALSO BE **CONFUSING AND UNRELIABLE...**

...WHICH IS WHY THEY CAN GET US INTO **ALL KINDS OF TROUBLE.**

MY **TEMPER** HITS ME LIKE A TON OF BRICKS...

...WHENEVER I SEE THE COLOR **RED.**

UM, YOU'RE FIRED!

IN THIS CHAPTER, WE'RE GOING TO LEARN HOW **PSYCHOLOGISTS** THINK ABOUT EMOTIONS, BY ASKING **THREE QUESTIONS.**

WHAT ARE THEY?

ARE THEY **UNIVERSAL?**

AND **WHY DO WE HAVE THEM?**

LET'S START WITH THE FIRST QUESTION, **WHAT ARE EMOTIONS?**

THE EARLIEST **MODERN THEORY OF EMOTION** WAS OUTLINED IN THE 19TH CENTURY BY **WILLIAM JAMES** AND **CARL LANGE.**

FORMALLY, THE **JAMES–LANGE THEORY OF EMOTION** STATES THAT EVENTS IN THE WORLD...

...LEAD TO **PHYSICAL CHANGES INSIDE OUR BODIES...**

OUR HEART RATES ARE ELEVATED...
WE'RE SWEATING...

...AND EMOTION IS THE **AWARENESS** OF THOSE CHANGES.

...WE MUST BE SCARED!

EVENT
PHYSICAL AROUSAL
Emotion

IN THESE TERMS, **ANY TIME WE EXPERIENCE EMOTION...**

...IT'S BECAUSE **SOME PHYSIOLOGICAL SYSTEM INSIDE OUR BODY HAS BEEN TRIGGERED.**

I'M FULL OF LUST!
I'M NOT!

YOUR HEART RATE IS ELEVATED.
YOUR ADRENAL SYSTEM IS IN OVERDRIVE.
YOURS ISN'T.

THIS SURPRISING THEORY RAISES AN **IMPORTANT QUESTION...**

I **POKE YOU,**
YOU **CRY,**
YOU **FEEL SAD.**
FASCINATING!

WHICH COMES FIRST...

...THE **EMOTION** OR THE **AROUSAL?**

...WHICH WE CAN **TEST!**

ALTHOUGH IT MIGHT SEEM LIKE COMMON SENSE THAT **EMOTIONS PROVOKE BODILY CHANGES...**

...IT TURNS OUT THAT THE **OPPOSITE** MAY ACTUALLY BE TRUE.

WHEN I SEE A GORILLA, I GET SCARED...

...SO I RUN!

YOU GOT SCARED **BECAUSE** YOU STARTED RUNNING WHEN YOU SAW THE GORILLA!

IN OTHER WORDS, WHILE WE TEND TO THINK THAT OUR EMOTIONS **CAUSE** OUR BODIES TO REACT...

I'M SMILING **BECAUSE I'M HAPPY.**

MY BLOOD IS BOILING **BECAUSE I'M ANGRY.**

...THE JAMES–LANGE THEORY SUGGESTS THAT **OUR BODIES REACT FIRST.**

ACTUALLY, YOU'RE HAPPY **BECAUSE** YOU'RE SMILING!

ACTUALLY,YOU'RE ANGRY **BECAUSE** YOUR BLOOD IS BOILING!

TO TEST THIS IDEA, PSYCHOLOGISTS USE **FACIAL FEEDBACK STUDIES.**

USING ONLY A **PENCIL...**

...WE CAN MAKE YOU ADOPT **DIFFERENT FACIAL EXPRESSIONS...**

...THEN **OBSERVE** HOW YOU **FEEL.**

LET'S SEE HOW THEY WORK.

RESEARCHERS HAVE FOUND THAT IF YOU SIMPLY MAKE PEOPLE HOLD A PENCIL **HORIZONTALLY BETWEEN THEIR TEETH**...

...THEY REPORT **POSITIVE EMOTIONS.**

THIS FORCES YOU TO FLEX YOUR **ZYGOMATICUS MUSCLES**, THE SAME MUSCLES YOU USE WHEN YOU SMILE.

I **LIKE** OTHER PEOPLE **MORE!**
THIS BOOK IS **HILARIOUS!**
PENCILS TASTE **AWESOME!**

ALTERNATELY, IF YOU CHANGE THE POSITION OF THE PENCIL, SO THEY HOLD IT **BETWEEN THEIR LIPS**...

...THEY REPORT **NEGATIVE EMOTIONS.**

THIS FORCES YOU TO EXERT YOUR **PLATYSMA AND DEPRESSOR ANGULI ORIS** MUSCLES, YOUR FROWNING MUSCLES.

I **DON'T** LIKE YOU.
THIS BOOK **ISN'T VERY FUNNY.**
PENCILS TASTE **TERRIBLE!**

FINALLY, IF YOU CAN SOMEHOW GET THEM TO **FURROW THEIR BROW**...

...IT LEADS TO **CONFUSION AND/OR ANXIETY.**

CORRUGATOR MUSCLES.

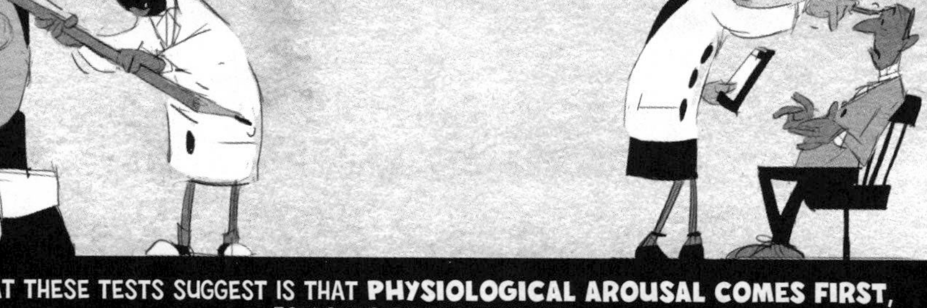
HOW DO YOU **FEEL?**
PLEASE **STOP.**

WHAT THESE TESTS SUGGEST IS THAT **PHYSIOLOGICAL AROUSAL COMES FIRST**, FOLLOWED BY THE EMOTION.

OUR PHYSIOLOGICAL PERCEPTION **PRECEDES OUR MENTAL AWARENESS!**

SMILING MAKES YOU **HAPPY**...
...AND FROWNING MAKES YOU **SAD!**

BUT THERE'S **MORE TO IT** THAN JUST THAT.

WHILE THE JAMES–LANGE THEORY SUGGESTS THAT **PHYSIOLOGICAL AROUSAL** AND **EMOTIONS** GO HAND IN HAND...

...MORE RECENT THEORIES STRESS THE FACT THAT EMOTIONS ALSO SEEM TO **REQUIRE COGNITIVE INTERPRETATION.**

DUH!

I LUST AFTER YOU WITH MY HEART **AND** MY MIND.

IN PARTICULAR, THE **SCHACHTER–SINGER THEORY** ACCOUNTS FOR THE FACT THAT THE **SAME BODILY RESPONSES...**

...CAN **STIMULATE DIFFERENT EMOTIONS** IN **DIFFERENT CIRCUMSTANCES.**

OUR **HEART RATES ARE BOTH ELEVATED...**
...AND WE'RE BOTH **SWEATING...**

...BUT I'M **SCARED...**
...AND I'M **IN LOVE!**

IN THESE TERMS, OUR EMOTIONAL RESPONSE IS INFLUENCED **NOT** JUST BY OUR **PHYSIOLOGICAL RESPONSE...**

...BUT **ALSO** BY **HOW WE INTERPRET** THE SITUATION WE'RE IN.

IF WE INJECT YOU WITH **EPINEPHRINE**, YOUR HEART RATE WILL BECOME ELEVATED...
...AS YOUR **ADRENAL SYSTEM** GOES INTO **OVERDRIVE.**

THEN, IF WE SHOW YOU A PICTURE OF A **GORILLA**, YOU'LL FEEL **SCARED...**
...BUT IF WE SHOW YOU A PICTURE OF A **HOT PERSON**, YOU'LL FEEL **HORNY.**

EVENT → PHYSICAL AROUSAL → INTERPRETATION → Emotion

Fear

Lust

ONE OF THE **CLASSIC STUDIES** THAT SUPPORTS THE SCHACHTER–SINGER THEORY IS THE

DUTTON AND ARON BRIDGE STUDY.

A **WOMAN** APPROACHED SOME MEN WHILE THEY WERE ON A **SCARY BRIDGE**...

HERE'S MY NUMBER...
MY HEART IS POUNDING.
MY PALMS ARE SWEATY.

...AND SOME OTHER MEN 10 MINUTES **AFTER THEY'D GOTTEN OFF OF IT.**

...CALL ME IF YOU WANT TO TALK.
MY PALMS AREN'T SWEATING ANYMORE.

WHAT DUTTON AND ARON DISCOVERED IS THAT THE MEN IN THE FIRST GROUP

WERE MUCH **MORE LIKELY TO CALL HER!**

SHE'S THE **BOMB!**
65% OF US CALLED.

MEH.
30% OF US CALLED.

OF COURSE **ALL** THE MEN **DIDN'T RESPOND IN THE SAME WAY.**

I'M SORRY.
WHAT CAN I SAY?
CHASMS JUST **TURN ME OFF.**

BUT THE POINT IS THAT THEIR EMOTIONAL RESPONSE WAS **HIGHLY INFLUENCED BY THEIR CIRCUMSTANCES.**

WE TURNED **FEAR** INTO **LUST!**
THAT'S WHY I TAKE MY DATES TO **SCARY MOVIES!**

THIS BRINGS US TO OUR NEXT BIG QUESTION, **ARE EMOTIONS UNIVERSAL?**

DO PEOPLE **EVERYWHERE** EXPERIENCE THE **SAME EMOTIONS**...
...REGARDLESS OF THEIR **CULTURE** AND **LANGUAGE**...
...OR **LIVING ENVIRONMENT?**

IN FACT, PSYCHOLOGISTS ARE IN GENERAL AGREEMENT THAT THERE ARE PROBABLY ABOUT **SEVEN DISTINCT EMOTIONS** RECOGNIZABLE TO EVERYONE AROUND THE WORLD.

HAPPINESS

SADNESS

ANGER

FEAR

DISGUST

SURPRISE

CONTEMPT

AND ALTHOUGH THE **PRECISE NUMBER IS OPEN TO DEBATE**...

WE SHOULD BREAK HAPPINESS INTO **DIFFERENT PARTS**...
...LIKE **JOY** AND **SATISFACTION** AND **CONTENTMENT!**
AND WHAT ABOUT THE DISTINCT **FEAR OF BEING RUBBED WITH A PENCIL?!**
...THERE IS SOME PRETTY GOOD **EVIDENCE** FOR THE UNIVERSALITY OF **AT LEAST THESE SEVEN.**

THE EVIDENCE FOR UNIVERSALITY COMES FROM A FEW SOURCES. **FIRST**, PEOPLE IN ALL CULTURES HAVE **SIMILAR FACIAL EXPRESSIONS**...

...AND WILL **RELIABLY IDENTIFY EMOTIONS** IN PHOTOS OF PEOPLE THAT LOOK NOTHING LIKE THEM.

IF YOU SHOW ANYBODY THIS PICTURE OF AN ANGRY ESKIMO...
...NOBODY WILL THINK SHE'S HAPPY.

SECOND, THERE'S EVIDENCE THAT **LINKS DIFFERENT EMOTIONS BACK TO SPECIFIC PHYSIOLOGICAL RESPONSES.**

WHENEVER ANYONE ANYWHERE IS SCARED, THE AMYGDALA IN THEIR BRAIN LIGHTS UP.

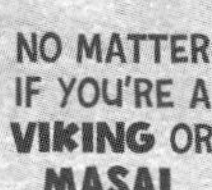
ANGER IS ALWAYS ASSOCIATED WITH AN INCREASED HEART RATE.
NO MATTER IF YOU'RE A VIKING OR MASAI.

FINALLY, ALL LANGUAGES HAVE **DISTINCT WORDS** FOR THESE 7 EMOTIONS.

WHY WOULD THEY HAVE A WORD FOR IT IF THEY DIDN'T EXPERIENCE IT?

AND ALTHOUGH SOME LANGUAGES DO HAVE WORDS FOR EMOTIONS THAT SEEM TO BE **NON–UNIVERSAL**...

"HAGAII."
"MEHAMEHA."
"SCHADENFREUDE."

...OR **UNTRANSLATABLE**...

"LITOST" IS A CZECH WORD THAT COMBINES GRIEF, REMORSE, AND LONGING...
...BUT YOU HAVE TO BE ABLE TO HOWL LIKE AN ABANDONED DOG TO CONVEY IT.

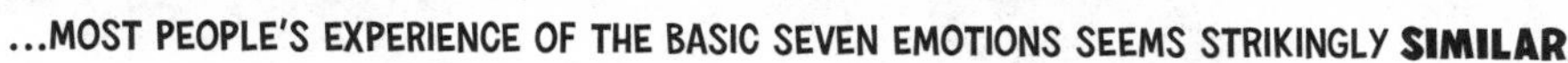

...MOST PEOPLE'S EXPERIENCE OF THE BASIC SEVEN EMOTIONS SEEMS STRIKINGLY **SIMILAR.**

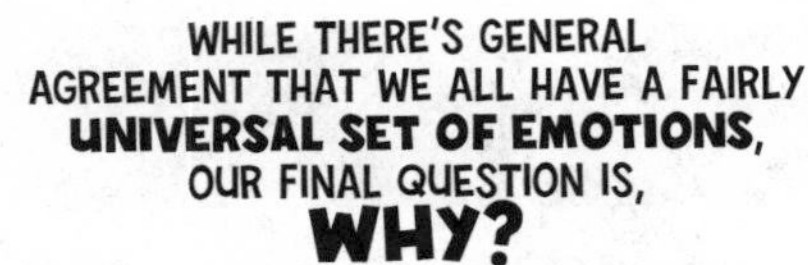
WHILE THERE'S GENERAL AGREEMENT THAT WE ALL HAVE A FAIRLY **UNIVERSAL SET OF EMOTIONS,** OUR FINAL QUESTION IS, **WHY?**

TELL ME CAPTAIN, **WHY DO YOU HAVE FEELINGS?**
WHAT DO YOU MEAN, SPOCK?
THE PRIMARY ANSWER IS THAT EMOTIONS HELP US **MAKE SNAP JUDGMENTS.**
EMOTIONS SEEM TO ME TO BE **HIGHLY ILLOGICAL.**
AH!
IN FACT, THERE'S EVIDENCE THAT IT TAKES **LESS THAN 100 MILLISECONDS** TO FORM AN EMOTIONAL IMPRESSION...
CAPTAIN, WHAT SEEMS TO BE THE **PROBLEM?**
THAT'S **FAST.**
...WHICH INDICATES THAT THEY ARE GOOD AT GUIDING OUR BEHAVIOR IN SITUATIONS WHERE WE NEED TO REACT **BEFORE WE HAVE TIME TO THINK ABOUT IT.**
MAYBE THEY'RE NOT SO **ILLOGICAL** AFTER ALL.
BURP!
BUT THAT'S NOT THE WHOLE STORY.

EMOTIONS HAPPEN FAST, BUT THEY CAN ALSO **LINGER LONG AFTER CONSCIOUS MEMORY HAS FADED.**

I DON'T KNOW WHERE WE ARE, BUT I FEEL LIKE SOMETHING **BAD** HAPPENED HERE.

ONE CLEVER WAY TO TEST THIS IS TO **SHOW A PICTURE OF A BLOODTHIRSTY MURDERER** TO A PERSON WHO HAS **AMNESIA.**

THIS MAN DID **HORRIBLE, UNSPEAKABLE THINGS.**

THEN, IF YOU **WAIT 5 MINUTES** OR SO...

...THE AMNESIAC WON'T **RECALL THE FACE...**

...BUT WILL **RETAIN A LINGERING EMOTIONAL IMPRESSION OF IT!**

HAVE YOU SEEN THIS PICTURE BEFORE?
NO.

BUT I **DON'T LIKE HIM.**

THIS SAME SORT OF EFFECT WORKS ON PEOPLE WITH **HEALTHY MEMORIES...**

...IT JUST **TAKES LONGER...**

HAHA! I JUST **SWINDLED** YOUR **FAMILY** OUT OF ITS **FORTUNE!**

FOR SOME REASON, EVER SINCE I WAS A KID I HAVEN'T TRUSTED PEOPLE WHO WEAR **PLAID.**

...AND SEEMS TO INFLUENCE OUR JUDGMENTS **ABOUT OTHER PEOPLE** PARTICULARLY STRONGLY.

I DON'T KNOW WHY I DON'T LIKE **HIM,** BUT I'M SURE I HAVE A GOOD **REASON.**
YOU CAN READ MORE ABOUT THAT IN THE **CHAPTER ON STEREOTYPING.**

AS WE'VE SEEN, EMOTIONS HELP US **MAKE SNAP DECISIONS NOW...**

...AND THEY CAN **GUIDE OUR BEHAVIOR LATER.**

DO YOU **WANT** ME TO KEEP RUBBING THIS PENCIL ON YOUR FOREHEAD?
NO!

THAT'S WHY PSYCHOLOGISTS THINK OF EMOTIONS AS AN **IMPORTANT ADAPTIVE TOOL.**

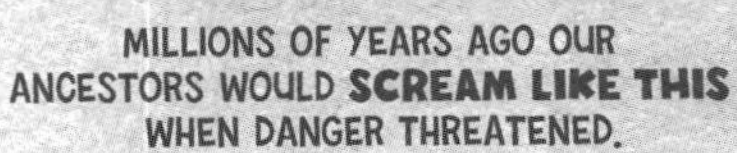
MILLIONS OF YEARS AGO OUR ANCESTORS WOULD **SCREAM LIKE THIS** WHEN DANGER THREATENED.

AAAIII!

AND IT WOULD CAUSE US TO **REACT LIKE THIS.**

HOWEVER, DESPITE THE FACT THAT EMOTIONS ARE CLEARLY IMPORTANT FOR OUR SURVIVAL, THEY'RE **NOT PERFECTLY RELIABLE.**

NOWADAYS WE HEAR **SOUNDS LIKE THIS** ALL THE TIME.

AAAIII!

AND THEY STILL MAKE US **REACT THE SAME WAY.**

THIS HELPS EXPLAIN BOTH WHY WE HAVE **VISCERAL NEGATIVE REACTIONS** TO PARTICULAR **SOUNDS...**

I FEEL **SCARED!**

YOU'RE IN NO PARTICULAR DANGER, I'M JUST **POUNDING ON THIS DRUM...**
...WHILE I **SCRAPE MY FINGERNAILS DOWN THIS CHALKBOARD.**

...AND WHY OUR EMOTIONAL RESPONSE CAN SOMETIMES **OVERPOWER OUR BETTER JUDGMENT.**

THIS HOUSE IS A **DUMP.**
BUT IF IT **SMELLS LIKE FRESHLY BAKED COOKIES,** MY CUSTOMERS ARE **LESS LIKELY TO NOTICE!**

IN PARTICULAR, THE DECEPTIVE PULL OF EMOTIONS CAN CAUSE **MAGICAL THINKING.**

THAT'S WHEN WE **KNOW** OUR BELIEFS ARE **UNREASONABLE...**

...BUT FEEL **COMPELLED TO FOLLOW THEM ANYWAY.**

I KNOW IT DOESN'T MAKE ANY DIFFERENCE...
...BUT I ALWAYS WEAR MY LUCKY HAT WHEN WE MAKE SACRIFICES TO THE VOLCANO.

FOR EXAMPLE, WHEN CONFRONTED WITH A SITUATION **LIKE THIS ONE...**

FIRST WE BUY A BRAND NEW TOILET, NEVER BEEN USED.
THEN WE POUR APPLE JUICE INTO IT...

...AND GRAB A CUP.

VOILA!
HAVE A DRINK!

...MOST PEOPLE **CAN'T BRING THEMSELVES TO ACT.**

CAPTAIN, YOUR EMOTIONS ARE OVERRIDING YOUR JUDGMENT.
THIS BEVERAGE IS QUITE REFRESHING.
WHAT CAN I SAY, I'M ONLY HUMAN.

EMOTIONS ARE **PREDICTABLY UNRELIABLE** IN SEVERAL OTHER WAYS AS WELL.

POSITIVITY BIAS DESCRIBES THE FACT THAT PEOPLE TEND TO REMEMBER THE PAST AS **BETTER THAN IT REALLY WAS.**

WHEN I WAS A BOY WE HAD TO WALK TO SCHOOL IN THE SNOW WITHOUT SHOES OVER HOT COALS, **BOTH WAYS!**
MAN THOSE WERE THE **GOOD OLD DAYS.**

IN FACT, IF YOU ASK PEOPLE TO MAKE **DIARY ENTRIES** IN WHICH THEY **RECORD THE EMOTIONAL INTENSITY OF CERTAIN EVENTS IN THEIR LIVES...**

THIS ICE CREAM CONE?
8

THIS PARTY?
7

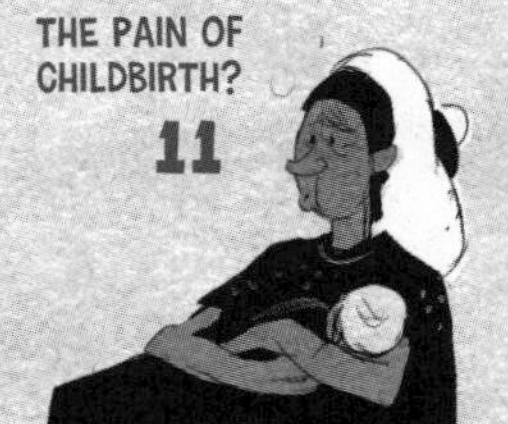
THE PAIN OF CHILDBIRTH?
11

THE TRAUMA OF BEING RUBBED BY A PENCIL?
9

...THEY WILL PREDICTABLY GIVE **LOWER INTENSITY RATINGS AS TIME PASSES!**

THAT ICE CREAM 10 YEARS AGO?
6

THAT PARTY?
5

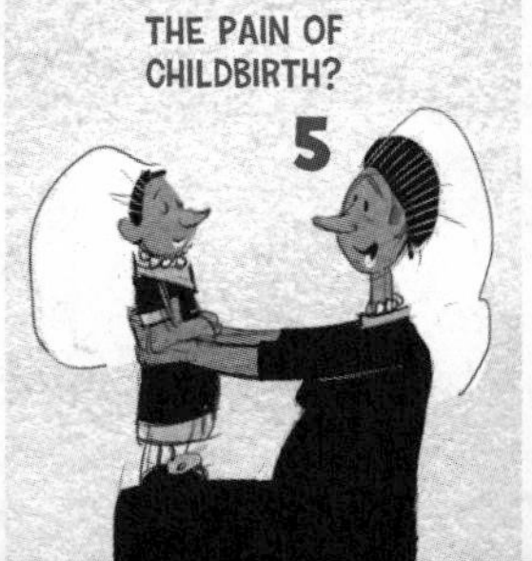
THE PAIN OF CHILDBIRTH?
5

4

TESTS LIKE THIS SUGGEST THAT **ALL EMOTIONAL MEMORIES FADE OVER TIME...**

...BUT THAT **NEGATIVE EMOTIONS** FADE **MORE QUICKLY...**

ACCORDING TO MY **DIARY**, I USED TO FEEL LIKE A **10...**
...BUT **THAT'S NOT HOW I REMEMBER IT.**

DON'T YOU REMEMBER THE **PAINS OF CHILDBIRTH?**
NEVERMIND THAT, LET'S HAVE ANOTHER ONE!

...AND AS A RESULT, OUR OVERALL MEMORIES TEND TO BE **MORE POSITIVE.**

PEOPLE VIEW THE PAST THROUGH **ROSE-COLORED GLASSES.**

DURATION NEGLECT, ON THE OTHER HAND, DESCRIBES THE WAY IN WHICH WE PREDICTABLY **FORGET THE DURATION** OF EMOTIONAL EXPERIENCES...

HOW LONG HAVE YOU BEEN HERE?

I DONNO.

...BUT INSTEAD REMEMBER THEIR **PEAK INTENSITY** AND **FINAL INTENSITY.**

FOR EXAMPLE, IF YOU GET A BUNCH OF PEOPLE TO **HOLD THEIR HANDS IN ICE WATER FOR EXACTLY 5 MINUTES...**

...THEN GET **SOME OF THEM** TO PUT THEIR HANDS IN **SLIGHTLY LESS COLD WATER** FOR AN **ADDITIONAL 30 SECONDS...**

...THAT SECOND GROUP WILL RATE THE **OVERALL EXPERIENCE** AS **LESS PAINFUL!**

8
6

IN SITUATIONS LIKE THIS, WHEN ASKED TO RATE THE OVERALL EXPERIENCE WITH NUMBERS, PEOPLE WILL GENERALLY **AVERAGE THE PEAK AND THE END.**

THIS SEEMS TO BE ESPECIALLY TRUE OF **HEDONIC EXPERIENCES,** WHICH INVOLVE PLEASURE OR PAIN.

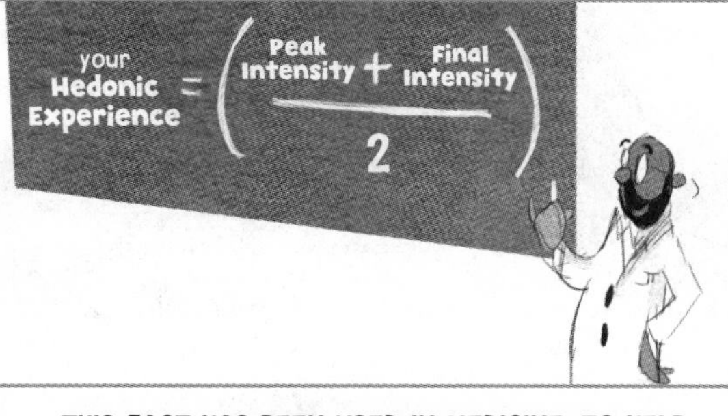

your Hedonic Experience = (Peak Intensity + Final Intensity) / 2

AS A RESULT, YOU CAN BIAS PEOPLE'S MEMORIES ABOUT HOW BAD OR GOOD AN EXPERIENCE IS BY **CHANGING THE LAST FEW MOMENTS OF IT.**

THIS FACT HAS BEEN USED IN MEDICINE, TO HELP LESSEN THE PAIN ASSOCIATED WITH CERTAIN **UNCOMFORTABLE MEDICAL PROCEDURES.**

AFTER I TORTURE MY STUDENTS, I **GIVE THEM ICE CREAM...**
...SO THEY'LL REMEMBER THE EXPERIENCE **FONDLY.**

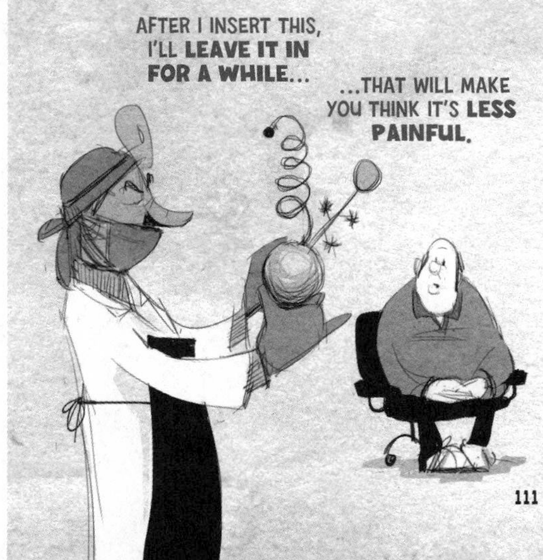

AFTER I INSERT THIS, I'LL **LEAVE IT IN FOR A WHILE...**
...THAT WILL MAKE YOU THINK IT'S **LESS PAINFUL.**

IN THIS CHAPTER WE'VE SEEN HOW EMOTIONS ARE **PRECEDED BY PHYSIOLOGICAL CHANGES**...

WHEN I CUT ONIONS, I **CRY**...
...WHICH MAKES ME FEEL **SAD**.
THAT'S JAMES–LANGE!

...BUT ALSO INFLUENCED BY OUR **COGNITIVE INTERPRETATION** OF THOSE CHANGES.

IT'S OK DADDY, I CAN TURN THEM INTO TEARS OF **LAUGHTER** BY MAKING **FART NOISES**.
THAT'S SCHACHTER–SINGER!

WE'VE LEARNED HOW EMOTIONS **HELP US REACT QUICKLY** TO IMPORTANT EVENTS...

RUN, SPOCK!
BUT CAPTAIN, THAT WOULD BE ILLOGICAL. HE'S SO **CUTE**.

...AND THAT THEY TEND TO **LINGER LONGER THAN OUR CONSCIOUS MEMORIES.**

I CAN'T REMEMBER HOW I KNEW THOSE THINGS WERE **DANGEROUS**.

IN SUM, OUR EMOTIONS ARE **VITAL TOOLS THAT HELP US MAKE SENSE OF THE CRAZY THINGS THAT HAPPEN TO US...**

...EVEN THOUGH THEY SOMETIMES **LEAD US ASTRAY**.

I THINK I'M IN **LOVE**.
THAT'S JUST BECAUSE I'M MAKING YOU **THINK YOUR HEART IS RACING**.

CHAPTER 7
MOTIVATION

WHAT'S YOUR **MOTIVATION?**
YOUR CHARACTER WANTS TO **PROVE TO THE WORLD** THAT HIS **FEAR OF GIANT SPIDERS** IS **JUSTIFIED** AND...
NO, I MEANT WHAT'S **MY** MOTIVATION?
WHY AM I WASTING MY TIME ON THIS STUPID MOVIE?

ALL SORTS OF THINGS **MOTIVATE OUR BEHAVIOR.**

WILL WORK FOR MONEY
WILL WORK FOR LOVE
WILL LOVE FOR MONEY

ONE OF THE EARLIEST ATTEMPTS TO **CLASSIFY OUR MOTIVATIONS** WAS ABRAHAM MASLOW'S **HIERARCHY OF NEEDS.**

AT THE BOTTOM OF THE PYRAMID ARE THE MOST **BASIC NEEDS...**

...WHICH INCLUDE THINGS **NECESSARY FOR SURVIVAL.**

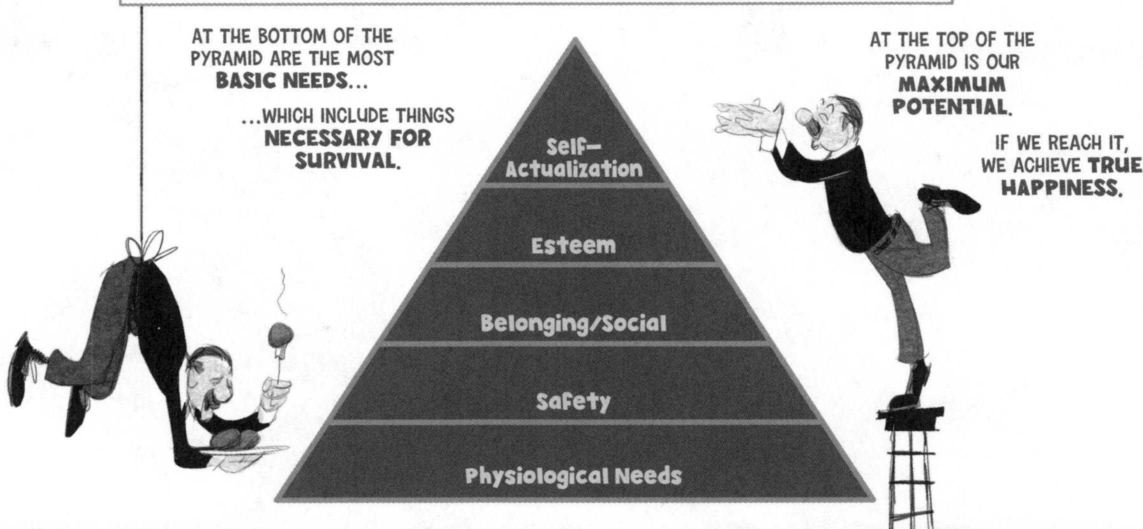
Self-Actualization
Esteem
Belonging/Social
Safety
Physiological Needs

AT THE TOP OF THE PYRAMID IS OUR **MAXIMUM POTENTIAL.**

IF WE REACH IT, WE ACHIEVE **TRUE HAPPINESS.**

ACCORDING TO MASLOW, WE **START AT THE BOTTOM...**

I'M MOTIVATED BY **HUNGER** AND **THIRST** AND **WARMTH** AND **OXYGEN.**

...AND **WORK OUR WAY TO THE TOP.**

I'M MOTIVATED BY **POETRY** AND **MUSIC** AND **TRUTH** AND **SCENTED CANDLES.**

AND IT'S **ONLY AFTER WE'RE SATISFIED ON ONE LAYER THAT WE MOVE UPWARD.**

AFTER I'VE **EATEN...**
...I'LL **ENSURE MY SAFETY...**
...THEN I'LL FIND **LOVE...**
...AND GET A **PROMOTION...**
...SO I CAN **ACHIEVE ENLIGHTENMENT.**

OF COURSE THIS MODEL IS **OVERLY SIMPLISTIC.**
NO MORE WRITING **POETRY IN THE TRENCHES!**
YOU'RE **NOT ALLOWED TO SKIP STEPS.**
ALTHOUGH IT CAN HELP US SORT THROUGH SOME OF OUR MANY **CONTRADICTORY MOTIVATIONS...**
I CRAVE STABILITY **AND** EXCITEMENT!
...IT DOESN'T ACCOUNT FOR THE FACT THAT WE REGULARLY PRIORITIZE HIGHER ORDER MOTIVATIONS **AT THE EXPENSE OF** LOWER ONES.
I WON'T EAT THAT BECAUSE IT'S **NOT SAFE.**
I WON'T EAT IT BECAUSE IT'S **NOT COOL.**
I WON'T EAT IT BECAUSE I HAVE **LOW SELF ESTEEM.**
I'M FASTING FOR MY **RELIGION.**
NEVERTHELESS, LET'S USE THE **BASE** OF MASLOW'S PYRAMID AS A **JUMPING—OFF POINT...**
...BECAUSE PEOPLE DO **TEND** TO **PRIORITIZE SAFETY AND FOOD.**
I'M **NOT** JUMPING IN...
...UNTIL I'M **SURE** THERE ARE **NO SHARKS.**

FOR STARTERS, WHAT MOTIVATES US TO **EAT?**

THIS MAY SEEM LIKE A **SIMPLE QUESTION,** BUT THERE'S **NO SIMPLE ANSWER.**

WE EAT TO **SURVIVE!**
DUH.

THEN WHY **CAN'T I STOP EATING?**

FOR EXAMPLE, THERE ARE **BIOLOGICAL SIGNALS** THAT TELL US WHEN WE'RE **FULL.**

SATIATION HORMONES ARE SECRETED BY OUR **INTESTINES** AND **FAT CELLS.**

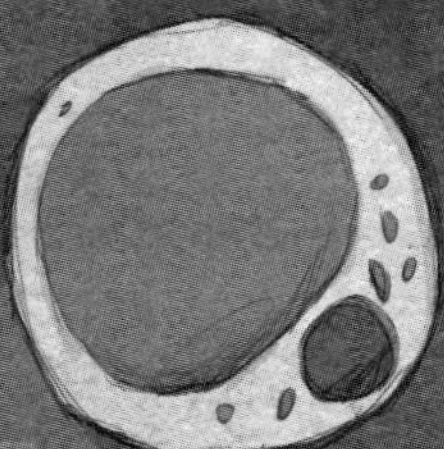

TELL CENTRAL COMMAND TO **STOP EATING!**
INCREASE **PYY!**
INCREASE **LEPTIN!**

BUT THEY'RE **EASILY SWAYED** BY **PSYCHOLOGICAL SIGNALS...**

FOR EXAMPLE, IF YOU **CHANGE THE LABEL** ON A DRINK...

...IT'LL **CHANGE HOW WE INTERPRET THE EXPERIENCE.**

Indulgent!
Low Calorie!

CENTRAL COMMAND THINKS THIS SHAKE IS "**LOW CALORIE.**"
SO LET'S EAT **MORE!**

...WHICH ARE **MUCH STRONGER.**

THOSE HORMONES ARE **NO MATCH** FOR THE SMELL OF **GREASE, AND SALT, AND SUGAR.**

GIMME **ANOTHER DOZEN.**
AND IF THEY'RE **"LOW CALORIE"**, BETTER GIMME **TWO.**

IN FACT, WHEN WE'RE TRYING TO **FIGURE OUT IF WE'RE FULL...**

...WE TEND TO **GUESS** BASED ON **HOW MUCH FOOD IS WITHIN REACH.**

YOU'RE STILL HUNGRY?
I MUST BE...
...THE BUFFET IS STILL OPEN.

IF YOU **MOVE OUR FOOD**, WE'LL **EAT LESS.**

IF YOU **HIDE OUR FOOD**, WE'LL **STOP EATING.**

OH, CANDY DISH...
...WHY DID YOU LEAVE ME?

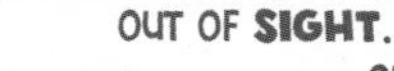

OUT OF SIGHT...
...OUT OF MIND...
...OUT OF BELLY.

AND, AS SHOWN IN ONE **CLASSIC STUDY**, IF YOU **REFILL OUR FOOD WITHOUT US KNOWING...**

...WE **WON'T KNOW WHEN TO STOP.**

WHEN WE SERVED SOUP FROM A BOWL THAT REFILLED ITSELF INVISIBLY...
...PEOPLE ATE 73% MORE SOUP!

OOF, MAYBE MY EYES ARE BIGGER THAN MY STOMACH.

THAT'S WHY **ONE GOOD WAY TO LOSE WEIGHT** IS TO SIMPLY USE **SMALLER PLATES.**

I'M ON THE PALEO CARBO DETOX LIQUID ANTI-GLUTEN GRAPEFRUIT DIET.

I'M ON THE EAT LESS FOOD DIET.

WHILE OUR **BASIC MOTIVATIONS** ARE COMPLICATED BY HOW OUR **BIOLOGY** AND **PSYCHOLOGY** INTERACT...

MY **MIND SAYS CHOCOLATE FROSTED...**

...MY **BELLY SAYS BEAR CLAW.**

...OUR **HIGHER ORDER MOTIVATIONS** ARE **NO SIMPLER.**

MY MOTIVATION TO **EAT** DEPENDS ON **THE SIZE OF MY PLATE...**

...AND MY MOTIVATION TO DATE A GUY DEPENDS ON **THE SIZE OF HIS WALLET.**

FOR EXAMPLE, ACCORDING TO SOME ECONOMIC THEORY, WE'RE **EXTRINSICALLY MOTIVATED...**

"EXTRINSIC" MEANS **"COMING FROM THE OUTSIDE."**

...SO WE DO THINGS **SIMPLY TO GAIN EXTERNAL REWARDS...**

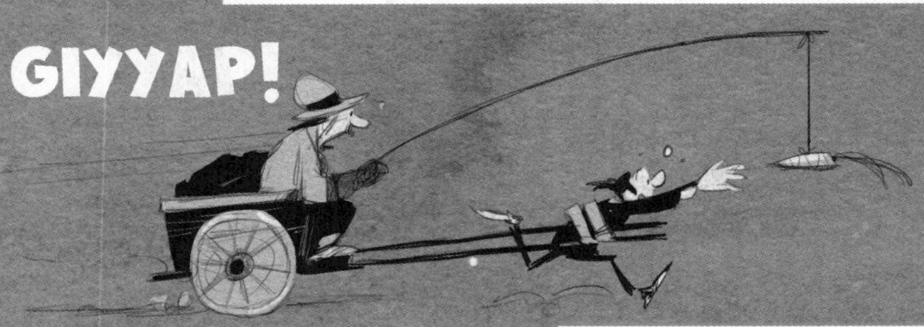

GIYYAP!

...AND **AVOID EXTERNAL PUNISHMENTS.**

GIYYAP!

BUT THAT'S **WAY TOO SIMPLISTIC.**

ALTHOUGH REWARDS AND PUNISHMENTS **CLEARLY INFLUENCE US...**

...THEY OFTEN **DON'T WORK AS INTENDED.**

I'M **ONLY** DOING THIS **FOR THE CARROTS.**

I DON'T EVEN **LIKE CARROTS.**

SLIGHT **DIFFERENCES** IN THE **WAY REWARDS ARE DISTRIBUTED...**

...CAN INSPIRE **UNINTENDED CONSEQUENCES.**

I'LL PAY YOU **BY THE HOUR.**

THEN I'LL **WORK SLOWER** TO **GET MORE MONEY.**

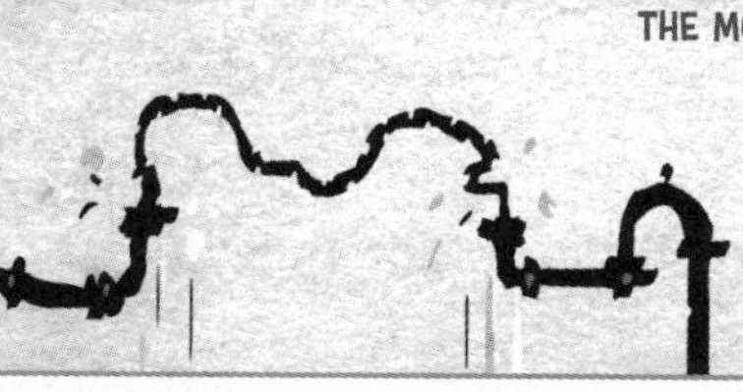
I'LL PAY **BY THE COMPLETED PROJECT.**

THEN I'LL **TAKE SHORTCUTS** TO GET THE MONEY FASTER.

THIS AFFECTS EVERYTHING FROM **PLUMBING** TO **EDUCATION POLICY...**

WE'LL PUNISH YOUR SCHOOL **IF YOUR KIDS FAIL THE STATE EXAMS.**

THEN WE'LL **EXPEL THE WEAKEST STUDENTS.**

...AND JUST ABOUT EVERYTHING ELSE WE DO IN THE **REAL WORLD, OUTSIDE THE LABORATORY.**

EVERYTHING WAS MUCH SIMPLER **IN THE BOX.**

SOME ATTEMPTS TO CREATE MOTIVATION CAN HAVE THE **EXACT OPPOSITE EFFECT** FROM THE ONE INTENDED.
I SAID GO **THAT** WAY!
I HATE **CARROTS!**

FOR EXAMPLE, SOMETIMES **PAYING PEOPLE** ACTUALLY **DE-MOTIVATES THEM.**

KIDS USUALLY NEED NO INCENTIVE TO **DOODLE...**
...BUT WHEN WE PAID THEM TO DOODLE, THEY **STOPPED** WHEN THE **PAYMENTS STOPPED.**
WHY DON'T YOU **DOODLE ANYMORE?**
SHOW ME THE MONEY!
IT'S THE **OVERJUSTIFICATION EFFECT.**

AND SOMETIMES **FINING PEOPLE** INSPIRES THEM TO **DO EXACTLY WHAT YOU WANTED TO AVOID.**

AT OUR DAYCARE, PARENTS WERE ARRIVING **LATE** TO GRAB THEIR KIDS...

...BUT WHEN WE STARTED CHARGING THEM FOR IT, THEY **DID IT MORE OFTEN.**

WHY ARE YOU SO **LATE?**

BECAUSE I'M **PAYING YOU FOR THE PRIVILEGE.**

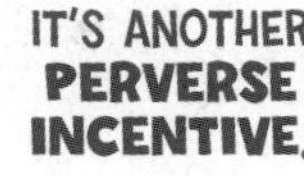
IT'S ANOTHER **PERVERSE INCENTIVE.**

PART OF THE DIFFICULTY IS THAT WE SEE INCENTIVES **THROUGH THE LENS OF OUR OWN EXPERIENCES...**

...WHICH CAN INCLUDE INTERTWINED LAYERS OF **SOCIAL MEANING.**

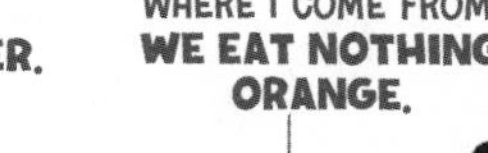

MY DESPICABLE FATHER WAS A **CARROT FARMER.**
WHERE I COME FROM, **WE EAT NOTHING ORANGE.**

SOCIAL MEANING CAN EASILY MAKE AN **INCENTIVE...**

HEY BABY, WANNA **SHAG AT MY PLACE?**
I'LL **PAY FOR THE CAB.**

...FEEL LIKE A **PUNISHMENT...**

I'M NOT A **PROSTITUTE!**

...AND **VICE VERSA.**

YOU WERE DISRESPECTFUL.
GO TO **DETENTION!**

HE'S SUCH A **BAD BOY!**
[SIGH]
SORRY LADIES, I'M **NEEDED AT THE OFFICE.**

CLEARLY, TO EXPLAIN HOW WE RESPOND TO **EXTERNAL MOTIVATIONS...**

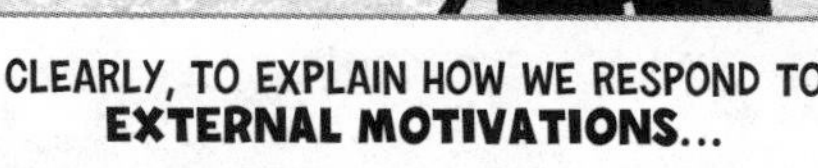

...WE NEED TO TAKE INTO ACCOUNT **INTERNAL ELEMENTS** AS WELL.

I HAVE TO **PAY HIM TO STUDY...**
...BUT HE **SHOOTS HOOPS FOR FREE.**

WELCOME TO THE **NCAA!**

SELF–DETERMINATION THEORY ATTEMPTS TO SORT THROUGH THE MIX OF FACTORS THAT **MOTIVATE US INTRINSICALLY.**

"INTRINSIC" MEANS **"COMING FROM THE INSIDE."**

I WON'T PULL **UNTIL I'M READY TO PULL.**

THE IDEA HERE IS THAT WE HAVE **THREE FUNDAMENTAL AIMS:**

WE ASPIRE TO **FORM STRONG SOCIAL BONDS...**

WE CALL THIS **RELATEDNESS.**

I CRAVE **ESTEEM.**
I JUST **DON'T WANNA BE LONELY.**

...TO HAVE **CONTROL OVER OUR LIFE AND ACTIONS...**

WE CALL THIS **AUTONOMY.**

I CRAVE **FREEDOM.**

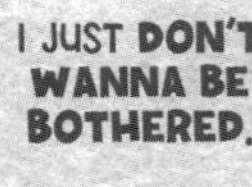
I JUST **DON'T WANNA BE BOTHERED.**

...AND TO **ACHIEVE SKILL AND MASTERY OVER TASKS.**

WE CALL THIS **COMPETENCE.**

I DREAM ABOUT **BEING GOOD AT THINGS.**
PASS THE **REMOTE CONTROL.**

ACCORDING TO THE THEORY, **INTERNAL MOTIVATION** WILL BE **GREATEST** WHEN **ALL THREE** AIMS ARE **WITHIN REACH.**

FOR EXAMPLE, WE'RE **MOST MOTIVATED TO LEARN SOMETHING IF OUR FRIENDS CARE ABOUT IT...**

COME ON, LET'S INTEGRATE!
BEATS BEING ALONE.

...AND WE HAVE **INFLUENCE OVER THE PROCESS...**

COME ON, LET'S TAKE DERIVATIVES!

SURE, BUT AFTER WE TAKE A BREAK.

...AND A SENSE OF **WHAT IT MEANS TO GET GOOD AT IT.**

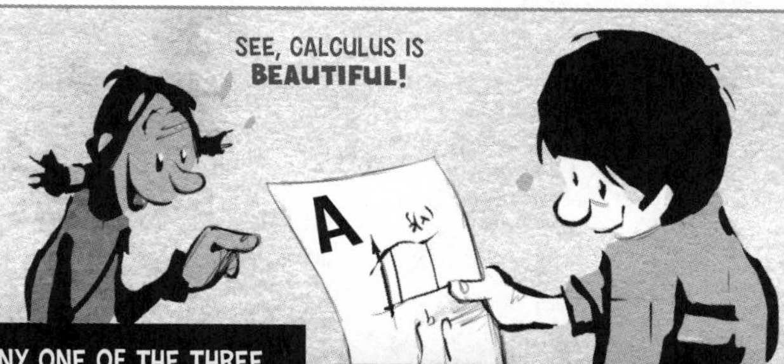
SEE, CALCULUS IS BEAUTIFUL!
A

ON THE FLIP SIDE, IF ANY ONE OF THE THREE **ESCAPES US...**

...IT CAN **DESTROY OUR MOTIVATION.**

EVERYONE ELSE LOVES MATH...
...BUT YOU SUCK AT IT.

HAVE YOU SEEN THE REMOTE CONTROL?

ONE WAY TO TEST MOTIVATION IS TO LOOK AT HOW WE RESPOND TO **EXPLICIT GOALS...**

...AND HOW **ALTERING THOSE GOALS CHANGES OUR BEHAVIOR.**

JUST TAKE IT ONE STEP AT A TIME.

BE THE BEST MULE EVER!

RESEARCHERS HAVE SHOWN HOW **"PERFORMANCE GOALS"...**

...AND **"MASTERY GOALS"...**

I WANNA BAKE 100 LOAVES OF BREAD PER WEEK.

I WANNA BE A GREAT BAKER.

...TEND TO INSPIRE **RADICALLY DIFFERENT OUTCOMES** IN THE **SHORT TERM...**

MISSION ACCOMPLISHED!

MY EXPERIMENT IS A DISASTER.

...AND THE **LONG TERM.**

SAME OLD, SAME OLD.

I'VE CREATED PERFECTION!

THEY'VE ALSO SHOWN HOW DIFFERENT GOALS **CHANGE WHAT WE NOTICE...**

THAT'S AN INTERESTING DRESS.
THAT'S AN INTERESTING BOOK.
THAT'S AN INTERESTING BODY.

...AND WHAT WE **CHOOSE.**

I WANNA EAT WHAT TASTES BEST.

I WANNA EAT WHAT'S HEALTHIEST.

THE WAY OUR GOALS **GUIDE US** IS **USUALLY A GOOD THING...**

...BUT THEY **DON'T ALWAYS WORK AS INTENDED.**

KEEP YOUR EYES ON THIS PRIZE...
...AND YOU WON'T BE DISTRACTED BY THAT PRIZE.

I HONESTLY THOUGHT I WAS AIMING FOR THE TARGET.

ONE PARTICULARLY PERNICIOUS EXAMPLE OF THIS IS **SELF-HANDICAPPING:**

IF WE'RE **ENGAGED IN A TASK...**

I'M PICKING UP GIRLS.

...BUT OUR PRIMARY GOAL IS ACTUALLY TO **PROTECT OUR SELF ESTEEM...**

I'LL BE DEVASTATED IF I FAIL.

...WE SOMETIMES **SABOTAGE OUR OWN SUCCESS...**

HEH HEH...
...HI CAN I HAVE YOUR PHONE NUMBER?
NOPE.

...TO INSULATE OURSELVES FROM THE **FEELING OF FAILURE.**

PHEW!
SHE MUST NOT LIKE THE HAT.

WHILE THIS CAN ALSO MAKE SUCCESS FEEL **SWEETER...**

...IT MAKES **FAILURE FAR MORE LIKELY.**

SHE SAID YES...
...EVEN WITH THE HAT!
SHE MUST REALLY LIKE ME!
SHE WAS BEING SARCASTIC, BRO.

SO, WHEN WE'RE NOT **HANDICAPPING OURSELVES**...

I ALWAYS USE **THIS CLUB**...
...SO PEOPLE WILL BLAME **THAT** WHEN I SUCK.

...WHICH GOALS **WORK THE BEST?**

SHOULD WE MAKE THE **HOLE BIGGER?**

LOTS OF EXPERIMENTS SHOW THAT **GENERIC GOALS**...

THEY TOLD ME TO **FOLD AS MANY AS I COULD** IN TWO MINUTES.
I FOLDED **2**.

...ARE **LESS EFFECTIVE** THAN **SPECIFIC GOALS**...

THEY TOLD ME TO FOLD **4** IN TWO MINUTES.
AND I DID IT!

...AND THE **MORE CHALLENGING** THE SPECIFIC GOAL, THE **BETTER!**

THEY TOLD ME TO FOLD **8**...
...AND I FOLDED **8**.
IT'S **GOAL-SETTING THEORY**.

BUT THERE'S A **LIMIT** TO HOW MUCH DIFFICULTY WE'LL TAKE...

YOU FOLD **31**.
THAT'S **TOO HARD**.
I **DON'T WANNA FAIL**.

...AND OUR **DISTANCE FROM THE GOAL** ALSO MATTERS.

IF I'D **ALREADY FOLDED 27**, I'D BE **EXCITED TO FINISH**.
BUT SINCE I'VE **ONLY DONE 10**, I'M **DEMOTIVATED**.

IT'S THE **GOAL GRADIENT HYPOTHESIS**.

WHICH EXPLAINS WHY, WHEN WE'RE **FACED WITH A DAUNTING TASK**...

WHAT MADE ME THINK I COULD **WRITE A NOVEL?**

...IT CAN HELP TO CREATE **SUBGOALS** THAT **BOLSTER** OUR SENSE OF **ACHIEVEMENT ALONG THE WAY**.

1. write list
2. eat sandwich
3. write novel

I'M, **2/3** OF THE WAY THERE ALREADY!

IT HELPS EVEN MORE TO **MAKE SPECIFIC PLANS** RELATING TO **SPECIFIC HURDLES** THAT WILL LIKELY GET IN OUR WAY.

AWESOME, IT'S **ANOTHER MIRAGE!**
THAT MEANS **KEEP CRAWLING!**

THESE PLANS TAKE THE FORM OF CONCRETE **IF—THEN SCENARIOS** ABOUT WHATEVER IT IS WE WANT TO CHANGE.

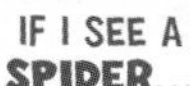

IF I SEE A **SPIDER...**
...I WILL **BREATHE SLOWLY.**

IF I SEE A **TWINKIE...**
...I WILL **NOT EAT IT.**

IT TURNS OUT THAT OUR **GOOD INTENTIONS** OFTEN FAIL BECAUSE THEY'RE **TOO VAGUE...**

MY NEW YEAR'S RESOLUTION...
...IS TO **HAVE A DIFFERENT NEW YEAR'S RESOLUTION NEXT YEAR.**

...AND ALL WE'RE MISSING IS **DETAILED INSTRUCTIONS FOR HOW TO CARRY THEM OUT.**

WE SHOULD GET **FLU SHOTS.**

IF YOU WRITE DOWN THE DATE AND TIME YOU'RE GONNA DO IT...
...YOU'RE **MORE LIKELY TO GET IT DONE.**

IT'S **IMPLEMENTATION INTENTIONS!**

DESPITE ALL THE **TRICKS** AND **TIPS** WE'VE SEEN IN THIS CHAPTER...

...MOTIVATION CAN STILL FEEL **ELUSIVE.**

I WANT **RESPECT**, **CONTROL**, AND **ACHIEVEMENT**...
...AND I WANT MY **GOALS WITHIN REACH.**

WOULD YOU PREFER CARROT **CAKE?**

HOWEVER, THERE IS **ONE APPROACH** WHICH **WORKS BETTER THAN ANY OTHER MOTIVATION.**

HOW DO YOU **GET TO CARNEGIE HALL?**

IT'S ALL ABOUT YOUR **HABITS.**

WHEN WE **PRACTICE** SOMETHING ENOUGH, **IT BECOMES AUTOMATIC...**

...AND THAT'S WHEN WE'RE **MOST LIKELY TO SUCCEED AT IT.**

I USED TO **PUT ONE FOOT IN FRONT OF THE OTHER...**

...NOW I JUST **WALK.**

NOW I DON'T EVEN **THINK** ABOUT **BRUSHING MY TEETH...**
...OR **PLAYING BEETHOVEN.**

SO, WHILE IT IS POSSIBLE TO CHANGE OUR BEHAVIOR BY **CREATING MOTIVATION...**

...IT IS MUCH MORE EFFECTIVE TO **CIRCUMVENT IT ALTOGETHER.**

GO GO RAH RAH RAH!

I'M TOTALLY **UNMOTIVATED...**
...BUT I **DO IT ANYWAY.**

CHAPTER 8

STRESS AND HEALTH

ALARM!

SO FAR, WE'VE FOCUSED MOSTLY ON OUR **MENTAL STATES...**

...BUT TO MAKE SENSE OF OURSELVES, WE NEED TO UNDERSTAND **OUR PHYSICAL STATES TOO.**

MY **MIND** SAYS "**STOP**"...
...BUT MY **BODY** SAYS "**GO.**"

ONE ESSENTIAL WAY OUR **MINDS AND BODIES INTERACT** IS THROUGH **STRESS.**

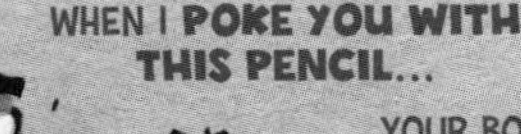
WHEN I **POKE YOU WITH THIS PENCIL...**
...YOUR BODY TELLS YOUR MIND TO **FREAK OUT!**

WHEN WE'RE **RELAXED...**

...OUR BODIES ARE CONTROLLED BY OUR **PARASYMPATHETIC NERVOUS SYSTEM...**

...WHICH HANDLES **RESTING AND DIGESTING.**

Decreased Heart Rate
Increased Digestion
ALSO KNOWN AS **FEEDING AND BREEDING.**

BUT WHEN THERE ARE **STRESSORS** AROUND...

...OUR BODIES ACTIVATE OUR **SYMPATHETIC NERVOUS SYSTEM...**

...WHICH HANDLES **FIGHTING AND FLIGHTING.**

Increased Heart Rate
Decreased Digestion
FREAK OUT!

TECHNICALLY, A **STRESSOR** IS ANYTHING THAT **CREATES A DEMAND ON THE BODY...**

I'M **HUNGRY.**

I'M **COLD.**

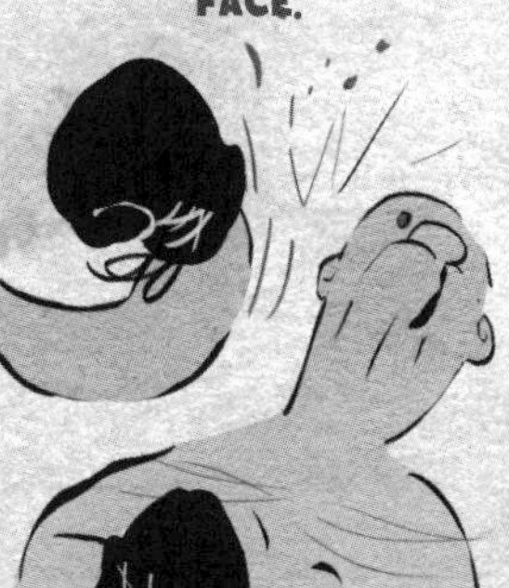
I'M BEING
HIT IN THE FACE.

I'M BEING
INJECTED WITH IRRITATING CHEMICALS!

...CAUSING OUR FIGHT OR FLIGHT RESPONSE TO **FIRE UP.**

I'M **TENSE.**

I'M **NERVOUS.**

I'M **ANGRY.**

I'M
INFLAMED.

BUT AS WE'LL SEE IN THIS CHAPTER, THAT RESPONSE **FIRES UP AT OTHER TIMES TOO...**

I FEEL LIKE I'M BEING **CHASED BY A GORILLA.**
AWESOME!

...WHETHER WE **LIKE IT OR NOT...**

I **CAN'T STOP** FEELING LIKE I'M BEING **CHASED BY A GORILLA.**

...AND THIS CAN HAVE **BAD CONSEQUENCES.**

CLEARLY OUR STRESS RESPONSE EVOLVED TO **KEEP US SAFE.**

BUT IN ADDITION TO **PHYSICAL STRESSORS...**

...WE **ALSO** EXPERIENCE **PSYCHOLOGICAL AND SOCIAL STRESSORS...**

YOU'RE LAME.

YOU'RE UGLY.

YOU'RE FIRED.

...EVEN WHEN THEY **HAVEN'T YET HAPPENED.**

THEY'RE GONNA THINK I'M LAME...
...AND UGLY...
...AND I'M GONNA GET FIRED.

AND THE CUMULATIVE EFFECT OF ALL THAT STRESS CAN CAUSE **HARM IN THE LONG TERM.**

FREAK OUT!

FREAK OUT!

FREAK OUT!

FREAK OUT!

CHRONIC STRESS CAN HAVE **SERIOUS HEALTH EFFECTS**:

WEAKENING OUR **MINDS**...

NO TIME TO **THINK**...

I NEED TO **ESCAPE**

...OUR **DIGESTION**...

NO TIME TO **ABSORB NUTRIENTS**...

...OUR **REPRODUCTION**...

NO TIME FOR **SEX**...

...OUR **IMMUNE SYSTEMS**...

NO TIME TO **HEAL**...

...AND EVEN **STUNTING OUR DEVELOPMENT**.

NO TIME TO **GROW**...

TO TOP IT OFF, OUR **BODY'S RESPONSE TO STRESS** CAN **ADD TO THE STRESS**...

I'M **STRESSED** ABOUT...

...ALWAYS BEING **STRESSED** ABOUT...

...ALWAYS BEING **STRESSED** ABOUT...

...ALWAYS BEING **STRESSED** ABOUT...

IT'S A FEEDBACK LOOP.

...AND CAUSE **MORE DAMAGE** THAN THE ORIGINAL SOURCE OF STRESS.

MY HEART IS ALWAYS BEATING LIKE A **ROCK BAND**.

WE **MEASURE STRESS** BY OBSERVING **ULCERS**...

...SAMPLING THE HORMONE **CORTISOL**...

...TAKING **BLOOD PRESSURE**...

...AND ASKING **QUESTIONS.**

HAVE YOU EXPERIENCED ANY DISCOMFORT LATELY?
LET ME TELL YOU.

THESE MEASUREMENTS SHOW THAT **SOME PEOPLE** ARE **NATURALLY MORE HIGH STRUNG**...

...THAN **OTHERS**...

I'M TYPE A! I'M NOT PATIENT! I WANNA WIN! I CAN'T RELAX!
IS THAT A SNAKE?!
PASS THE REMOTE CONTROL.

...AND **MORE LIKELY** TO EXPERIENCE **STRESS RELATED ILLNESS.**

WHERE'D HE GO?
HOSPITAL.

BUT THESE MEASUREMENTS ALSO SHOW THAT A **MAJORITY OF AMERICANS** SUFFER FROM **UNHEALTHY LEVELS OF STRESS**...

WORK!
KIDS!
MONEY!
SEX!

...WHICH HAS **EVEN BROADER IMPLICATIONS** FOR **PUBLIC HEALTH**.

WHERE'D THEY GO?
HOSPITAL.

AND THAT RAISES THE **QUESTION:**

HOW ARE WE SUPPOSED TO **COPE?!**

FIRST AND FOREMOST, SIMPLY HAVING A SENSE OF **CONTROL OVER OUR LIVES** CAN BENEFIT OUR LONG TERM **HEALTH**.

I **WORRY LESS** IF I HAVE A **SPEAR**.

IN ONE SEMINAL STUDY, WHEN SOME **NURSING HOME RESIDENTS** WERE GIVEN **RESPONSIBILITIES**...

YOU CAN **SET YOUR OWN SCHEDULE!**
AND **TAKE CARE OF THESE PLANTS**.

...THAT OTHERS WERE **NOT**...

DON'T DO **ANYTHING**.
WE'LL TAKE CARE OF YOU.

...THEY **SURVIVED SIGNIFICANTLY LONGER!**

AFTER 18 MONTHS, THEIR ODDS OF DEATH WERE **CUT IN HALF!**
I PREFER **PLANTING DAISIES** TO **PUSHING THEM UP**.

WHICH SUGGESTS WAYS TO REMEDY STRESS WHEN THINGS **AREN'T QUITE SO DIRE**.

GIMME A **LEADERSHIP ROLE**...
...UNLESS YOU WANT ME TO BE A **STIFF** INSTEAD OF A **WORKING STIFF!**

SIMILAR RESULTS HAVE BEEN OBSERVED IN **RATS.**

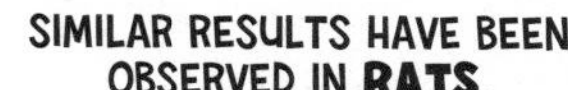

I'M SO **TIRED** OF THE **RAT RACE.**
TELL ME ABOUT IT.

RATS WHO RECEIVE **REPEATED RANDOM MILD ELECTRIC SHOCKS...**

ZZZT!

OUCH, MY **ULCER.**

...GET **WAY MORE STRESSED OUT** THAN THOSE WHO ARE **GIVEN A WARNING AHEAD OF TIME.**

HEAR THE CHIME? **BRACE YOURSELF!**

THAT **WASN'T** SO BAD.

AND RATS WHO HAVE THE **POWER TO STOP THE ZAPPING...**

...REDUCE THEIR STRESS LEVELS **EVEN MORE.**

WHEN IT STARTS,
I CAN PULL THE LEVER TO STOP IT!

WHEN IT STARTS, **I GET ZAPPED FOR THE SAME AMOUNT OF TIME...**
...BUT I **DON'T** GET A LEVER.

BEATS WORKING IN A **CUBICLE.**

OUCH, MY **ULCER.**

THIS SUGGESTS THAT A LARGE PART OF STRESS COMES FROM **UNPREDICTABILITY...**

THE REAL **TORTURE** ISN'T **WAITING FOR THE TRAIN...**
...IT'S **NOT KNOWING WHEN IT'LL COME!**

...AND THAT THE BEST SOLUTION IS **BEING ABLE TO DO SOMETHING ABOUT IT.**

I'M WAY MORE RELAXED WHEN I CAN **CHECK THE TIMETABLE ON MY PHONE.**

WHEREAS **FOREKNOWLEDGE** ALONE CAN REDUCE HOW MUCH STRESS WE FEEL...

IT'S MUCH EASIER TO **WAIT**...
...WHEN YOU KNOW **HOW LONG YOU HAVE TO WAIT.**

...SO CAN CERTAIN **INTERPRETATIONS.**

MY GLASS IS **HALF EMPTY.**
MY GLASS IS **HALF FULL.**

FOR EXAMPLE, WHEN **BAD THINGS** HAPPEN TO US...

YOU EACH **FAILED YOUR EXAM!**

...IT'S MUCH **MORE STRESSFUL** TO THINK THEY REFLECT **PERMANENT FAULTS IN OURSELVES...**

...THAN TO THINK THEY REFLECT **TEMPORARY BLIPS IN OUR FORTUNES.**

I **SUCK.**
Always
Forever
I'm Stupid
Inevitable
My Fault
F
I SHOULD **GO GET ICE CREAM.**
I'll Do Better Next Time.
I'm Lucky To Be Alive
The Test Was Unfair
@*&# Happens
F

THIS SUGGESTS THAT WE CAN BE **TRAINED TO RESPOND IN HEALTHIER WAYS...**

AT LEAST WE'RE NOT BEING **CHASED BY TIGERS!**
IT'S **COGNITIVE REAPPRAISAL!**

...THOUGH OBVIOUSLY THAT SORT OF THING **ISN'T SIMPLE.**

MORE **STRAIGHTFORWARD** WAYS TO REDUCE STRESS INCLUDE **MEDITATION...**

OMM.
OMM.

...EXERCISE...

OOF.
OOF.

...HUMOR...

A **RAT** AND A **YOGI** WALK INTO A BAR...

...AND **SOCIAL SUPPORT.**

OK, SO THAT'S NOT FUNNY BUT I **LOVE YOU ANYWAY.**

ALL OF WHICH HAVE **PROVEN BENEFITS TO OUR HEALTH...**

...AND **OUR COGNITIVE ABILITIES.**

I'M **NOT DEAD YET!**

AFTER I FINISH THIS **MAZE** I'M GONNA SOLVE **HILBERT'S PROBLEMS!**

WHICH BRINGS US TO SOMETHING **MYSTERIOUS.**

WE'VE SEEN SOME OF THE WAYS THAT **CHANGES IN OUR BODIES** CAN **INFLUENCE OUR MINDS...**

...BUT IS THE **OPPOSITE** TRUE?

JOGGING IS **GOOD FOR YOUR BRAIN!**

I WISH **CROSSWORD PUZZLES** WERE GOOD FOR MY **THIGHS.**

IN PARTICULAR, IS IT POSSIBLE TO IMPROVE ONE'S HEALTH THROUGH **BELIEF ALONE?**

IF YOU HAVE **FAITH,** GOD WILL **REWARD YOU...**
...WITH **SIX PACK ABS!**

ON THE ONE HAND, ALTHOUGH THERE IS **SOME EVIDENCE** THAT **RELIGIOUS FAITH** CAN **REDUCE STRESS...**

...THERE'S **SCANT EVIDENCE** THAT IT CAN ACTUALLY **HEAL ILLNESS.**

I'M HEALTHIER BECAUSE I **PLAY.**

I'M HEALTHIER BECAUSE I **PRAY.**

YOU MAY BE **MORALLY UPRIGHT...**
...BUT THAT WON'T IMPROVE YOUR **BACK PROBLEMS.**

ON THE OTHER HAND, THERE'S **LOTS OF EVIDENCE** THAT OUR **BELIEFS ABOUT PILLS** CAN HAVE **ASTONISHING CONSEQUENCES!**

STEP RIGHT UP AND GET YOUR **PLACEBO!**
GUARANTEED TO **REDUCE** YOUR **ACHES** AND **PAINS...**
...AND THE **AMOUNT OF MONEY IN YOUR WALLET.**

PLACEBOS, OF COURSE, **AREN'T SUPPOSED TO HAVE ANY EFFECTS.**

IT'S JUST **CHALK** AND **SUGAR.**

THEY'RE GIVEN TO PATIENTS **TO FOOL THEM.**

IT'S GOT **UNBELIEVABLE POWERS!**

BUT TIME AND AGAIN, THEY'VE BEEN SHOWN TO **INFLUENCE A HOST OF PHYSICAL SYMPTOMS AND ABILITIES.**

IT'S THE **ONLY PILL** WE KNOW OF THAT CAN **REDUCE NAUSEA, INSOMNIA, BLOOD PRESSURE, DEPRESSION**, AND **HEADACHES...**
...AND INCREASE NAUSEA, INSOMNIA, BLOOD PRESSURE, DEPRESSION, AND HEADACHES.

WHILE NOBODY SHOULD MISTAKE THESE RESULTS FOR **MEDICAL CURES...**

IT WORKS BECAUSE IT **GETS YOUR HOPES UP...**
...BUT DON'T LET THEM GET UP **TOO HIGH.**

...THEY DO INDICATE, ONCE AGAIN, THE POWERFUL INFLUENCE OF OUR **TOP DOWN ASSOCIATIONS.**

Relaxation
Trust
Pills Work
Medication
Science
Lab Coat
Ease
THE POWER OF THIS PILL...
...DEPENDS **ENTIRELY** ON WHAT YOU BELIEVE IT TO BE.

AND THERE'S MORE TO IT THAN **JUST PILLS.**

AS IT TURNS OUT, JUST AS OUR BELIEFS AND EXPECTATIONS **INFLUENCE OUR EXPERIENCES**...

...THEY ALSO **INFLUENCE OUR BODILY FUNCTIONS.**

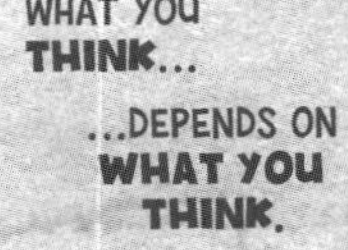
WHAT YOU THINK...
...DEPENDS ON WHAT YOU THINK.

THE EFFECT OF THIS DRINK...
...DEPENDS ON WHAT YOU THINK.

SOME STUDIES SHOW THAT IF WE'RE TOLD A **DRINK** IS **MORE EXPENSIVE**...

...WE TEND TO THINK IT **TASTES BETTER.**

AT $99.99...
...THIS WINE MUST BE FINE.

OTHER STUDIES SHOW THAT IF WE'RE TOLD A **HEALTH ELIXIR** IS **MORE EXPENSIVE**...

...WE TEND TO THINK IT **WORKS BETTER.**

THIS EXPENSIVE DRINK PREVENTS WORKOUT FATIGUE...

...AND SO DOES THIS CHEAP ONE.

I'M **ENERGIZED!**

I'M **EXHAUSTED.**

AND IF WE'RE TOLD A **MENTAL STIMULANT** IS **MORE EXPENSIVE**...

...IT ACTUALLY **DOES WORK BETTER.**

THIS EXPENSIVE DRINK IMPROVES MENTAL FUNCTIONING...

...AND SO DOES THIS CHEAP ONE.

"CEMLIAR RECU" IS AN ANAGRAM FOR "MIRACLE CURE"!

"COBELAP" IS AN ANAGRAM FOR...
...UM?

AND THEN THERE'S THE **THINK—DRINK EFFECT.**
I CALL THIS ONE THE **PLACEBO.**®
IF WE'RE TOLD A **DRINK CONTAINS ALCOHOL,** WHEN IT ACTUALLY DOESN'T...
...WE STILL BECOME **INTOXICATED.**
HAVE **ANOTHER ROUND ON US!**
SHANKTH.
I **LOVE** YOU, BRO!
WHO YOU LOOKING AT?
PHBPHBPBHBHHBB
THIS EFFECT IS **SO POWERFUL** THAT SOME RESEARCHERS THINK DRUNKENNESS OFTEN HAS AS MUCH TO DO WITH **EXPECTATIONS...**
...AS WITH **CHEMISTRY.**
THISH COCKTAIL ISH **POTHENT!**
WHASH **IN IT?**
LEMON JUICE, SIMPLE SYRUP, BITTERS, AND A SPLASH OF **PERFIDY.**
SO TOO, OUR PERENNIAL ENTHUSIASM FOR **MIRACLE CURES** AND **DIET FADS...**
...MAY DEPEND HEAVILY ON OUR **BELIEF THAT THEY WORK.**
I'M ON THE **PALEO DIET.**
AND I'M **GLUTEN FREE.**
ME TOO!
WHAT YOU **DIGEST** IS MOSTLY **BIOLOGY.**
BUT **HOW** YOU DIGEST...
...DEPENDS ON **WHAT YOU THINK.**

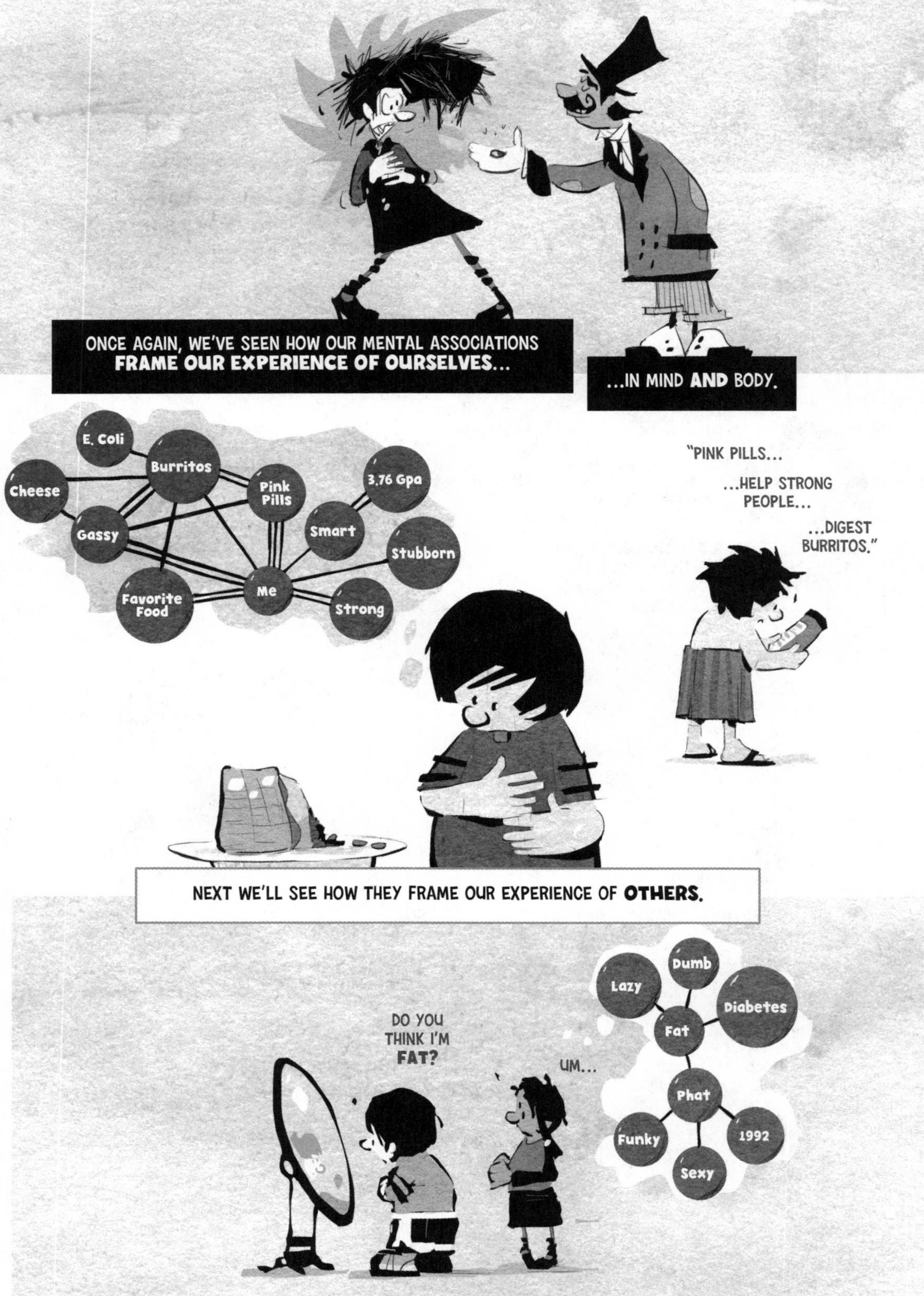
IN THIS CHAPTER, WE'VE COVERED THE **RAVAGES OF STRESS...**
...AND THE **POWER OF PLACEBOS.**
ONCE AGAIN, WE'VE SEEN HOW OUR MENTAL ASSOCIATIONS **FRAME OUR EXPERIENCE OF OURSELVES...**
...IN MIND **AND** BODY.
E. Coli
Burritos
Cheese
Pink Pills
3.76 Gpa
Gassy
Smart
Stubborn
Favorite Food
Me
Strong
"PINK PILLS...
...HELP STRONG PEOPLE...
...DIGEST BURRITOS."
NEXT WE'LL SEE HOW THEY FRAME OUR EXPERIENCE OF **OTHERS.**
DO YOU THINK I'M **FAT?**
UM...
Dumb
Lazy
Diabetes
Fat
Phat
Funky
1992
Sexy

PART THREE

MAKING SENSE OF EACH OTHER

CHAPTER 9
LANGUAGE

DRAW!

ALTHOUGH LANGUAGE IS OUR **PRIMARY TOOL FOR COMMUNICATION...**

...IT DOESN'T ALWAYS WORK **AS WE EXPECT.**

WE HAVE THE RIGHT TO BEAR ARMS!
DO YOU MEAN "BARE" AS IN NAKED...
...OR "BEAR" AS IN GRIZZLY?

IN FACT, CLOSE ANALYSIS SHOWS THAT THE THINGS WE SAY AND WRITE ARE ALMOST ALWAYS **AMBIGUOUS...**

THAT FAT CAT IS COLD!
DO YOU MEAN TEMPERATURE COLD...
...OR TEMPERAMENT COLD?

...SO MUCH SO THAT IT'S AMAZING WE **EVER** MANAGE TO **SUCCESSFULLY COMMUNICATE.**

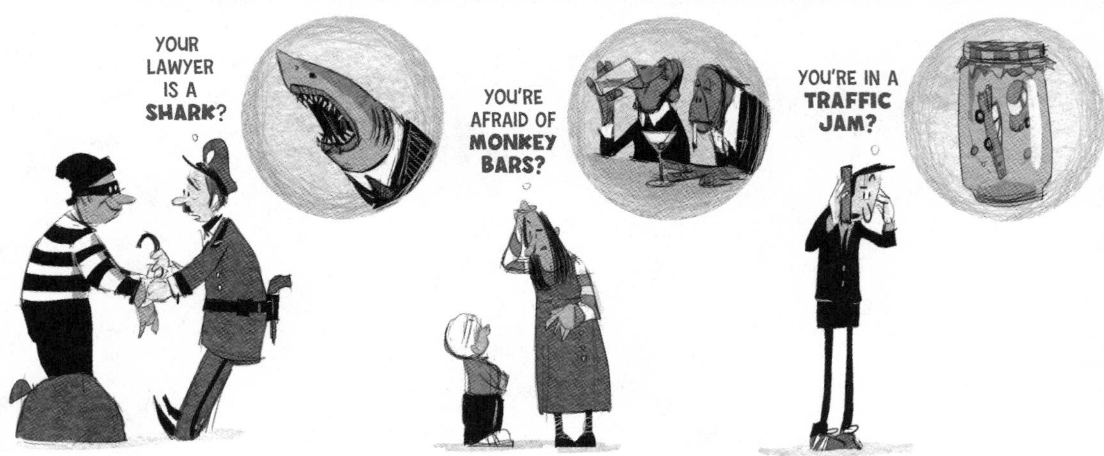

YOUR LAWYER IS A SHARK?
YOU'RE AFRAID OF MONKEY BARS?
YOU'RE IN A TRAFFIC JAM?

LANGUAGE IS CRAMMED WITH AMBIGUITIES THAT ARE **LEXICAL**...

MANY WORDS HAVE **MULTIPLE MEANINGS.**

TIME FLIES LIKE AN **ARROW**...
...**FRUIT FLIES** LIKE A **TOMATO.**

...AND **PHONETIC**...

SIMILAR SOUNDS CAN HAVE **MULTIPLE MEANINGS, TOO.**
LIKE "**TWO.**"

HI, MY NAME IS **MILTON AUGUST.**
NICE TO MEET YOU, MILT.
WHAT'S YOUR NAME IN **SEPTEMBER?**

...AND **STRUCTURAL.**

EVEN THE **SHAPE OF A SENTENCE** CAN **AFFECT ITS MEANING.**

LAST NIGHT I **SHOT AN ELEPHANT IN MY PAJAMAS**...

...HOW HE GOT IN MY **PAJAMAS** I'LL **NEVER KNOW.**

AND TO TOP IT OFF, PEOPLE DON'T ALWAYS **SAY WHAT THEY MEAN!**

THE SECRET OF LIFE IS **HONESTY AND FAIR DEALING**...
...IF YOU CAN **FAKE THAT,** YOU'VE **GOT IT MADE.**

AND YET, EVEN WHEN WE'RE BEING **POETIC** OR **IRONIC** OR **OBTUSE** WE STILL **MANAGE TO UNDERSTAND EACH OTHER...**

YO DOG, THAT **CLOWN** IS A **SHOE IN.**
BUT HE'S A **ONE TRICK PONY.**
AND PRETTY SOON HIS **CHICKENS WILL COME HOME TO ROOST.**

...AND THE BIG QUESTION IS, **HOW?**

WHEN ANYONE **SAYS ANYTHING...**
...THERE'S A **CRAZY ARRAY** OF **POSSIBLE MEANINGS.**

SO HOW DO WE **CATCH THE RIGHT ONE?**

THE **SIMPLEST ANSWER** IS THAT WE MAKE USE OF **CONTEXT...**

...WHICH PROVIDES US WITH THE KIND OF **TOP-DOWN CUES** WE LEARNED ABOUT IN THE CHAPTER ON PERCEPTION.

YEP, MY LAWYER IS **DEFINITELY** A **SHARK.**

AHA!
BUT SINCE **SHARKS** LIVE **ONLY IN THE WATER...**
...AND **LAWYERS DON'T LIVE IN THE WATER...**
...HE CANNOT **LITERALLY** BE A SHARK.

WE GATHER THAT CONTEXT FROM THE **NEURAL NETS** WE LEARNED ABOUT IN THE MEMORY CHAPTER.

Ambulance
Suit
Sharp
Baby
Puppy
Serrated
Judge
Lawyer
Ruthless
Canine
Wolf
Shark
Teeth
Mean
Cruel
Swim
Jaws
Steven Spielberg
Ratatouille
Rats
Ocean
Pigeons
Pixar
Finding Nemo
Skinner Boxes

THE SOUNDS HIT OUR EARS, AND WE USE OUR NETWORK OF MEMORIES TO **INFER THE INTENDED MEANING.**

mylawyerisa**shark**
HE MAY BE **SHARP** AND **MEAN** AND **CRUEL**...
...BUT I'M CONFIDENT HE'S NOT **REALLY** A BLOODTHIRSTY MARINE PREDATOR.
BUT WHILE THIS PROCESS HELPS US **NARROW THINGS DOWN**...
Im**sickatheart**
I'M GUESSING YOU'RE **SAD**...
...BUT YOU'RE **NOT SAYING** YOU HAVE **HEART DISEASE.**
...IT **ISN'T TOTALLY RELIABLE.**

IN FACT, OUR RELIANCE ON CONTEXT OFTEN **BREAKS DOWN.**

I gave her cat food.
I'm glad I'm a man, and so is my wife.

FOR EXAMPLE, SOMETIMES WE ENCOUNTER **LANGUAGE ILLUSIONS,** WHERE OUR **INTERPRETATION CHANGES AS WE WADE FARTHER IN.**

Mary gave the child the dog bit a bandaid.

THAT SORT OF PHRASE IS AMBIGUOUS BECAUSE OF ITS **STRUCTURE...**

AT FIRST I THOUGHT **MARY** GAVE THE DOG TO THE CHILD.

BUT THEN I WONDERED **WHY WOULD A DOG BITE A BANDAID?**

...BUT LET'S NOT FORGET ALL THE OTHER **AMBIGUITIES** THAT CAN SCREW US UP.

THAT **WORD** IS CONFUSING.
THAT **SOUND** IS CONFUSING.
THAT **GUY** IS CONFUSING.
THAT **GAL** IS A LIAR!
WE NEED A **WAY OUT OF THIS MESS.**

THE POINT IS, WHAT ACTUALLY COMES OUT OF ANOTHER PERSON'S MOUTH IS **ALMOST ALWAYS AMBIGUOUS.**

yoostoopidcritinuzpeesofcrahplayzdumcheepidioteyewisheyenevermetyoo...
WHA?

SO TO MAKE SENSE OF IT WE EMPLOY **ANOTHER LAYER OF STRATEGY...**

hopeyerchildrenhavtooeatthestuffthatgrowzih meyeshoesyoocheatingsunovastinkingwahrthawg!
YOUR NEURAL NET ALONE ISN'T ENOUGH IF YOU CAN'T CATCH HER MEANING.

...BY MAKING CERTAIN **ASSUMPTIONS ABOUT COMMUNICATIVE INTENT.**

yoolowzyjurk
sdayawayfrumee
flippndipsteck

WHAT YOU HEAR...
...DEPENDS ON WHAT YOU THINK HER GOALS ARE.

IT'S A PROCESS PSYCHOLOGISTS CALL **PRAGMATICS.**

OR GRICEAN IMPLICATURE...
...NAMED AFTER THIS GUY...
...IF YOU REALLY MUST KNOW.

WHENEVER WE CONVERSE, WE USE **PRAGMATIC STRATEGIES** TO INTERPRET SOMEONE'S MEANING:

QUALITY
WE ASSUME THAT PEOPLE ARE **TELLING US THE TRUTH**.
EXCEPT IF WE KNOW THEY'RE **LYING**, OF COURSE.

I'M SO HUNGRY I COULD **EAT A HORSE**.
AHA!
BUT SINCE YOU'RE NOT **LITERALLY** A SHARK...
...YOU MUST BE SPEAKING **FIGURATIVELY!**

RELATION
WE ASSUME CONVERSATIONS **MAKE SENSE**.
SO IF WE HEAR **GAPS IN MEANING** WE FILL THEM IN.

HOW DO YOU LIKE **BEING MARRIED?**
WELL...
...I LOVE MY **CHILDREN**.
DADDY, WHY **DOESN'T MOMMY LIKE YOU?**

QUANTITY
WE EXPECT TO GET THE RIGHT AMOUNT OF INFORMATION.
SO IF WE GET NOT ENOUGH...
...OR TOO MUCH...
...WE SEARCH FOR A REASON.

IT'S MONDAY, WHY'D YOU GIVE ME A TICKET?
No Parking On Sundays
IT DOESN'T SAY YOU CAN PARK HERE MONDAYS.

MANNER
WE EXPECT CLARITY.
SO IF WE SENSE AMBIGUITY WE TRY TO FIND A MOTIVE FOR IT.

WELL...
...HE'S NOT NECESSARILY NOT HANDSOME.
JUST HOW UGLY IS HE?

ALL THAT HAPPENS NOT JUST AS WE **LISTEN** BUT ALSO AS WE **TALK.**

MY SPEECH HAS **LOUSY QUALITY...**
...DISJOINTED RELATION...
...OVERWHELMING QUANTITY...
...AND MY **MANNER IS BIZARRE.**
WHAT AM I **TRYING TO SAY?**

beeyoordehohnleewunfoorme**eyewoodnehverlookatanudderman**azlohngazeyelive

FOR THE MOST PART THOUGH, WE'RE **UNAWARE** THAT WE DO THIS **COMPLEX AND INTERTWINED INTERPRETATION** IN THE COURSE OF EVERYDAY CONVERSATION.

ALL I'M TRYING TO DO IS **SPEAK TO YOU!**
ALL I'M TRYING TO DO IS **INFER YOUR MEANING!**
ACTUALLY, YOU'RE BOTH TRYING TO **BREAK UP!**

WHICH MAKES IT ALL THE MORE AMAZING THAT **CHILDREN** LEARN IT SO QUICKLY.

SANTA WON'T GIVE YOU A PRESENT **IF YOU'RE NOT GOOD,** SHNOOKUMS.
ITS OK DADDY...
...I CAN TELL YOU **REALLY MEAN** THAT SANTA **WILL** GIVE ME A PRESENT **IF I'M GOOD.**

THERE ARE **COMPETING THEORIES** ABOUT **HOW WE LEARN LANGUAGE.**

IT'S NATURE!
IT'S NURTURE!

SOME PEOPLE THINK WE MUST HAVE AN **INNATE ABILITY FOR IT...**

...WHILE OTHERS INSIST WE **LEARN IT ON THE FLY.**

WE ALL SHARE A UNIVERSAL GRAMMAR!

THEN WHY ARE LANGUAGES ALWAYS CHANGING?

HOWEVER, LET'S **SIDESTEP** THOSE **RAGING DEBATES...**

LANGUAGE IS TOO ERROR PRONE TO LEARN BY LISTENING!
LANGUAGE IS TOO ERROR PRONE TO BE INNATE!

...AND FOCUS MORE CLOSELY ON HOW WE LEARN **WORDS** IN PARTICULAR...

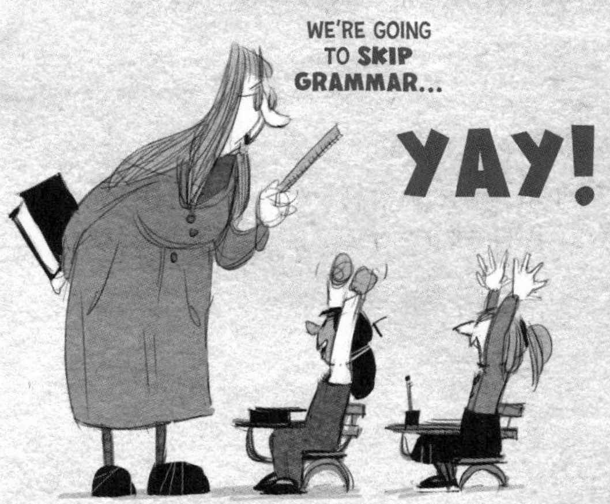

WE'RE GOING TO SKIP GRAMMAR...
YAY!

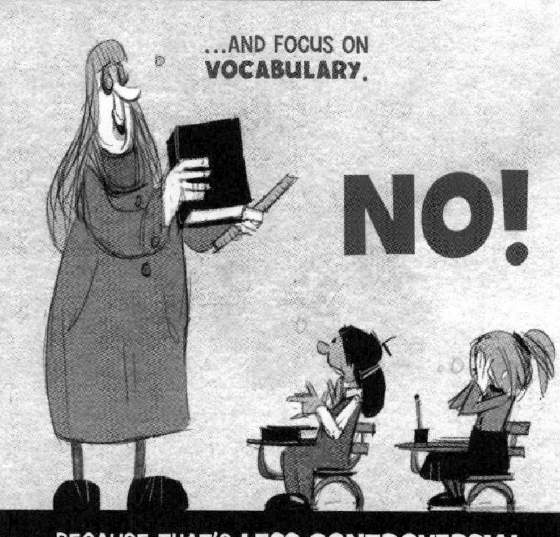

...AND FOCUS ON VOCABULARY.
NO!

...BECAUSE THAT'S **LESS CONTROVERSIAL.**

TO UNDERSTAND WORDS, WE HAVE TO **DISTINGUISH THEM FROM THE OVERALL FLOW OF LANGUAGE.**

Gehtoffameyelegidontwannabetouchedrightnow!
I LOVE YOU TOO, DADDY.

HOWEVER, WHEN WE ZOOM IN ON **SOUNDWAVES** OF HOW WE **ACTUALLY TALK...**

SAY "WHERE ARE THE SILENCES?"
wherearethesilences?

...WE SEE MULTIPLE **PAUSES** THAT MAKE IT HARD TO TELL WHERE **ONE WORD ENDS** AND **ANOTHER BEGINS.**

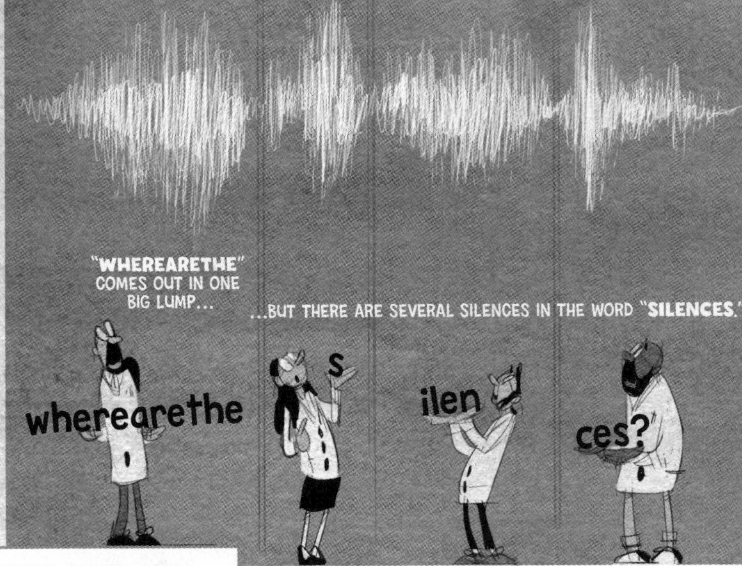
"WHEREARETHE" COMES OUT IN ONE BIG LUMP...
...BUT THERE ARE SEVERAL SILENCES IN THE WORD "SILENCES."
wherearethe
s
ilen
ces?

AND THE QUESTION IS, IN THIS **GARBLED RIVER OF SPEECH...**

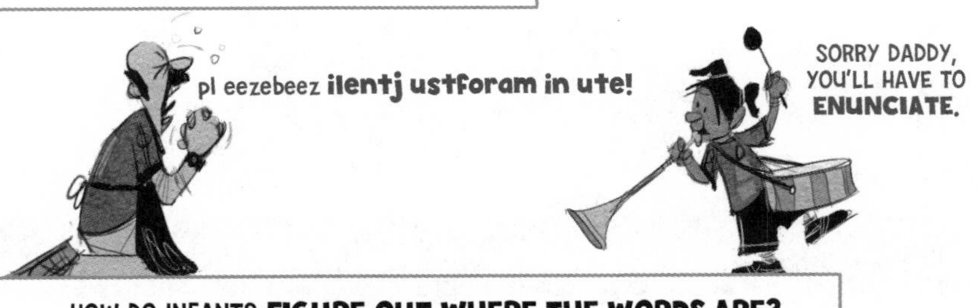
pl eezebeez ilentj ustforam in ute!
SORRY DADDY, YOU'LL HAVE TO ENUNCIATE.

...HOW DO INFANTS **FIGURE OUT WHERE THE WORDS ARE?**

wenwesp eak weyallt enddobem ooshym outh ed.
WHAT'D SHE SAY?
WHEN WE SPEAK, WE ALL TEND TO BE MUSHY MOUTHED.

ONE WAY WOULD BE TO LISTEN FOR **STATISTICAL REGULARITIES**...

FOR EXAMPLE, WHEN I SAY...
...your**sugardaddy**gives**sugarcookies**withhigh**sugarcontent**tohis**sugarplumfairy**...
...THE SOUND "**GAR**" **ALWAYS** FOLLOWS THE SOUND "**SHU**"...
...BUT THE SOUND THAT FOLLOWS "**GAR**" VARIES BETWEEN "**DA**," "**COO**," "**CON**," AND "**PLUM**."

...BECAUSE THEY INDICATE **WHICH SYLLABLES ARE MOST LIKELY TO FORM WORDS.**

"shu"
"gar"
"gar"
"da"
"coo"
"con"
"plum"
THE **ODDS ARE 1/1** OF MOVING FROM "SHU" TO "GAR"...
...BUT THE **ODDS ARE ONLY 1/4** OF MOVING FROM "GAR" TO EITHER "DA," "COO," "CON," OR "PLUM."
SO "**SHUGAR**" IS **MORE LIKELY TO BE A WORD**...
...THAN "**GARCOO**," OR "**GARPLUM**."

BUT DO INFANTS **ACTUALLY DO THAT?**

I'LL PUT MY MONEY ON "SHUGAR."
IT'S **STATISTICAL INFERENCE!**

SHOCKINGLY, THE ANSWER IS YES!

MY BABY IS A **POET**.
MY BABY IS AN **ARTIST**.
MY BABY IS A **STAR**.
ACTUALLY, ALL YOUR BABIES ARE **STATISTICIANS**.

TO **TEST** WHETHER WE'RE AWARE OF **STATISTICAL PATTERNS** AS WE **LEARN WORDS**...

...PSYCHOLOGISTS PLAYED A STRING OF **FAKE THREE-SYLLABLE WORDS REPEATEDLY AND RANDOMLY** TO SOME INFANTS...

GO-LA-TI, BI-DA-KU, RE-ME-FA, RE-ME-FA, GO-LA-TI, RE-ME-FA, BI-DA-KU, GO-LA-TI, GO-LA-TI

...THEN **WAITED UNTIL THEY GOT BORED.**

WHAT ARE **THOSE SOUNDS?**
THEY DON'T MEAN **NOTHIN'**.

THEN THE PSYCHOLOGISTS **CHANGED THE ORDER OF THE SYLLABLES** WITHIN THE WORDS...

FA-GO-DA, ME-TI-BI, LA-KU-RE, LA-KU-RE, FA-GO-DA, LA-KU-RE, ME-TI-BI, FA-GO-DA, FA-GO-DA

...AND DISCOVERED THAT THE BABIES GOT **TEMPORARILY INTERESTED AGAIN.**

WHAT ARE THOSE **DIFFERENT SOUNDS?**

THEY DON'T MEAN **NOTHIN'**, **EITHER.**

AT THE VERY LEAST, THIS SHOWS THAT BABIES **NOTICE WHEN TRANSITIONAL PROBABILITIES CHANGE**...

FA-GO-DA IS JUST AS **MEANINGLESS** AS GO-LA-TI.
DUH!

...BUT COULD IT EXPLAIN **MORE** ABOUT HOW WE LEARN LANGUAGE?

YOU MIGHT THINK THERE ARE **TOO MANY WORDS** IN ENGLISH TO POSSIBLY LEARN THEM ALL THIS WAY.

WHAT DOES **INELUCTABLE KUMQUAT QUAGMIRE** MEAN?
IT MEANS **"GET A DICTIONARY,"** NITWIT.

HOWEVER, BY PUTTING **AUDIO RECORDERS** ON BABIES...

...PSYCHOLOGISTS DISCOVERED THAT MOST OF WHAT THEY HEAR COMES FROM A SET OF ONLY **200 WORDS.**

I'LL GET **ALL** YOUR LINGUISTIC INPUT ON THIS FLASH DRIVE!
DO YOU HAVE A **WARRANT** FOR THAT?
AND I'M LIKE **THIS** AND HE'S ALL LIKE **THAT** AT THE PLACE AND SHE GOES **WAY ALL LIKE IF HE'S THERE** HOW COME SHE HAS HIS **THING** ON LIKE HER YOU KNOW...

ONCE THOSE 200 WORDS ARE LEARNED, CHILDREN CAN, THEORETICALLY, **BOOTSTRAP UP** TO LEARN THE REST.

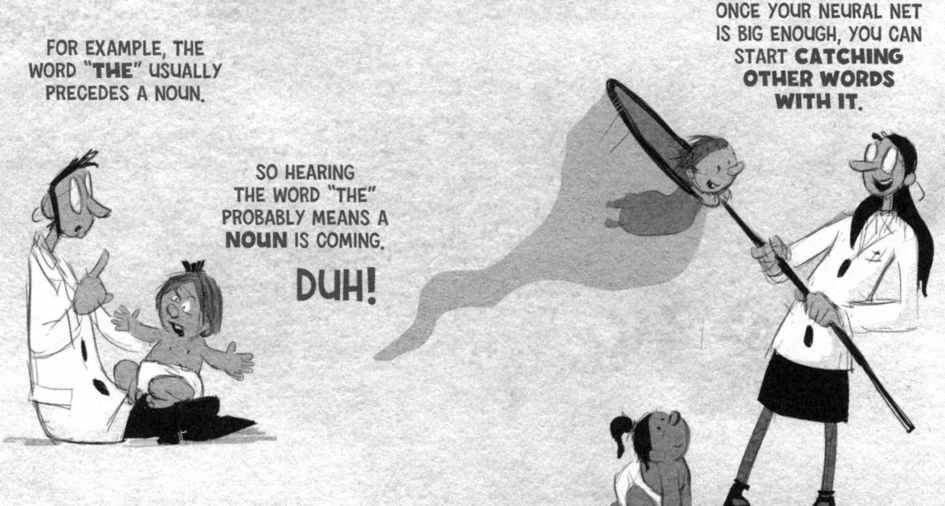

FOR EXAMPLE, THE WORD **"THE"** USUALLY PRECEDES A NOUN.
SO HEARING THE WORD "THE" PROBABLY MEANS A **NOUN** IS COMING.
DUH!
ONCE YOUR NEURAL NET IS BIG ENOUGH, YOU CAN START **CATCHING OTHER WORDS WITH IT.**

BUT LET'S FINISH WITH A QUESTION THAT'S **EVEN MORE CONTROVERSIAL.**

ONCE WE'VE **LEARNED A LANGUAGE...**

...HOW DOES IT **FRAME OUR EXPERIENCES?**

I USED TO THINK IN **DIAPERS...**
...BUT NOW I **THINK IN WORDS.**
AND **ARBITRARY FEATURES** OF THE **LANGUAGE YOU SPEAK...**
...INFLUENCE THE **WAY THAT YOU THINK!**

THIS LINE OF QUESTIONING, DEVELOPED BY THE LINGUIST **BENJAMIN WHORF** IN THE EARLY 1900'S...

I CALL IT **LINGUISTIC RELATIVITY!**

...HAS INSPIRED LOTS OF **FANCIFUL THEORIES...**

OPPRESSED PEOPLES, HAVING NEVER HEARD THE WORD "**FREE**"...

...WILL **NEVER FIGHT TO DEMAND THEIR FREEDOM...**
...OR SCOUR THE INTERNET **LOOKING FOR GOOD DEALS.**

...CONTENTIOUS ARGUMENTS...

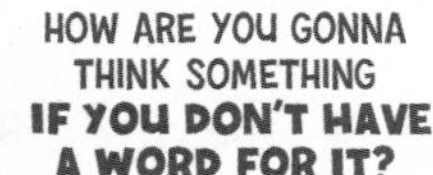
HOW ARE YOU GONNA THINK SOMETHING **IF YOU DON'T HAVE A WORD FOR IT?**

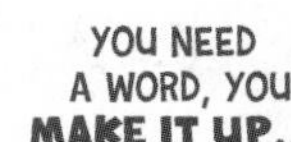
YOU NEED A WORD, YOU **MAKE IT UP...**

...LIKE "**POOPINATOR!**"
THAT'S MY NEW WORD FOR **YOU!**

Language Determines Thought!

Language Reflects Thought!

...AND, FORTUNATELY FOR US, **INTERESTING RESEARCH.**

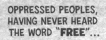

TO TEST HOW **GRAMMAR** MIGHT **INFLUENCE EXPERIENCE**...

NOW LET'S DO GRAMMAR **AND** VOCABULARY!
GROAN.

...RESEARCHERS FOUND WORDS IN **SPANISH** AND **GERMAN** THAT ARE **FEMININE** IN ONE LANGUAGE AND **MASCULINE** IN THE OTHER.

IN **SPANISH** "KEY" IS **FEMININE:** "LA LLAVE"...
...BUT IN **GERMAN** IT'S **MASCULINE:** "DER SCHLÜSSEL."

IN **SPANISH** "BRIDGE" IS **MASCULINE:** "EL PUENTE"...
...BUT IN **GERMAN** IT'S **FEMININE:** "DIE BRÜCKE."

THEN THEY ASKED BILINGUAL SUBJECTS TO **DESCRIBE THOSE OBJECTS IN ENGLISH** AND DISCOVERED THAT THE GENDERS ASSOCIATED WITH THE WORDS **INFLUENCED THEIR DESCRIPTIONS.**

IT'S **INTRICATE, LOVELY,** AND **LITTLE.**
IT'S **HARD, HEAVY,** AND **JAGGED.**

IT'S **STURDY, TOWERING,** AND **BIG.**
IT'S **BEAUTIFUL, ELEGANT,** AND **SLENDER.**

REMEMBER, THIS RESEARCH IS **CONTROVERSIAL**...

LANGUAGE MAKES THEM **SEE THINGS DIFFERENTLY!**
NO!
IT ONLY MAKES THEM **SAY** THINGS DIFFERENTLY!

...BUT IT SHOULD REMIND US OF SOMETHING **IMPORTANT.**

LANGUAGE IS LIKE THE **OTHER COGNITIVE TOOLS** WE'RE LEARNING ABOUT.

EVEN AS THESE TOOLS HELP US **EXTRACT ORDER** FROM THE **CHAOS AND AMBIGUITY** ALL AROUND US...

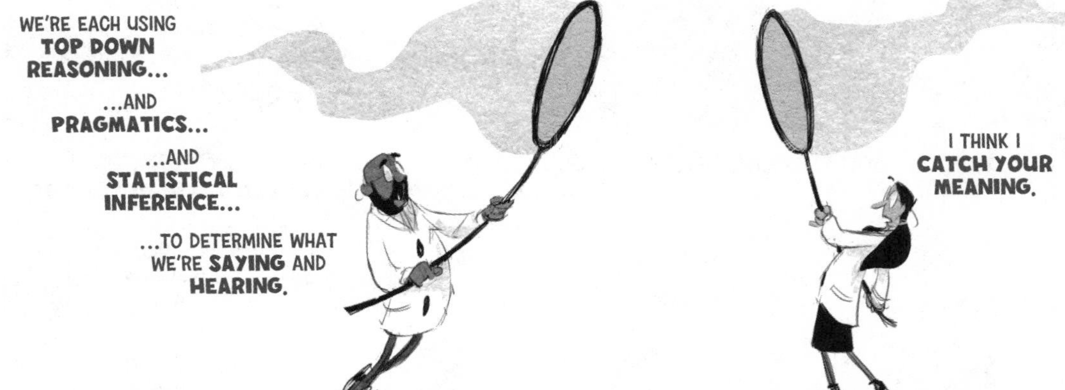
WE'RE EACH USING **TOP DOWN REASONING...**
...AND **PRAGMATICS...**
...AND **STATISTICAL INFERENCE...**
...TO DETERMINE WHAT WE'RE **SAYING** AND **HEARING.**
I THINK I **CATCH YOUR MEANING.**

...THEY ALSO, INEVITABLY, **INFLUENCE OUR INTERPRETATION OF EVERYTHING WE ENCOUNTER.**

DRAW!
DUCK!

CHAPTER 10
PERSONALITY

ANOTHER WAY TO **MAKE SENSE OF OTHER PEOPLE**...

...IS TO **DESCRIBE THEM.**

LOOK AT THOSE ANGRY WEIRDOS.

YOU BILIOUS, SYCOPHANTIC, NINCOMPOOP!

YOU SOLIPSISTIC TURKEY WITCH!

BUT UNDER THE SURFACE OF OUR **INSULTS**...

...**ENDEARMENTS**...

...AND **GOSSIP**...

fungal
obnoxious
strange
unhinged
selfish
indulgent
glaring
doltish
foolish
groping

nice
serene
generous
thoughtful
noble
ingenious
snuggly
cupcake
honey

plastic
overprotective
eccentric
gob-smacked
spartan
corrupt
peculiar
remedial
scamming

...HOW MANY **DISTINCT PERSONALITY TRAITS** ACTUALLY EXIST?

THEY SAY I'M ANXIOUS AND HIGH-STRUNG AND EMOTIONAL AND MELODRAMATIC AND TEMPESTUOUS...
...WHAT DO YOU THINK THEY MEAN?

TO ANSWER THIS QUESTION, EARLY PERSONALITY PSYCHOLOGISTS COMPLILED **HUGE LISTS OF ADJECTIVES...**

abrasive
abrupt
absolutist
abstemious
active
acute
adoring
adept
adaptable
adrift
adroit
aesthetic
affecting
afeared
ageless
aggressive
aglow
aimless
altruistic

...THAT WE **COMMONLY USE** TO **CLASSIFY EACH OTHER.**

adjustable

aloof

THEN, WITH SOME **CLEVER INSIGHTS...**

...AND **STATISTICAL INGENUITY...**

MANY OF THESE WORDS MEAN **APPROXIMATELY THE SAME THINGS!**
chummy
sociable

THESE WORDS SHARE **COMMON FACTORS.**

kind
nice
friendly
affable
amiable
benevolent

...THEY **NARROWED THEM DOWN TO FIVE.**

MOST OF THE VARIANCE IN PERSONALITY CAN BE DESCRIBED IN THESE **FIVE DIMENSIONS.**

Conscientiousness
Agreeableness
Neuroticism
Openness
Extroversion

THEY SPELL **CANOE...**

...OR **OCEAN.**

ACCORDING TO THE **BIG FIVE THEORY**, THE BEST WAY TO **EVALUATE OUR PERSONALITIES** IS TO SEE **WHERE WE STAND ON EACH OF 5 SCALES.**

WE EACH HAVE ALL 5 TRAITS TO GREATER OR LESSER DEGREES.

CONSCIENTIOUSNESS
IS A MEASURE OF OUR **RIGOR, SELF-DISCIPLINE,** AND **ORGANIZATION.**

I'M HERE FOR MY 7 PM RESERVATION.

YEAH BUT IT'S 6:45!
UM, I THINK I HAVE A 6 PM RESERVATION?

more ←→ less

AGREEABLENESS
IS A MEASURE OF OUR **COOPERATIVENESS, GENEROSITY,** AND **FRIENDLINESS.**

CAN ANYBODY SPARE A DOLLAR?

SURE. HERE'S MY ATM CARD, THE PIN IS 1492.
PLUS, DO YOU NEED A RIDE, OR SOME FOOD OR A MASSAGE OR...?

NO!

more ←→ less

NEUROTICISM
IS A MEASURE OF HOW WE EXPERIENCE **EMOTIONS**, PARTICULARLY **NEGATIVE ONES.**

I'M **UNCOMFORTABLE!**
I'M **NERVOUS!**
HOW DO I KNOW HE'S NOT A **TERRORIST**, THE WAY HE LOOKED AT ME WITH HIS **PEN** LIKE HE'S GONNA **LUNGE** ACROSS AND **STAB ME** IN MY CHEST!

NO WORRIES, MAN.

more ← → less

OPENNESS
IS A MEASURE OF HOW WE APPROACH **NEW EXPERIENCES.**

ANYBODY WANNA TRY SOME **DEEP FRIED GRASSHOPPER KIMCHI PIEROGIES?**

more ← → less

EXTROVERSION
IS A MEASURE OF OUR **PREFERENCE FOR THE COMPANY OF OTHERS.**

PARTY ON!

SSHHHHHH

more ← → less

KEEP IN MIND THAT THE **BIG FIVE** ARE **PREDOMINANTLY STABLE.**

I'M LIKE THIS AT 3 PM **AND** AT 3 AM.

IN 10 YEARS, I'LL **STILL BE ME.**

WHILE THEY DO **SHIFT A BIT OVER THE COURSE OF OUR LIVES...**

...THEY REMAIN **STEADY WITHIN US** EVEN WHEN OUR CIRCUMSTANCES GUIDE US TO BEHAVE DIFFERENTLY.

CONSCIENTIOUSNESS TENDS TO **RISE WHEN WE'RE YOUNG...**
..., AND **DECLINE AS WE GET OLD.**

AS WE'LL SEE IN **CHAPTER 11...**
...EVEN **EXTROVERTS** ARE **QUIET IN THE LIBRARY.**

SHSHSHSH!

SO IT'S BEST TO THINK OF THEM AS **TRAITS**, NOT **SKILLS.**

I **PREFER SOLITUDE...**
...BUT THAT DOESN'T MEAN YOU'RE **BAD AT SOCIALIZING.**
I **LOVE TO PARTY...**
...BUT THAT DOESN'T MEAN YOU'RE **GOOD AT IT.**

CRUCIALLY, THEY'RE ALSO **VALUE FREE**, THOUGH THAT CAN BE **HARD TO BEAR IN MIND.**

A SPONTANEOUS, CRITICAL, RELAXED, HABITUAL, INTROVERT...
...IS **NO BETTER** THAN A CONSCIENTIOUS, AGREEABLE, NEUROTIC, OPEN-MINDED, EXTROVERT.

BECAUSE THE 5 DIMENSIONS ARE **RELIABLE...**

SEE? THAT OLD BAT HAS **ALWAYS** BEEN MORE AGREEABLE THAN ME!

...AND CAN BE USED TO **MAKE ACCURATE PREDICTIONS ABOUT US...**

IF YOU WANT TO KNOW ABOUT **KERBLEKIZHOUBOU FOOD...**

...ASK **CHELSEA** INSTEAD OF **DAVE**, SHE'S MUCH MORE **OPEN.**

...THEY'RE **USEFUL FOR DOING SCIENCE.**

WE CAN USE THEM TO PERFORM **TESTS!**

AN **EXTROVERT** AND A **NEUROTIC** CLIMB INTO A **SKINNER BOX...**

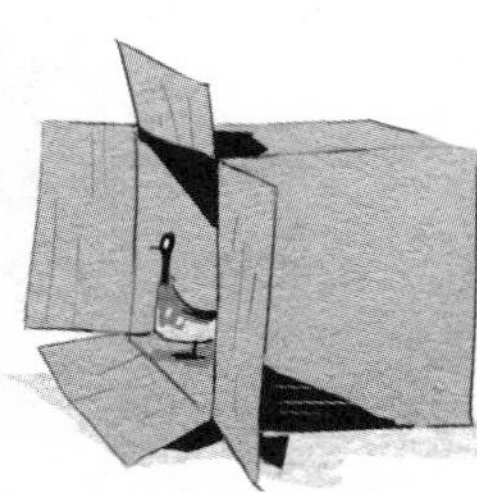

THAT SEPARATES THEM FROM THE **BOGUS PSYCHOLOGICAL CATEGORIES** PROMOTED IN THE PAST...

I DIDN'T DO THE DISHES BECAUSE I'M **PHLEGMATIC, CHOLERIC, SANGUINE, AND MELANCHOLIC!**

YOU **HIPPOCRITE!**

...AND ON THE **INTERNET...**

MY **OPPENKLEINER® PERSONALITY TYPE®** IS **ACFG®...**
...WHICH STANDS FOR **AWESOME, COOL, FANTASTIC, GREAT!**

...WHICH **DON'T HAVE PREDICTIVE POWER.**

MY HOROSCOPE SAYS I SHOULDN'T FEEL AFRAID TO **SWIM UPSTREAM.**
MINE SAYS I SHOULD **GROWL MORE.**

WHILE THE BIG 5 WORK THE **BEST** AT PREDICTING DIFFERENCES IN OUR BEHAVIOR...

IN THE **LONG RUN**, THEY'RE OUR **MOST CONSISTENT TRAITS.**

...THERE ARE **OTHER PERSONALITY TRAITS** THAT BEAR **SCIENTIFIC SCRUTINY.**

FOR EXAMPLE, WE HAVE MEASURABLE DIFFERENCES IN **MACHIAVELLIANISM...**

THAT'S NOT FAIR, YOU **CHEATED!**

YUP, AND I **WON!**

...AUTHORITARIANISM...

WHY ARE YOU **STANDING ON MY FACE?**
DON'T ASK QUESTIONS, **I'M THE BOSS.**

...NARCISSISM...

I **HATE MIRRORS.**

MOST PEOPLE COULDN'T ROCK THIS HAT.
BUT **I CAN!**

...AND EVEN **HUMOR STYLE.**

THE **HAT** SAID TO THE **TIE:**
YOU HANG AROUND HERE, I'LL **GO ON A HEAD.**

POOT POOT
POOT POOT
POOT POOT
POOT POOT

WE ALSO VARY IN THE **SOURCES OF OUR MOTIVATION.**

I'M THE KING OF THE MOUNTAIN!
I'M NOT PLAYING.

SOME PEOPLE ARE MORE DRIVEN BY **ACHIEVEMENT...**

I HOPE I GET A B+.

IF I ONLY GET A B+ I'LL KILL MYSELF!

...OTHERS BY **COGNITIVE CHALLENGES...**

MAZES GIVE ME A HEADACHE.

I LOVE THE CROSSWORD...
...EVEN THOUGH I SUCK AT IT.

...OR BY **AVOIDING UNCERTAINTY.**

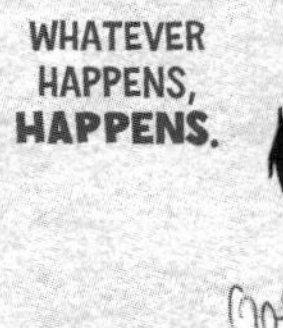

WHATEVER HAPPENS, HAPPENS.
FIRST I'LL MAJOR IN MARINE BIOLOGY, THEN GET A JOB AT THE AQUARIUM, THEN MARRY AN ICHTHYOLOGIST.

AND SOME PEOPLE TEND TO **SEEK POSITIVE RESULTS...**

...WHEREAS OTHERS TEND TO **AVOID NEGATIVE ONES.**

GET OUT THERE SO WE WIN!

GET OUT THERE SO WE DON'T LOSE!
IT'S REGULATORY FOCUS.

JUST AS WE ARE **DRIVEN TOWARD DIFFERENT ENDS**...

I WANT TO **RULE THE WORLD.**
I WANT TO **DRAW THIS FLOWER.**

...SOME OF US ARE BETTER AT **WAITING FOR THEM.**

I WANT IT ALL, AND I WANT IT **NOW!**
THE SUN'LL COME OUT... ...**TOMORROW.**

IN A CLASSIC STUDY, **WHEN YOUNG CHILDREN WERE PUT IN A ROOM ALONE WITH MARSHMALLOWS...**

IF YOU CAN WAIT 15 MINUTES, I'LL **DOUBLE THE MARSHMALLOWS.**

...SOME OF THEM COULD **RESIST**...

THAT'S A LONG TIME TO **SIT ON YOUR HANDS.**

...OTHERS **NOT SO MUCH.**

AND THIS GAP IN ABILITY TO **DELAY MARSHMALLOW GRATIFICATION** PREDICTED SAT SCORES AND BODY MASS INDEX **14 YEARS LATER!**

DUDE, YOU BETTER **START STUDYING.**

THERE'S ALSO EVIDENCE THAT WE HAVE **DIFFERENT MINDSETS ABOUT OUR SKILLS.**

I'M A **NATURAL.**

I'M A **PRODUCT OF HARD WORK.**

FOR EXAMPLE, SOME OF US TEND TO THINK OUR **INTELLIGENCE** IS **FIXED**...

...AND OTHERS TEND TO THINK IT'S **MALLEABLE...**

I'M **GOOD AT THIS.**

I'M GETTING **GOOD AT THIS.**

...AND THAT DISTINCTION PREDICTS **HOW WE RESPOND TO SETBACKS...**

IF HE'S **STRUGGLING...**

...HE'LL **GIVE UP.**

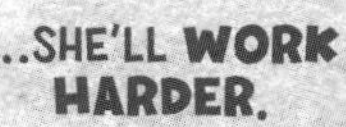
IF SHE'S **STRUGGLING...**

...SHE'LL **WORK HARDER.**

...AND WHAT **GOALS** WE GIVE OURSELVES.

HE ONLY DOES THE **THINGS HE'S GOOD AT.**

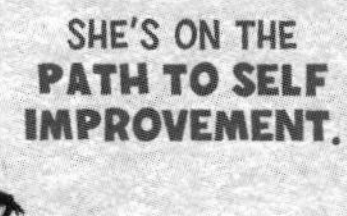
SHE'S ON THE **PATH TO SELF IMPROVEMENT.**

OTHER RESEARCH SUGGESTS WE HAVE **DIFFERENT MINDSETS FOR DIFFERENT SUBJECTS.**

I'M A **NATURALLY GIFTED UNICYCLIST...**
...BUT MY **JUGGLING** IS THE **PRODUCT OF HARD WORK.**

CLEARLY, OUR **PERSONALITIES ARE COMPLICATED...**

I SCORED **HIGH ON THE BIG 5!**
IT'S **NOT A COMPETITION...**
...YOU **FIXED-MINDSET NARCISSIST.**

...BUT THAT DOESN'T KEEP US FROM FORMING **QUICK JUDGMENTS ABOUT ONE ANOTHER...**

...WHETHER OR NOT THEY'RE **ACCURATE.**

HE'S SO **EASYGOING...**
...AND SUCH A **GOOD LISTENER!**
ACTUALLY HE'S A **PSYCHOPATH.**

PLENTY OF EXPERIMENTS SHOW THAT WE START ASSESSING EACH OTHER **VERY QUICKLY...**

...BUT WE ALSO **REFINE OUR ASSESSMENTS** OVER TIME AS WE **OBSERVE MORE DETAILS.**

IT ONLY TAKES **HALF A SECOND FOR HER** TO KNOW SHE **DOESN'T TRUST YOU.**

HE LIKES TO PRETEND HE'S A JERK...
...BUT INSIDE HE'S GOT A **HEART OF GOLD.**

WHICH RAISES THE QUESTION: **WHAT SHOULD WE LOOK FOR?**

DO YOU THINK HE'D MAKE A **GOOD HUSBAND?**
LET'S **BREAK INTO HIS HOME TO FIND OUT.**

AS WE MOVE THROUGH THE WORLD, WE **LEAVE BEHIND CLUES ABOUT OUR PERSONALITIES.**

IN PSYCHOLOGY JARGON, THESE INCLUDE **IDENTITY CLAIMS...**

THESE ARE WAYS WE CONSCIOUSLY BROADCAST WHO WE ARE...
...BY DRESSING IN A PARTICULAR STYLE...
...OR EXHIBITING PATRIOTISM...
...OR DISPLAYING TROPHIES...
...OR OTHERWISE SHOWING OFF OUR VALUES.

...AND **FEELING REGULATORS...**

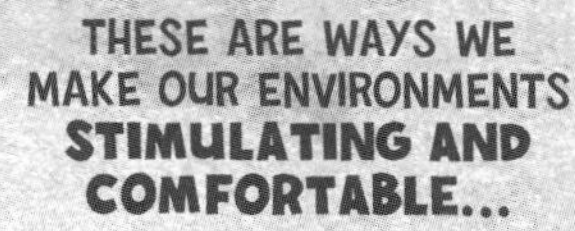

THESE ARE WAYS WE MAKE OUR ENVIRONMENTS STIMULATING AND COMFORTABLE...

...BY ARRANGING FAMILY PHOTOS NEAR OUR BEDSIDE...
...OR STORING MEMENTOS IN OUR DESK...

...OR PAINTING OUR WALLS IN COLORS WE LIKE...
...OR OTHERWISE NESTING.

...AS WELL AS MORE GENERAL **BEHAVIORAL RESIDUE.**

THESE ARE THE UNCONSCIOUS WAYS WE MAKE AN IMPACT.

HE'S MESSY.
HE'S CLEAN.

HE CHEWS WITH HIS MOUTH OPEN.

THESE **PERSONALITY CLUES** PERVADE OUR **LIVING SPACES**...
THIS GUY'S PLACE IS A **PIG STY**:
LOW CONSCIENTIOUS-NESS!
...OUR **COMMUNICATIONS**...
...AND OUR **HABITS.**

THIS GAL POSTS PHOTOS OF **DESOLATE LANDSCAPES** WITH **NO PEOPLE IN THEM**:

INTROVERT!

THIS GUY LISTENS TO **SNOOP DOGG, WILLIE NELSON,** AND **PDQ BACH**:

OPEN!

IN FACT, WE DEPOSIT THEM JUST ABOUT **EVERYWHERE IMAGINABLE.**

LET'S SEE WHAT WE CAN LEARN BY **LOOKING IN HIS TRASH!**

THEY ARE LIKE THE DATA WE USE TO **SNIFF EACH OTHER OUT.**

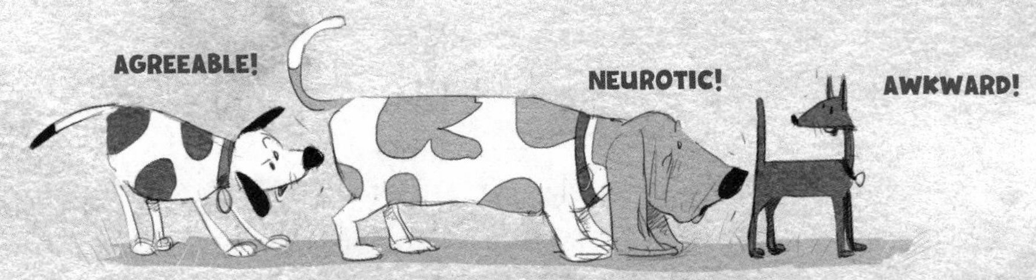
AGREEABLE!
NEUROTIC!
AWKWARD!

AND IT TURNS OUT THAT THE **ACCURACY OF OUR IMPRESSIONS** ABOUT EACH OTHER **DEPENDS ON WHERE WE SNIFF.**

IF YOU REALLY WANT TO KNOW HOW **OPEN** SHE IS...

...SNIFF HER **DOG HOUSE,** NOT HER **BUTT.**

FOR EXAMPLE, WE'RE BETTER AT ASSESSING **OPENNESS** BY SNOOPING THROUGH SOMEONE'S **BEDROOM...**

...THAN BY ACTUALLY **MEETING THEM.**

HE LIKES TO **EXPLORE NEW THINGS...**
...I CAN TELL BECAUSE OF THESE **TRAVEL STICKERS...**
...BUT HE **DIDN'T MENTION IT.**

AND WE'RE BETTER AT ASSESSING **CONSCIENTIOUSNESS** BY LOOKING AT SOMEONE'S **BLOG...**

...THAN BY LISTENING TO THEIR **FAVORITE MUSIC.**

SHE'S **ORDERLY...**
...YOU CAN TELL BY HER **USE OF GRAMMAR.**
THOUGH YOU'D NEVER GUESS IT FROM HER TASTE FOR **DEATH METAL.**

AND ALTHOUGH WE'RE GENERALLY GOOD AT ASSESSING **EXTROVERSION...**

...WE HAVE NOTABLE **BLINDSPOTS** IN OUR ABILITY TO SNOOP OUT **AGREEABLENESS** AND **NEUROTICISM.**

HE'S A **PARTY ANIMAL...**
...YOU CAN TELL FROM THE WAY HE **MAKES COPIES.**
PEOPLE DON'T **BROADCAST THEIR GENEROSITY...**
...OR **ADVERTISE THEIR ANXIETIES.**

OF COURSE OUR JUDGMENTS CAN **BE WRONG.**

I WAS SO SURE, BASED ON THE **COLOR OF HER COLLAR...**
...THAT SHE WAS **COMPASSIONATE AND AGREEABLE.**
ACTUALLY SHE'S **A BAD DOG...**
...THAT'S WHY SHE'S **IN THE DOGHOUSE.**

WE LOOK TO OUR PERSONALTIES TO EXPLAIN THE **VARIATIONS BETWEEN US.**

IT'S PART OF MY **IDENTITY.**

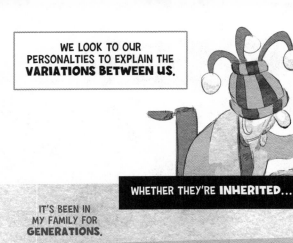

WHETHER THEY'RE **INHERITED...**

IT'S BEEN IN MY FAMILY FOR **GENERATIONS.**

...OR **LEARNED...**

OF COURSE MY WIFE WAS **SUPPORTIVE,** TOO.

...THEY GIVE US A PRETTY GOOD WAY TO PREDICT OUR BEHAVIOR OVER THE **LONG RUN.**

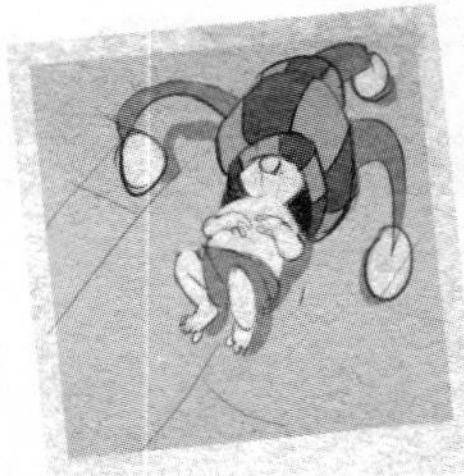

I'VE **ALWAYS** BEEN **DIFFERENT.**

BUT AS WE'LL SEE IN THE NEXT CHAPTER, IF THERE'S **ONE THING** THAT MAKES US MORE **SIMILAR** THAN WE ARE DIFFERENT...

...IT'S THAT WE ARE **CREATURES OF CIRCUMSTANCE.**

FREE ICE CREAM IF YOU WEAR A **SILLY HAT!**

CHAPTER 11
SOCIAL INFLUENCE

I'M USUALLY **PUNCTUAL**, BUT NOT TODAY...

ALL OF OUR BEHAVIOR IS
HEAVILY INFLUENCED BY OUR CIRCUMSTANCES.

I WANNA BE AN **ARTIST!**

SHE'S GONNA NEED **SUPPORTIVE PARENTS...**
...AND **PAINT.**

NEVERTHELESS, WHEN WE
ACCOUNT FOR OTHER PEOPLE'S ACTIONS,
WE TEND TO **IGNORE THAT FACT...**

...AND OVEREMPHASIZE THE
INFLUENCE OF **PERSONALITY.**

WHY DID HE **STEAL MY ORANGES?**
MAYBE BECAUSE HE WAS **STARVED** AND THE **FRUIT WAS HANGING LOW** AND HE **DIDN'T REALIZE THEY WERE YOURS?**
NAH! HE MUST BE A **CRIMINAL!**

THIS BIAS IS SO POWERFUL, IT HAS BEEN DUBBED THE
FUNDAMENTAL ATTRIBUTION ERROR.

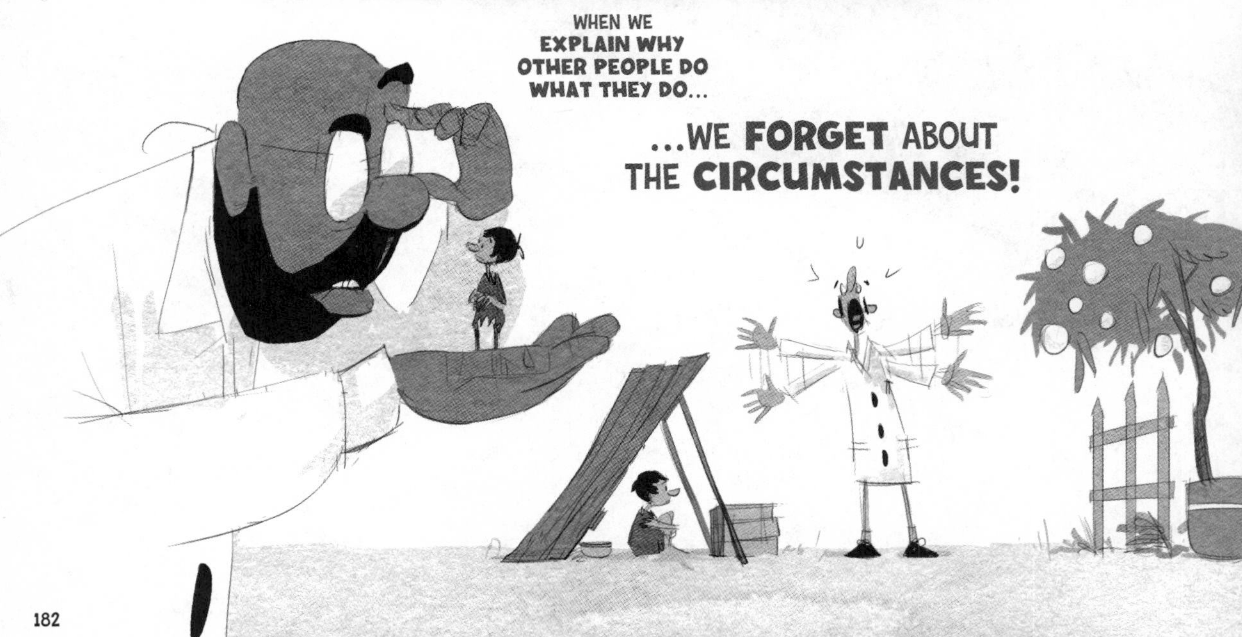
WHEN WE **EXPLAIN WHY OTHER PEOPLE DO WHAT THEY DO...**
...WE **FORGET** ABOUT THE **CIRCUMSTANCES!**

ALTHOUGH WE TEND TO BE AWARE OF HOW **SITUATIONS** AFFECT **OUR OWN ACTIONS...**

...WE **DON'T HAVE THAT INSIGHT ABOUT OTHER PEOPLE.**

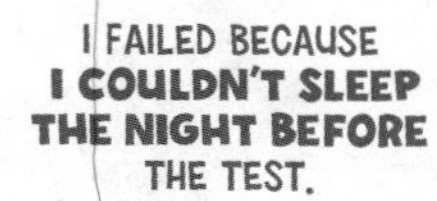

I FAILED BECAUSE **I COULDN'T SLEEP THE NIGHT BEFORE** THE TEST.

F

SHE MUST **NOT CARE ABOUT HER STUDIES.**

SO IN THIS CHAPTER WE'RE GOING TO EXPLORE **HOW CIRCUMSTANCES INFLUENCE US.**

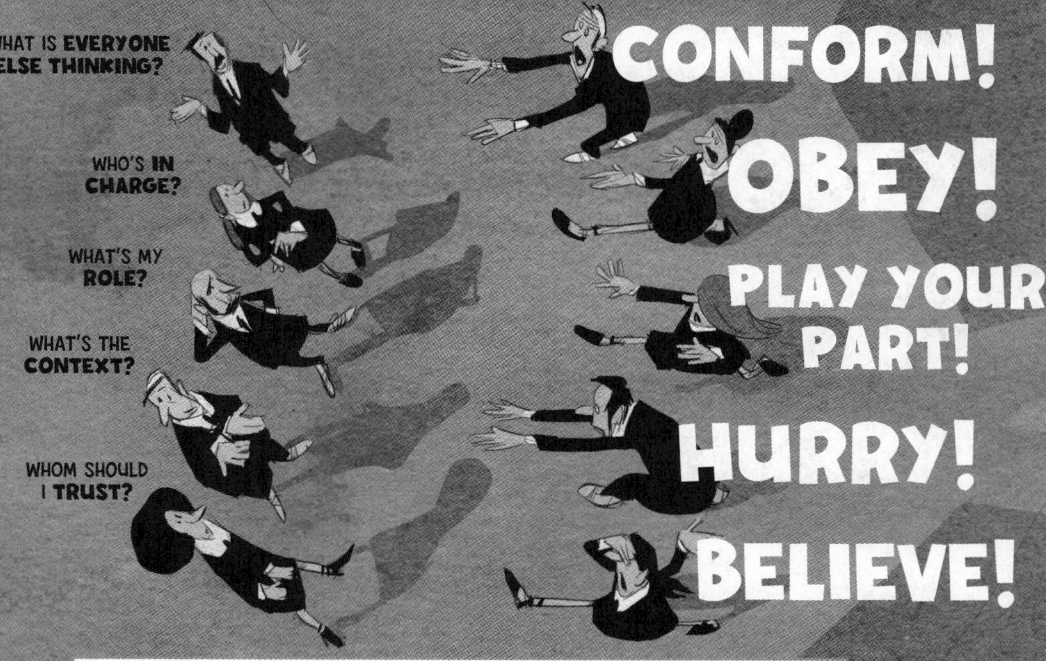

WHAT IS **EVERYONE ELSE THINKING?**
WHO'S **IN CHARGE?**
WHAT'S MY **ROLE?**
WHAT'S THE **CONTEXT?**
WHOM SHOULD I **TRUST?**
CONFORM!
OBEY!
PLAY YOUR PART!
HURRY!
BELIEVE!

WE'LL MOSTLY FOCUS ON **SOCIAL SITUATIONS,** BECAUSE THEIR INFLUENCE IS THE **MOST REMARKABLE.**

I THOUGHT I WAS **THINKING FOR MYSELF.**
OH, NO...
... WE WERE **DOING YOUR THINKING FOR YOU.**

CONFORMITY

WHAT'S **EVERYONE ELSE THINKING?**

WE ALL KNOW WHAT IT'S LIKE TO BE INFLUENCED BY WHAT OTHER PEOPLE **WEAR**...

EVERYBODY WEARS **THESE!**
OK!

...AND HOW THEY **ACT**.

EVERYBODY WALKS **THIS WAY!**
I THINK I GOT IT.

BUT THE URGE TO **CONFORM TO SOCIAL NORMS** IS EVEN **STRONGER** THAN WE USUALLY EXPECT...

EVERYBODY THINKS 2+2=5.
ER...
...WELL...
...THEN THERE **MUST BE SOMETHING TO THAT IDEA,** I GUESS.

...AS SHOWN IN A SEMINAL STUDY BY **SOLOMON ASCH**.

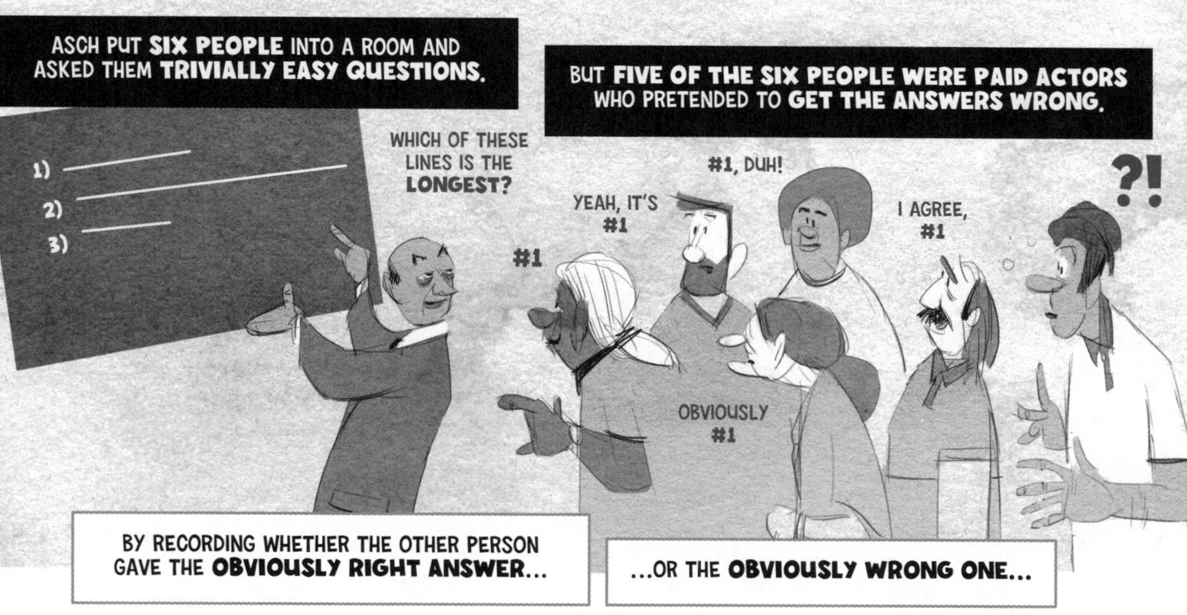
ASCH PUT **SIX PEOPLE** INTO A ROOM AND ASKED THEM **TRIVIALLY EASY QUESTIONS.**
BUT **FIVE OF THE SIX PEOPLE WERE PAID ACTORS** WHO PRETENDED TO **GET THE ANSWERS WRONG.**
1)
2)
3)
WHICH OF THESE LINES IS THE **LONGEST?**
#1
YEAH, IT'S #1
#1, DUH!
OBVIOUSLY #1
I AGREE, #1
?!
BY RECORDING WHETHER THE OTHER PERSON GAVE THE **OBVIOUSLY RIGHT ANSWER...**
...OR THE **OBVIOUSLY WRONG ONE...**

UH...
...NUMBER...
...ER...
...ONE I GUESS.
...ASCH DISCOVERED THAT ONLY A **FEW OF US ARE IMMUNE FROM THE PRESSURES OF THE GROUP...**

MOST PEOPLE WENT WITH THE GROUP AT LEAST ONCE DURING THE STUDY!
...EVEN WHEN IT CAUSES US TO **OVERRIDE OUR BETTER JUDGMENT.**

NOWADAYS **EVERYBODY** WEARS **THESE...**
...AND WALKS **THIS WAY...**
...AND TENDS TO **AGREE WITH THEIR TWITTER FEED.**

COMPLIANCE

WHO'S IN CHARGE?

SIMILARLY, MOST OF US HAVE A **RESPECT FOR AUTHORITY** THAT CAN **QUICKLY GET OUT OF HAND.**

TO STUDY THIS, **STANLEY MILGRAM** PUT PEOPLE IN A ROOM WITH AN **AUTHORITY FIGURE** AND A "**TEACHING MACHINE.**"

THEY WERE TOLD THE MACHINE WOULD DELIVER **ELECTRIC SHOCKS** TO A STRANGER...

HI, I'M A SCIENTIST.
AND THIS IS AN EDUCATIONAL TOOL.

...TO HELP THEM **LEARN STUFF.**

HE'LL BE IN ANOTHER ROOM.

IF HE FAILS THE MEMORY TEST, PRESS **THIS.**

ZZZAP!

OW!
ZZZAP!

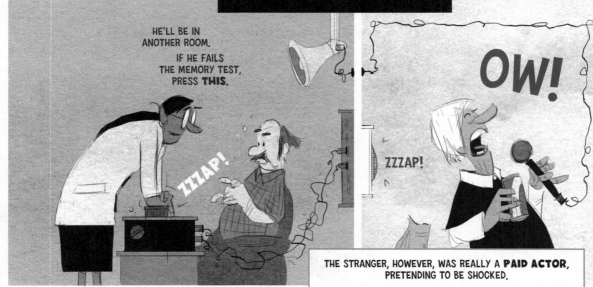

THE STRANGER, HOWEVER, WAS REALLY A **PAID ACTOR,** PRETENDING TO BE SHOCKED.

EACH TIME THE "LEARNER" GOT THE **WRONG ANSWER** ON A WORD TEST...

...THE "TEACHER" WAS ORDERED TO **INCREASE THE VOLTAGE.**

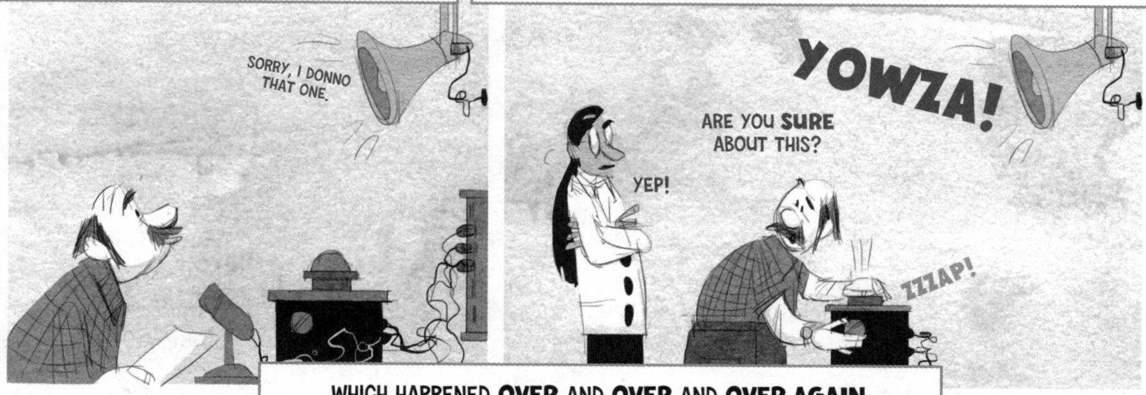
SORRY, I DONNO THAT ONE.
YOWZA!
ARE YOU **SURE** ABOUT THIS?
YEP!
ZZZAP!

WHICH HAPPENED **OVER** AND **OVER** AND **OVER AGAIN.**

HELP!
IT'S **ESSENTIAL.**
REALLY?
ZZZAP!
STOP!
MOS' DEF.
UM?
ZZZAP!
TURN IT **UP TO ELEVEN!**
HEART ATTACK!
ZZZAP!

SHOCKINGLY, NEARLY TWO-THIRDS OF PARTICIPANTS CONTINUED TO OBEY THE ORDER **EVEN WHEN THE DOSAGE REACHED LETHAL LEVELS.**

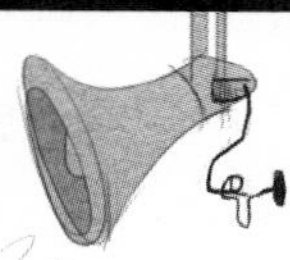
THIS MAKES ME FEEL REALLY **UNCOMFORTABLE.**
IMAGINE HOW IT MAKES ME FEEL!

JUST **DO IT!**
ZZZAP!

WHICH HELPS EXPLAIN MANY **REAL WORLD TRAGEDIES.**

OUCH, **PLEASE STOP.**
SORRY, I'M **FOLLOWING ORDERS.**

SOCIAL ROLES

WHAT'S **MY** PART?

JUST LIKE ACTORS **PLAY THEIR PARTS ON A STAGE**, PEOPLE **FULFILL THEIR ROLES IN EVERYDAY LIFE...**

OH THAT THIS TOO TOO SOLID **FLESH** WOULD **MELT**.

OH THAT THIS TOO TOO TAXING **SHIFT** WOULD **END**.

...AND THIS TOO CAN HAVE **EXTREME CONSEQUENCES.**

TALK TO THE **BADGE**, KID.

ONE OF THE MOST **DISTURBING** EXPERIMENTS ABOUT THIS WAS THE **STANFORD PRISON STUDY...**

HEY **MAN**.

HEY **DUDE**.

...WHERE STUDENT VOLUNTEERS WERE **RANDOMLY ASSIGNED** TO ACT AS **PRISONERS OR GUARDS...**

HERE'S YOUR **ID NUMBER** AND **CELL BLOCK**.
GET IN LINE FOR **DELOUSING**.

HERE'S YOUR **BATON** AND **DARK GLASSES**.
KEEP **THEM IN LINE**.

...TO SEE HOW THOSE ROLES **INFLUENCED THEIR BEHAVIOR.**

UNFORTUNATELY, DESPITE THE FACT THAT EVERYONE KNEW IT WAS **ROLE PLAY...**

HEY **MAN.**

HEY **DUDE.**

...THE VOLUNTEERS' BEHAVIOR BECAME **SO DISTURBING SO QUICKLY...**

SLEEP ON THE **CONCRETE!**
POOP IN **THIS!**
WE'RE **REVOLTING!**
NO KIDDING, GO TO **SOLITARY!**
YOU'RE **NOTHING MORE THAN YOUR NUMBER!**

...THAT THE EXPERIMENT HAD TO BE **PREMATURELY STOPPED.**

I'M GONNA **BEAT** THE ***&#$ OUT OF YOU!**

ABORT! ABORT!

AND IF THESE **PRETEND ROLES** CAN CAUSE SUCH **WRETCHED BEHAVIOR** AMONG OTHERWISE FRIENDLY PEOPLE...

SORRY ABOUT THAT, MAN.
YEAH, I'M SORTA **EMBARRASSED,** DUDE.

...WHAT HAPPENS WHEN THE ROLES ARE **REAL?**

THIS ISN'T **MAKE BELIEVE.**

SITUATIONAL CONSTRAINTS

WHAT'S THE **CONTEXT?**

WE'VE SEEN HOW OUR BEHAVIOR IS HEAVILY INFLUENCED BY OUR **RELATIONSHIPS...**

...BUT IT'S ALSO **CONSTRAINED BY OUR CIRCUMSTANCES.**

ON **WEEKENDS,** I'M IN **COMMAND.**

AT **WORK,** I'M **SUBMISSIVE.**

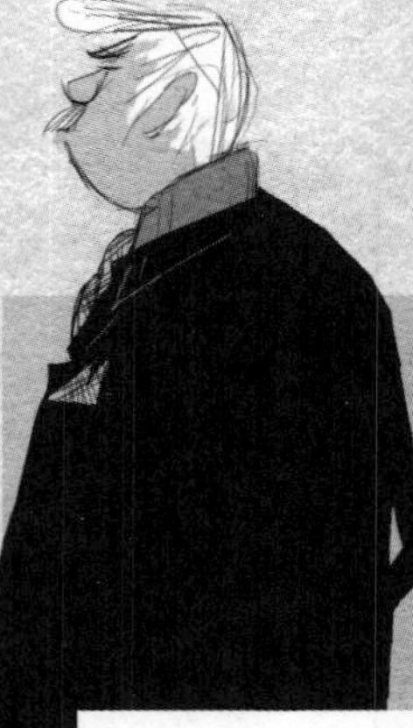

FOR EXAMPLE, TO TEST HOW SIMPLY **BEING HURRIED** CAN ALTER OUR ACTIONS...

...**JOHN DARLEY** AND **DANIEL BATSON** RECRUITED **PRIESTS IN TRAINING...**

WE'RE DEVOTING OURSELVES TO **HELPING OTHERS.**

...TO WRITE A SERMON ON THE **PARABLE OF THE GOOD SAMARITAN.**

I WILL ASSIST THIS **DECREPIT MAN.**
HELP!

THE PARTICIPANTS WERE TOLD THEY NEEDED TO DELIVER THEIR SERMONS **IN A NEARBY BUILDING**...

...BUT ONLY **SOME OF THEM** WERE TOLD THEY **HAD TO RUSH**...

YOU'RE
LATE!
HURRY!
HELP!

...AND THAT ALONE MADE THEM **LESS LIKELY** TO **HELP A DECREPIT MAN** STRATEGICALLY PLACED IN THEIR WAY.

SORRY, I'M LATE,
GOTTA HURRY.

IN THIS CASE, THE **SITUATION** WAS MORE INFLUENTIAL THAN THEIR **PERSONALITY**...

BEING
HURRIED...
...MAKES YOU
ACT LESS HOLY!

...AND LIFE IS **FULL OF SIMILAR EXAMPLES**.

YOU'RE EATING
NORWOOKIAL
FOOD?
YOU MUST BE
OPEN TO NEW
EXPERIENCES.
NAH, I'M
STARVING.

PERSUASION

WHOM SHOULD I **TRUST?**

FINALLY, WHILE WE MAY BE **INCLINED** TO **BEHAVE ONE WAY...**

...WE CAN OFTEN BE **PERSUADED TO BEHAVE IN ANOTHER.**

I ALWAYS **DO WHAT I WANT.**

I'M **CHARMING.**

I'LL **DO WHATEVER YOU SAY.**

SOMETIMES WE'RE PURSUADED BY **IMPORTANT NEW INFORMATION.**

THAT **ARGUMENT** TIPS THE BALANCE IN YOUR FAVOR.

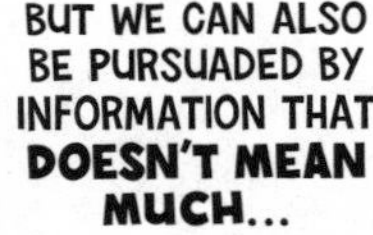

BUT WE CAN ALSO BE PURSUADED BY INFORMATION THAT **DOESN'T MEAN MUCH...**

...JUST BECAUSE IT **GRABBED OUR ATTENTION...**

...AND BY ASSERTIONS THAT DON'T ACTUALLY **MEAN ANYTHING AT ALL...**

...JUST BECAUSE THEY **SOUND LIKE EXPLANATIONS.**

POLLS SHOW THAT THE **STANDARD DEVIATION OF MURDERS IS INCREASING!**

SOUNDS **IMPORTANT...**
...MUST BE.

YOU SHOULD **BELIEVE IN ME** BECAUSE I'M **SOMEONE YOU CAN BELIEVE IN!**

SOUNDS **CONVINCING...**

...MUST BE.

PLUS, WE'RE SUCKERS FOR ANYTHING WE THINK IS **SCARCE.**

THIS IS YOUR **ONLY CHANCE** TO GET ONE OF THESE!

SOUNDS **RARE...**
...I'LL BUY IT!

OBVIOUSLY, APPEALS ARE MORE EFFECTIVE IF THEY'RE MADE BY **ATTRACTIVE** AND **SOCIABLE PEOPLE...**

THAT **PERFUME** TIPS THE BALANCE IN HER FAVOR.

...BECAUSE ALL OF US WANT TO **FIT IN.**

I LIKE YOU.
I BELIEVE YOU.

THAT'S WHY WE RESPOND TO **RECIPROCITY...**

I **SCRATCHED YOUR BACK...**
...NOW WILL **YOU SCRATCH MINE** AND OPEN AN ACCOUNT WITH US?
OK.

...AND OFFERS TO MAKE **CONCESSIONS.**

I OFFERED IT FOR **$500,000** AND YOU REJECTED ME.
I'LL COMPROMIZE BY LOWERING THE PRICE TO **$300,000.**

I'D BETTER ACCEPT OR I'LL **SEEM LIKE A JERK.**

IT'S ALSO WHY, IF YOU WANT TO **PROMOTE A CERTAIN BEHAVIOR...**

...IT HELPS SIMPLY TO CLAIM THAT **OTHER PEOPLE ARE ALREADY DOING IT...**

...AND TO BE AS **SPECIFIC AS POSSIBLE.**

WE WANT PEOPLE TO **RECYCLE** MORE.

80% of People Already Recycle...
...That Brand of Soda Can.

PERSUASION CON'T.

PERHAPS THE MOST FASCINATING PERSUASION TECHNIQUE RELIES ON OUR STRONG DESIRE TO **FEEL CONSISTENT.**

I CAN'T BELIEVE YOU CONVINCED ME TO DO **THIS.** I MUST **NOT BE AFRAID OF ROLLER COASTERS AFTER ALL! AAAAAHHHHH!!!**

IN PREVIOUS CHAPTERS, WE'VE SEEN HOW THIS DESIRE INFLUENCES OUR **COGNITION...**

YOU BELIEVE YOUR NEURAL NET MAKES SENSE...
...SO YOU IGNORE EVIDENCE THAT CONTRADICTS WHAT YOU BELIEVE.
IT'S CONFIRMATION BIAS!

...AND OUR **METACOGNITION.**

I BELIEVE I'VE ALWAYS KNOWN THAT!

IT'S HINDSIGHT BIAS!

BUT IT ALSO INFLUENCES OUR **SENSE OF OUR OWN BEHAVIOR.**

I BELIEVE THAT MY BELIEFS AND MY BEHAVIOR LINE UP NICELY.

THAT'S WHY, WHEN WE'RE **MAKING CHOICES,** WE'LL OFTEN **LET OUR PREVIOUS BEHAVIOR GUIDE US.**

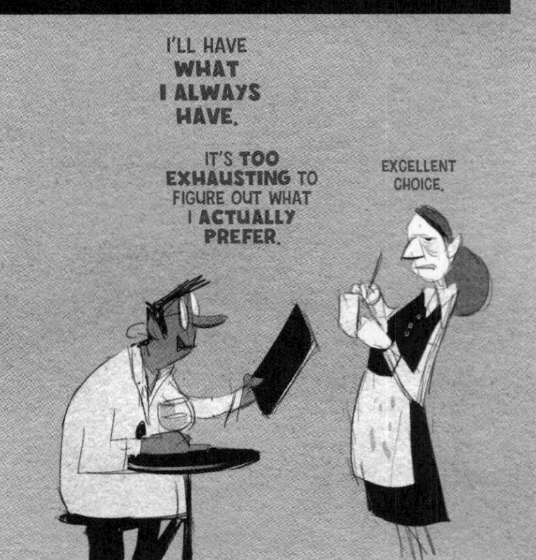
I'LL HAVE WHAT I ALWAYS HAVE.
IT'S TOO EXHAUSTING TO FIGURE OUT WHAT I ACTUALLY PREFER.
EXCELLENT CHOICE.

HOWEVER, IF OUR BEHAVIOR AND OUR BELIEFS **DON'T LINE UP**, IT CREATES **COGNITIVE DISSONANCE**...

...WHICH WE **LIKE TO AVOID**.

I'M **NOT** THE SORT OF PERSON WHO DOES **THIS**!
MY **HEAD HURTS**!

SO, WHEN **CIRCUMSTANCES** CAUSE US TO **CHANGE OUR BEHAVIOR**...

...WE'LL OFTEN **CHANGE OUR ATTITUDES TO FIT**.

I HAD TO START SHOPPING AT **GRANOLA MART®** BECAUSE IT'S **ON MY WAY TO MY NEW JOB**.

MAYBE IT'S NOT **INFESTED WITH COMMIE PINKOS** AFTER ALL.

AND THIS FACT CAN BE USED TO **PERSUADE US OF THINGS**.

IF YOU WANT PEOPLE TO COMMIT TO SOMETHING **BIG**, **BUT THEY DON'T WANT TO...**

Buy Our Book!
WOULD YOU PUT **THIS** ON YOUR LAWN?
ARE YOU **CRAZY?**

...YOU CAN START BY ASKING THEM FOR **A SMALLER SOMETHING**...

WOULD YOU PUT **THIS** ON YOUR LAWN?
UM, **OK**.
Buy Our Book!

...BECAUSE THEIR ORIGINAL "NO" CAN OFTEN BE OVERCOME WITH **LITTLE STEPS** THAT MAKE THEM FEEL LIKE THEY'RE WALKING TOWARD **"YES."**

Buy Our Book!
NOW WOULD YOU PUT **THIS** ON YOUR LAWN?

OK, BUT ONLY BECAUSE I'M **CONSISTENT**.
Buy Our Book!

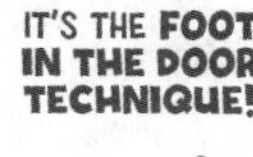

IT'S THE **FOOT IN THE DOOR TECHNIQUE!**

IN SUM, WHILE **PERSONALITY** IS LIKE AN **AVERAGE ACCOUNTING OF OUR DIFFERENCES...**

...WE TEND TO **MAKE TOO MUCH OF IT.**

SOME PEOPLE ARE MORE LIKE THIS...
...AND SOME ARE MORE LIKE THIS.

BUT ALL OF US ARE MORE ALIKE THAN WE ARE DIFFERENT.

AND TO BETTER UNDERSTAND **WHY PEOPLE BEHAVE AS THEY DO,** WE HAVE TO LOOK AT THEIR **CIRCUMSTANCES...**

DANGER! pit ahead
WE'RE NOT STUCK DOWN THERE...
...BECAUSE WE ADAPT OUR BEHAVIOR TO FIT THE SITUATION!

...ESPECIALLY THE **SOCIAL ONES.**

WHY ARE YOU IN HERE?
EVERYONE ELSE WAS JUMPING IN.

NEXT, WE'LL LOOK AT **OTHER** KINDS OF **MISTAKES WE MAKE WHEN JUDGING EACH OTHER.**

CHAPTER 12

STEREOTYPES AND GROUPS

IN THE THINKING CHAPTER, WE LEARNED HOW WE **GROUP OBJECTS TOGETHER** TO **SAVE MENTAL ENERGY...**

Bark
Green
Plants
Trees
Leaves
Pot
Grow Up High
Hairy
Hippies
Smelly
Peace
Free Love

TREES HAVE **BRANCHES** AND **LEAVES** AND **GROW UP HIGH.**

IT'S THE **PRINCIPLES OF COGNITIVE ECONOMY!**

...AND BY NOW IT SHOULD BE NO SURPRISE THAT WE **DO THIS WITH PEOPLE TOO.**

HIPPIES ARE **SMELLY** AND **HAIRY** AND **GROW UP HIGH.**

IT'S **STEREOTYPING!**

A **STEREOTYPE** IS A **SET OF ASSOCIATIONS** THAT WE HOLD ABOUT MEMBERS OF A **PARTICULAR GROUP.**

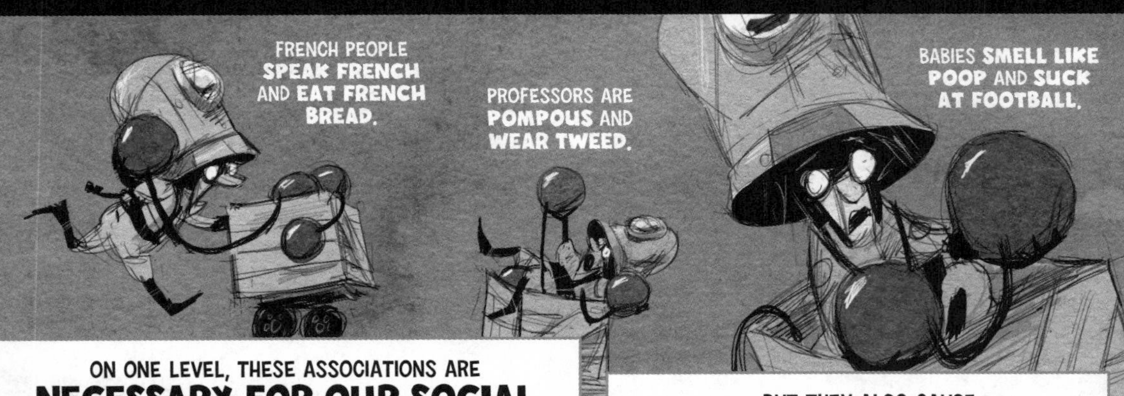
FRENCH PEOPLE **SPEAK FRENCH** AND **EAT FRENCH BREAD.**
PROFESSORS ARE **POMPOUS** AND **WEAR TWEED.**
BABIES **SMELL LIKE POOP** AND **SUCK AT FOOTBALL.**

ON ONE LEVEL, THESE ASSOCIATIONS ARE **NECESSARY FOR OUR SOCIAL FUNCTIONING...**

...BUT THEY ALSO CAUSE **ALL KINDS OF PROBLEMS.**

I USE MY KNOWLEDGE OF YOUR GROUP TO HELP ME **PREDICT THINGS ABOUT YOU...**
...LIKE **WHAT LANGUAGE YOU SPEAK...**

...AND WHETHER YOU'RE **LESS IMPORTANT THAN I AM.**

FOR STARTERS, MANY STEREOTYPES **DON'T ACCURATELY REFLECT REALITY.**

FRENCH FRIES ARE **OILY**...

...FRENCH **PEOPLE** MUST BE TOO!

AND WHEN THEY DO, WE OFTEN **INTERPRET THEM TOO BROADLY.**

SHORT PEOPLE **CAN'T REACH THE ATM**...
...WE **SHOULDN'T TRUST THEM WITH MONEY.**

BECAUSE WE OFTEN BUILD OUR STEREOTYPES **WITH VERY LIMITED EVIDENCE...**

THE FIRST **PIRATES** I MET **HAD BEARDS**...

...SO NOW I THINK **ALL PIRATES** HAVE **BEARDS.**

...THEY CAN HAVE **TERRIBLE CONSEQUENCES.**

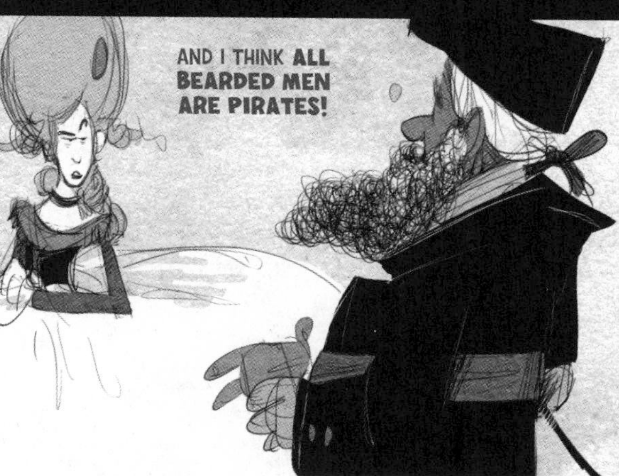
AND I THINK **ALL BEARDED MEN ARE PIRATES!**

IN THIS CHAPTER WE'RE GOING TO **MAKE SOME SENSE OF THIS MESS...**

YOU'RE IN THE **GIRL GROUP.**
AND I'M IN THE **SMART GROUP.**

...BY EXAMINING **HOW SOCIAL GROUPINGS AFFECT US...**

...AND THE **PEOPLE WE LUMP TOGETHER.**

Like Art
Prefer Pink
Barbie
Girls
Bad At Math
Sugar
Nice
Spice
I'M **SMARTER** THAN YOU THINK I AM.
YEAH, WELL YOU'RE ALSO SMARTER THAN **YOU** THINK YOU ARE!
Prefer Blue
Like Sports
G.I. Joe
Boys
Good At Science
Snips
Tails
Snails

LIKE OUR OTHER MENTAL ASSOCIATIONS, STEREOTYPES EXERT **TOP DOWN INFLUENCE** ON **WHAT WE SEE...**
...AND **WHAT WE REMEMBER**, AND **WHAT WE TALK ABOUT**.
Dresses in Black
Scary
Witch
Eats Orphans
BACK IN MY DAY, THE SCHOOLS WERE RUN BY **WITCHES**.
THOSE WERE **NUNS**, DAD!
Dresses in Black
Scolds Kids
Nun
Feeds Orphans
THEY HELP US SORT THROUGH THE **AMBIGUITIES** WE ENCOUNTER.
Ax
Crazy Maniac
Red Blood
Scary
WHEW, I WAS **SCARED FOR A MINUTE.**
Ax
Lumber-Jack
Red Plaid
Monty Python
UNFORTUNATELY, BECAUSE THEY ALSO **GUIDE OUR PERCEPTIONS OF OTHER PEOPLE'S BEHAVIOR...**
...IN THE WRONG CIRCUMSTANCES, THESE ASSOCIATIONS CAN CREATE **TRAGIC MISUNDERSTANDINGS.**
I'M GONNA NEED **BACKUP**.
This Housing Project
Guns
High Crime
Dark Hallway
Fear
Cops & Robbers
Our Home
"Bang!"
Play Gun
Hand Gun

THIS POWERFUL INFLUENCE HAS BEEN **SHOWN REPEATEDLY IN THE LABORATORY.**

HOW WE **INTERPRET OTHER PEOPLE'S BEHAVIOR...**
...DEPENDS ON WHAT **GROUP** WE THINK THEY BELONG TO.

FOR EXAMPLE, IF YOU PUT PEOPLE IN A ROOM AND ASK THEM TO **INTERPRET AN AMBIGUOUS STORY...**

WHY DO YOU THINK "HE **LEERED AT HER** AS HE **SWAYED ACROSS THE FLOOR?"**

...THEIR RESPONSES WILL BE **INFLUENCED BY SUBTLE CUES RELATED TO STEREOTYPES...**

...EVEN WHEN THEY'RE **UNAWARE OF IT.**

BY THE WAY, HIS NAME WAS **"BORIS."**
HE MUST BE AN **ALCOHOLIC COMMUNIST!**
Boris
USSR
Vodka
Russian
BY THE WAY, HIS NAME WAS **"GUIDO."**
HE MUST BE A **GANGSTER!**
Guido
Italian
Gangster
Accordion Theme From The GodFather

THIS **PRIMING EFFECT** HELPS EXPLAIN WHY STEREOTYPES **PERSIST IN THE FACE OF COUNTER-EVIDENCE.**

BY THE WAY, HE HAD A **BEARD.**
HE MUST BE A **PIRATE.**
ALL **BEARDED MEN** ARE **PIRATES!**
Beard
Can't Be Trusted
Pirate
Letch

GROUP ASSOCIATIONS ALSO INFLUENCE **CHAINS OF COMMUNICATION.**

PSSTPSST...
PSSTPSST...
PSSTPSST...
IT'S THE **TELEPHONE GAME** AGAIN!

WE CAN SEE THIS IN STUDIES ABOUT **RUMOR TRANSMISSION:**

IF YOU SHOW SOMEONE A **COUNTER-STEREOTYPICAL** PICTURE...

...AND ASK THEM TO DESCRIBE IT TO **SOMEONE WHO HASN'T SEEN IT...**

A **NUN** WITH A **GUN MUGGED** A **GANGSTER.**

...THEN ASK THAT PERSON TO DESCRIBE IT TO **ANOTHER...**

THERE WAS A **MUGGING** AND A **NUN** AND A **GANGSTER.**

...AND **SO ON...**

A **NUN** AND A **GUN** AND A **GANGSTER.**

...PRETTY SOON THE DETAILS WILL TEND TO **CONFORM TO SHARED STEREOTYPES.**

Mug
Gun
Mean
Gangster

AL CAPONE SHOT MOTHER TERESA!
MAKES SENSE.

Not witches
Peaceful
Meek
Nun

IN OTHER WORDS, WE TEND TO REINFORCE STEREOTYPES **JUST BY TALKING ABOUT EACH OTHER.**

THE **CLEAN-SHAVEN CAPTAIN COMMANDED THE CORSAIR.**
PASS IT ON...
PSSTPSST...
PSSTPSST...
PSSTPSST...
OF COURSE ALL **BEARDED MEN** ARE **PIRATES!**
EVERYONE KNOWS **THAT.**

THIS SORT OF **GROUP–BASED REASONING** IS HARD TO AVOID, AND IT CAN HAVE **INSIDIOUS SOCIAL REPERCUSSIONS.**
LOOK, IT'S A **PIRATE!**
ACTUALLY, IT'S **CONFIRMATION BIAS!**
FOR EXAMPLE, ONE CLASSIC STUDY SHOWED THAT EVEN **BOGUS CATEGORIES** CAN WORK LIKE **SELF–FULFILLING PROPHECIES.**

IF YOU **BELIEVE IT'S TRUE**, IT **WILL BECOME TRUE.**

TEACHERS WHO WERE TOLD THAT SOME STUDENTS IN THEIR CLASS WERE **"SPURTERS"**...
...EVEN THOUGH THE DESIGNATION HAD **NO BASIS IN REALITY...**

PSYCHOLOGICAL TESTS SHOW THAT JOHNNY IS **ABOUT TO GET MUCH SMARTER.**

SPURTER, **SHPLURTER.**
JOHNNY'S JUST ANOTHER KID.
...GAVE THOSE STUDENTS **MORE CARE AND ATTENTION...**
...WHICH CAUSED THEM TO **IMPROVE MORE THAN THEIR PEERS.**

JOHNNY, I EXPECT **GREAT WORK FROM YOU.**
HERE'S EVIDENCE THAT MERELY THINKING A STUDENT WILL IMPROVE CAN **ACTUALLY CAUSE THAT IMPROVEMENT.**

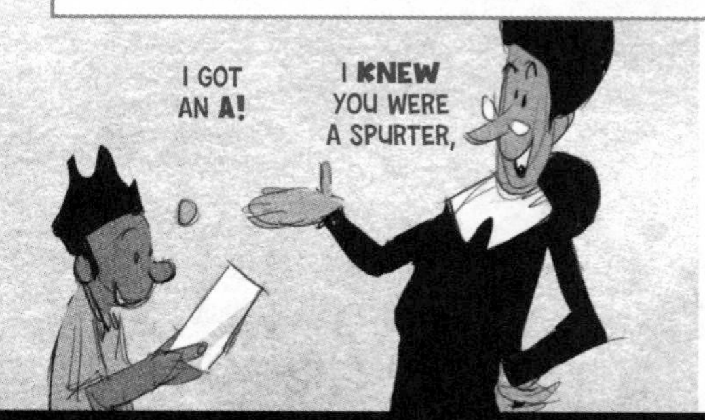
I GOT AN **A!**
I **KNEW** YOU WERE A SPURTER.
SADLY, STEREOTYPES ARE RARELY SO **POSITIVE.**

THE MIND IS A **POWERFUL THING.**

DANG, I ONLY GOT A **C!**

THAT'S BECAUSE YOU'RE **NOT A SPURTER.**

OBVIOUSLY, NEGATIVE STEREOTYPES ARE **TERRIBLE FOR THE PEOPLE BEING STEREOTYPED...**

...BUT THEY TOO CAN ACT LIKE **SELF–FULFILLING PROPHECIES.**

MY **APPLICATION** REJECTED...

MY **MORTGAGE** DENIED...

MY **CONTRIBUTIONS** MARGINALIZED...

...MAYBE PIRACY IS MY **ONLY OPTION.**

Rob From The Rich

Drunk

Bearded

Crazy

Pirates

Me?

Can't Be Taught

Can't Be Trusted

WHEN OUR **BELIEFS ABOUT WHAT OTHER PEOPLE THINK** LEAD TO **CHANGES IN OUR OWN BEHAVIORS...**

...IT CAN MAKE THOSE ORIGINAL BELIEFS **COME TRUE.**

SHE **DOESN'T LIKE ME,** SO **I AVOID HER.**

HE **NEVER TALKS TO ME,** SO **I DON'T LIKE HIM.**

IT'S A **FEEDBACK LOOP...**

THAT GRAY GUY IS **ACTING NERVOUS...**

...HE **MUST BE UP TO SOMETHING.** I'LL FOLLOW HIM.

THAT COP IS **FOLLOWING ME...**

...IT'S **MAKING ME NERVOUS.**

...THAT **GAINS POWER WHEN MORE PEOPLE GET INVOLVED.**

YOU PEOPLE **DON'T RESPECT US!**

ONE OF THE MOST PERNICIOUS SELF-FULFILLING PROPHECIES IS
STEREOTYPE THREAT.

THAT'S WHEN A NEGATIVE STEREOTYPE DIRECTED AT YOU...

EVERYONE KNOWS GRAY BOYS SUCK AT SPELLING.

...UNDERMINES YOUR PERFORMANCE...

HOW DO YOU SPELL "RACIAL INJUSTICE"?

UM...

...BY GIVING YOU AN **EXTRA THING TO WORRY ABOUT...**

IT'S ANOTHER THING TO JUGGLE!

"Ratial"?
"Racial"?
"Rashal"?

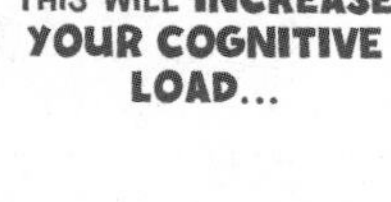
"SH" Sound

Everyone Thinks You Suck At Spelling!
THIS WILL INCREASE YOUR COGNITIVE LOAD...
...REDUCING YOUR AVAILABLE MENTAL ENERGY FOR THE TASK AT HAND.

...AND **SABOTAGING YOUR MOTIVATION.**

IF EVERYONE THINKS I'M NO GOOD AT IT...
...MAYBE I'M REALLY NOT.

RECALL THIS FROM THE CHAPTER ON MOTIVATION.

FORTUNATELY, WHILE THIS EFFECT **REINFORCES MANY INEQUITIES IN THE WORLD,**
IT CAN BE **OVERCOME.**

WHEN I WAS A KID, GIRLS SUCKED AT MATH AND SPORTS...
...BUT THOSE DAYS ARE OVER!

OUR **GROUP IDENTITIES**, OF COURSE, ARE **NOT ALL BAD**.
THIS SHIP IS **LIKE MY FAMILY**.
ARRRRRRRR

WE GROUP OURSELVES TO SHARE **COMMON INTERESTS**...

LET'S GO, **FIGHTIN' ACORNS!**

...**GOALS**...
LET'S **BREW**, BROS!

...**RELIGIOUS AFFILIATIONS**...
LET'S **GET INTO HEAVEN!**

...AND OTHER **SOCIAL SUPPORT NETWORKS**.
LET'S ALL HAVE A **MOMENT OF SILENCE** FOR GRAYBEARD'S DEAD PARROT.

UNFORTUNATELY, NO MATTER WHAT BRINGS US TOGETHER, WE'RE **STRONGLY** INCLINED TO **THINK MORE FAVORABLY ABOUT MEMBERS OF OUR OWN GROUP**...

...AND MORE **NEGATIVELY ABOUT OTHERS**.

US

THEM

PSYCHOLOGISTS HAVE STUDIED THIS BY GROUPING PEOPLE RANDOMLY...
HEADS ARE HATS, TAILS ARE NO HATS.
...THEN PLACING THEM IN SLIGHTLY COMPETITIVE SITUATIONS...
THE GROUP THAT CLEANS MY OFFICE BEST, WINS.
...AND OBSERVING AS THEY IMMEDIATELY START INTERPRETING THE SITUATION IN WAYS THAT ARE FAVORABLE TO THEIR OWN GROUP'S MEMBERS.
NO HAT KEVIN CLEANED A LARGER AREA...
...BUT HAT LUKE'S AREA WAS DIRTIER SO HE DESERVES MORE CREDIT.
Lazy
Rachel
Kevin
Tricky
Them
No Hats
Bad
Jose
Luke
Hard Working
Us
Honest
Hats
Good
PEOPLE THUS DIVIDED ARE ALSO BETTER AT NOTING PERSONAL DIFFERENCES INSIDE THEIR OWN GROUP...
...AND MORE LIKELY TO ASSUME OTHERS ARE ALL THE SAME.
HAT LUKE LIKES BURGERS.
HAT ANITA LIKES PIZZA.
ALL THE NO HATS ARE PROBABLY TACO LOVERS.
ALL OF WHICH, OF COURSE, MAKES IT EASIER FOR US TO BELIEVE NEGATIVE STEREOTYPES.
IF WE ASSUME THEY'RE ALL CLONES...
...WE WON'T BOTHER TELLING ONE FROM ANOTHER.

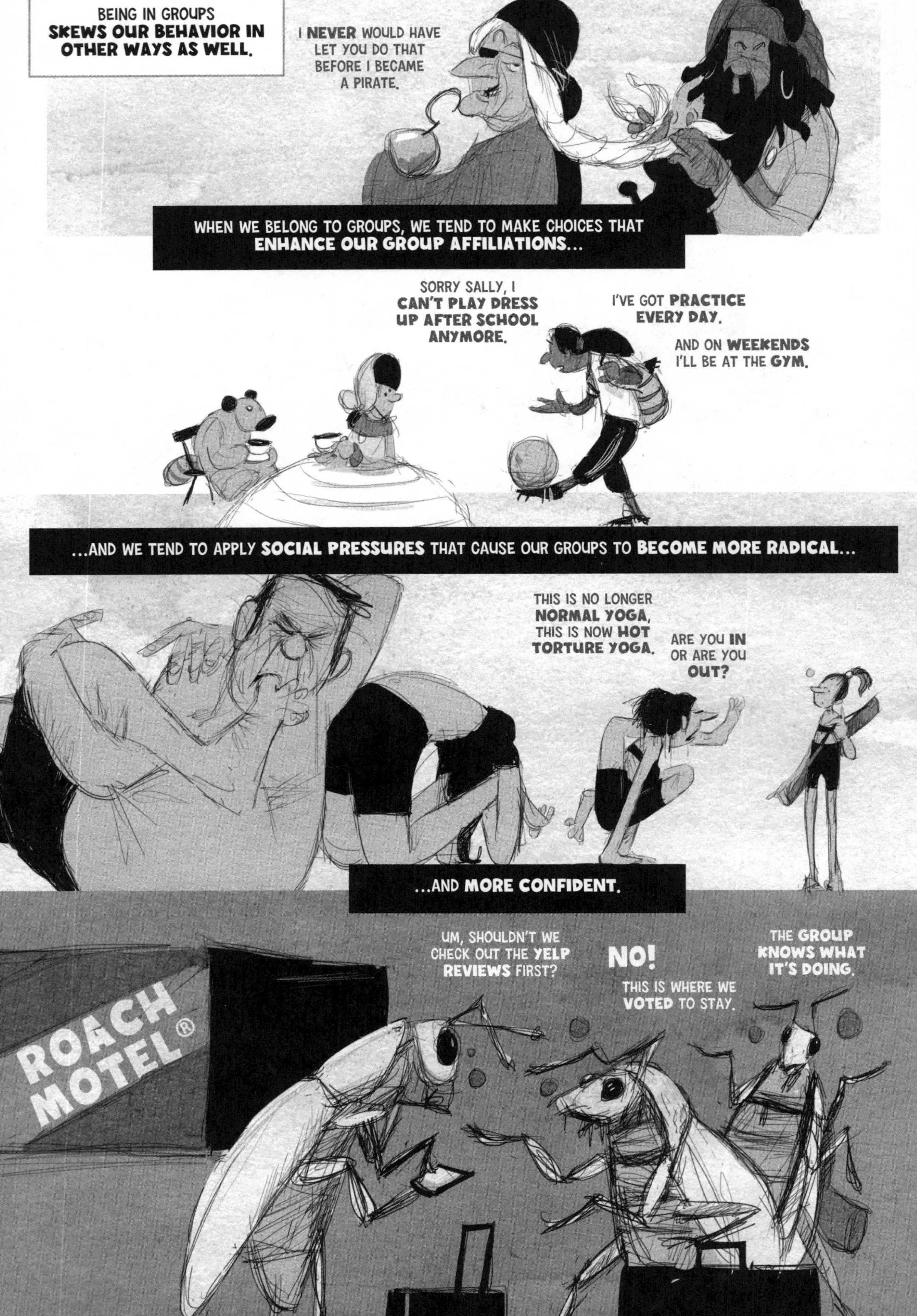
BEING IN GROUPS **SKEWS OUR BEHAVIOR IN OTHER WAYS AS WELL.**
I **NEVER** WOULD HAVE LET YOU DO THAT BEFORE I BECAME A PIRATE.
WHEN WE BELONG TO GROUPS, WE TEND TO MAKE CHOICES THAT **ENHANCE OUR GROUP AFFILIATIONS...**
SORRY SALLY, I **CAN'T PLAY DRESS UP AFTER SCHOOL ANYMORE.**
I'VE GOT **PRACTICE EVERY DAY.**
AND ON **WEEKENDS** I'LL BE AT THE **GYM.**
...AND WE TEND TO APPLY **SOCIAL PRESSURES** THAT CAUSE OUR GROUPS TO **BECOME MORE RADICAL...**
THIS IS NO LONGER **NORMAL YOGA,** THIS IS NOW **HOT TORTURE YOGA.**
ARE YOU **IN** OR ARE YOU **OUT?**
...AND **MORE CONFIDENT.**
UM, SHOULDN'T WE CHECK OUT THE **YELP REVIEWS** FIRST?
NO!
THIS IS WHERE WE **VOTED** TO STAY.
THE **GROUP KNOWS WHAT IT'S DOING.**
ROACH MOTEL®

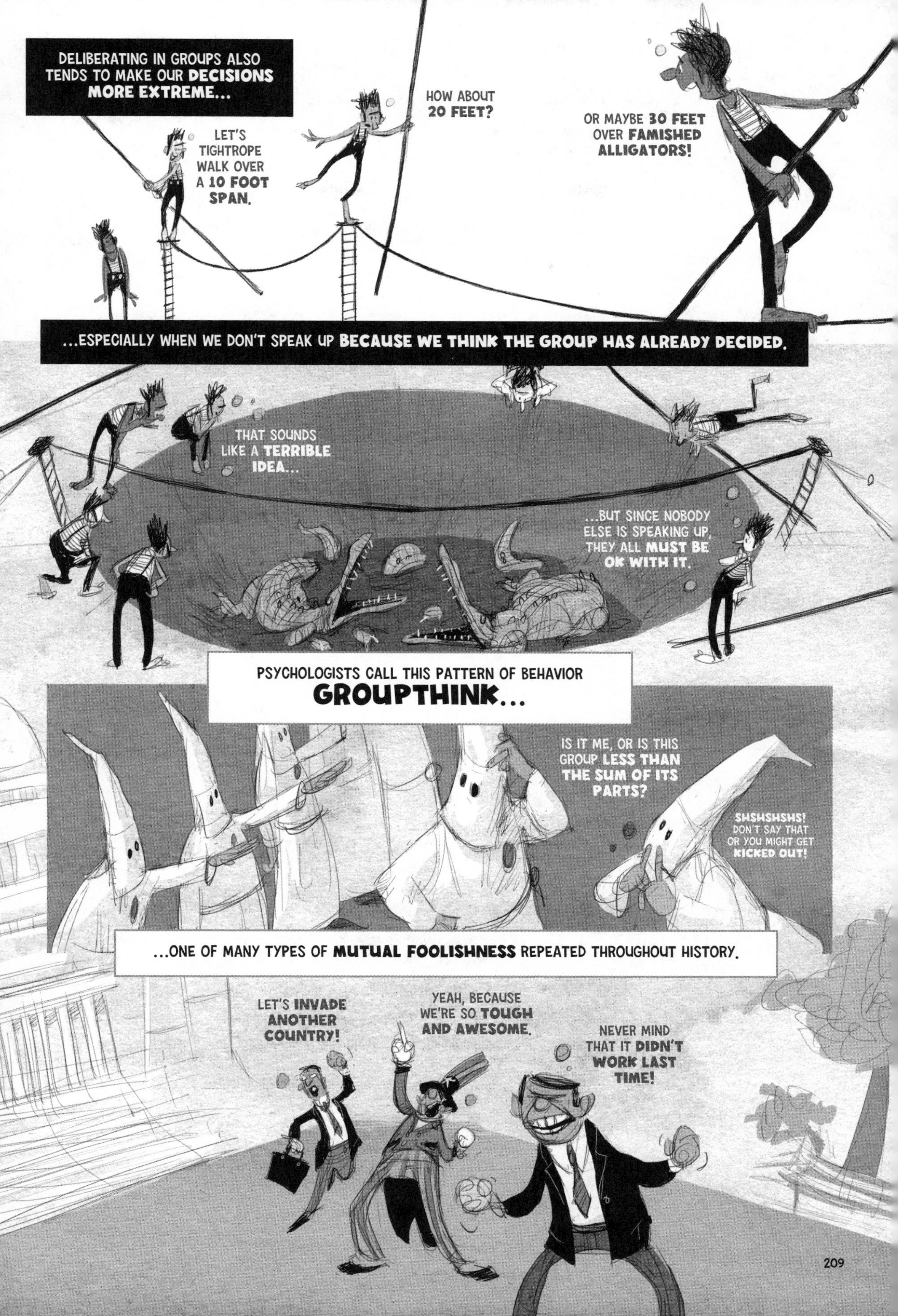
DELIBERATING IN GROUPS ALSO TENDS TO MAKE OUR DECISIONS MORE EXTREME...
LET'S TIGHTROPE WALK OVER A 10 FOOT SPAN.
HOW ABOUT 20 FEET?
OR MAYBE 30 FEET OVER FAMISHED ALLIGATORS!
...ESPECIALLY WHEN WE DON'T SPEAK UP BECAUSE WE THINK THE GROUP HAS ALREADY DECIDED.
THAT SOUNDS LIKE A TERRIBLE IDEA...
...BUT SINCE NOBODY ELSE IS SPEAKING UP, THEY ALL MUST BE OK WITH IT.
PSYCHOLOGISTS CALL THIS PATTERN OF BEHAVIOR GROUPTHINK...
IS IT ME, OR IS THIS GROUP LESS THAN THE SUM OF ITS PARTS?
SHSHSHSHS! DON'T SAY THAT OR YOU MIGHT GET KICKED OUT!
...ONE OF MANY TYPES OF MUTUAL FOOLISHNESS REPEATED THROUGHOUT HISTORY.
LET'S INVADE ANOTHER COUNTRY!
YEAH, BECAUSE WE'RE SO TOUGH AND AWESOME.
NEVER MIND THAT IT DIDN'T WORK LAST TIME!

ON SOME LEVEL, WE **CELEBRATE OUR OWN GROUPS** AND **MISTRUST OTHERS** BECAUSE THAT BEHAVIOR EVOLVED TO **HELP US SURVIVE.**

GET OUT THERE AND KILL 'EM!
GO SPOTS!
GO STRIPES!
RIP 'EM TO SHREDS!

ONE THEORY, CALLED THE **STEREOTYPE CONTENT MODEL...**

STEREOTYPES HAVE TWO PRIMARY DIMENSIONS...
...WARMTH AND COMPETENCE.

...EVEN SUGGESTS THAT A **BIG REASON** WE JUDGE OTHER GROUPS IS TO **PREDICT HOW THEY'D COMPETE AGAINST US.**

IF WE THINK OTHERS HAVE HIGH WARMTH AND LOW COMPETENCE...
...NO WORRIES!
IF WE THINK THEY HAVE HIGH COMPETENCE AND LOW WARMTH...
...BE AFRAID!
Warmth
Competence

WHATEVER THEIR RATIONALE, STEREOTYPES EMERGE FROM OUR **BASIC COGNITIVE ARCHITECTURE...**

...SO THEY'RE **VERY HARD TO ROOT OUT.**

Pity
Dumb
Warm
Won't Eat Me
Smart
Fear
Will Eat Me
Cold

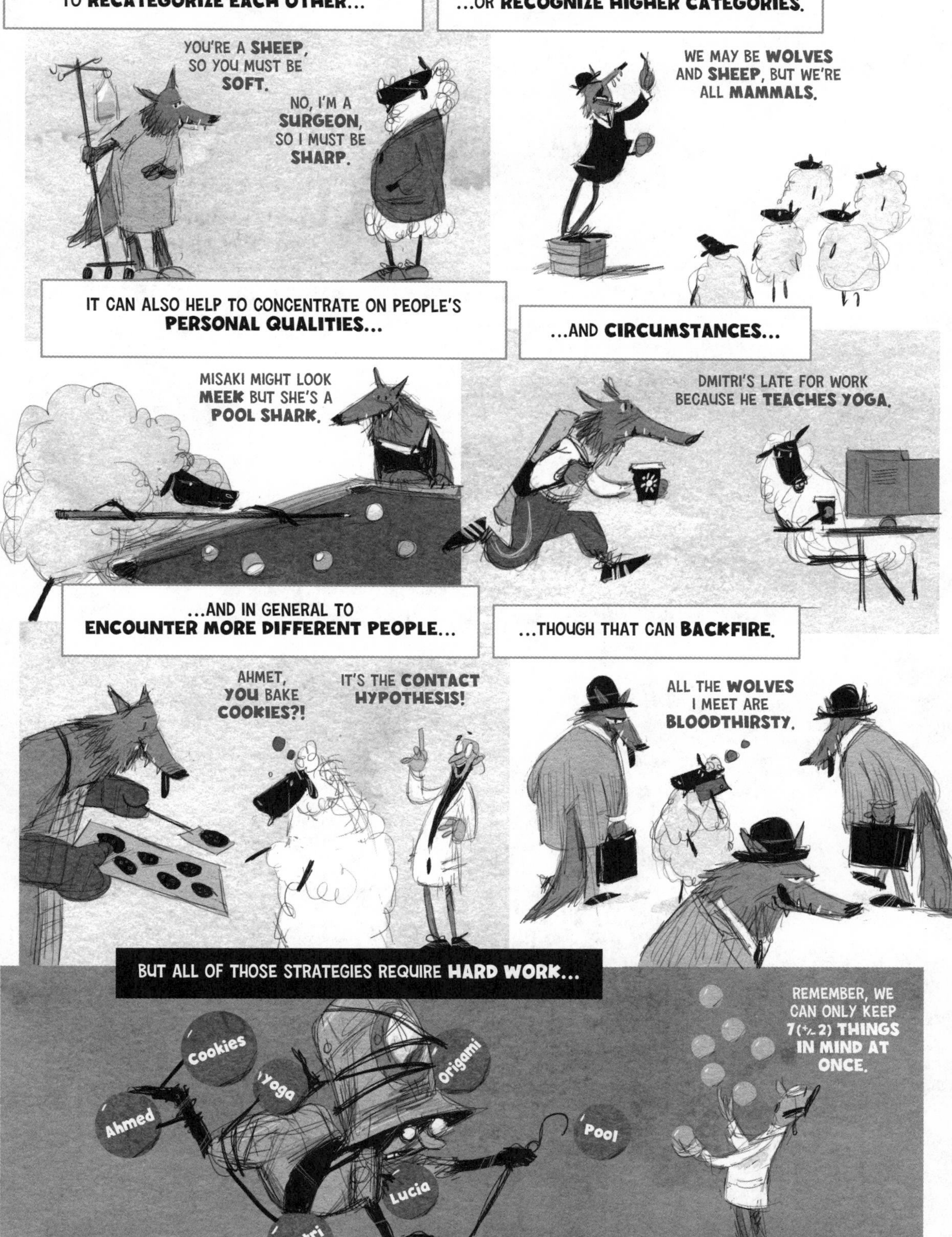
TECHNIQUES TO **REDUCE NEGATIVE STEREOTYPING** INCLUDE ENCOURAGING PEOPLE TO **RECATEGORIZE EACH OTHER**...
YOU'RE A **SHEEP**, SO YOU MUST BE **SOFT**.
NO, I'M A **SURGEON**, SO I MUST BE **SHARP**.
...OR **RECOGNIZE HIGHER CATEGORIES**.
WE MAY BE **WOLVES** AND **SHEEP**, BUT WE'RE ALL **MAMMALS**.
IT CAN ALSO HELP TO CONCENTRATE ON PEOPLE'S **PERSONAL QUALITIES**...
MISAKI MIGHT LOOK **MEEK** BUT SHE'S A **POOL SHARK**.
...AND **CIRCUMSTANCES**...
DMITRI'S LATE FOR WORK BECAUSE HE **TEACHES YOGA**.
...AND IN GENERAL TO **ENCOUNTER MORE DIFFERENT PEOPLE**...
AHMET, **YOU** BAKE **COOKIES?!**
IT'S THE **CONTACT HYPOTHESIS!**
...THOUGH THAT CAN **BACKFIRE**.
ALL THE **WOLVES** I MEET ARE **BLOODTHIRSTY**.
BUT ALL OF THOSE STRATEGIES REQUIRE **HARD WORK**...
Cookies
Yoga
Origami
Ahmed
Pool
Lucia
Dmitri
Misaki
REMEMBER, WE CAN ONLY KEEP 7(+/-2) **THINGS IN MIND AT ONCE**.
...SO WE MOSTLY **DON'T USE THEM**.

AS WE'VE SEEN IN THIS CHAPTER, STEREOTYPES AND GROUP ASSUMPTIONS ARE COGNITIVE SHORTCUTS THAT HELP US CONSERVE MENTAL ENERGY...
SORRY JENNY, I JUST DON'T HAVE ENOUGH BRAIN POWER TO LOVE YOU RIGHT NOW...
...SO I THINK OF YOU AS FOOD.
IT'S THE PRINCIPLES OF COGNITIVE ECONOMY.
...WHICH MEANS WE USE THEM MORE WHEN WE'RE CONFRONTED WITH SCARCITY.
IT'S NOT MY FAULT YOU MAKE ME FEEL HUNGRY!
I HAVE LIMITED FOOD, POLITICAL POWER, IMAGINATION, AND TIME.
SO, IF WE WANT TO FIGHT RACISM, SEXISM, RELIGIOUS VIOLENCE, AND ANY OTHER THORNY SOCIAL PROBLEMS THAT PIT GROUPS AGAINST EACH OTHER...
THE SHEEP SHALL LOVE THE WOLVES...
...AND THE CHICKENS SHALL LOVE THE FOXES...
...AND THE ELEPHANTS SHALL LOVE THE DONKEYS...
...WE'VE GOT A LOT OF WORK TO DO.
WE NEED TO REDUCE EVERYBODY'S COGNITIVE LOAD!

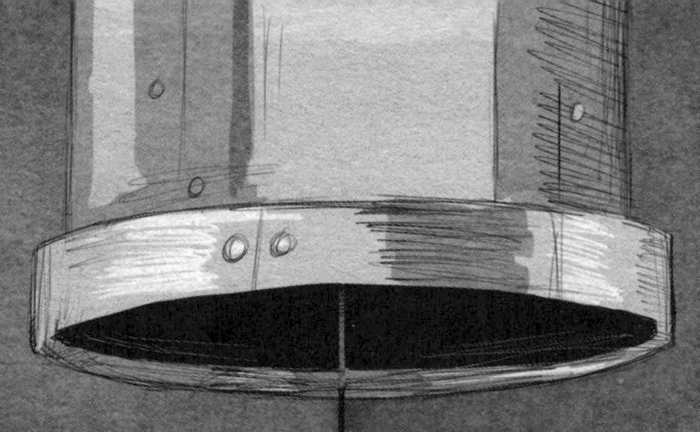

CONCLUSION

WHEN THINGS AREN'T WORKING

IN THIS BOOK, WE'VE ANALYZED A WIDE RANGE OF EXPERIENCES, INCLUDING HOW WE FORM MEMORIES...
YOU DROPPED THIS!
...DEVELOP FEELINGS...
MY BODY GETS ALL TINGLY WHEN I'M NEAR YOU.
...SHARE IDEAS...
DUCK!
...AND MAKE MISTAKES...
...AND MAKE MORE MISTAKES...
...AND SO ON.
THE AVAILABILITY HEURISTIC GIVES YOU A BAD IDEA...
...THEN CONFIRMATION BIAS GIVES YOU EVIDENCE TO SUPPORT IT...
...AND SOCIAL INFLUENCE HELPS YOU INFECT OTHER PEOPLE WITH IT.
BUT WE HAVEN'T COVERED ALL OF PSYCHOLOGY.
NOT EVEN CLOSE.
REMEMBER, PSYCHOLOGY DEALS WITH THE ENTIRE RANGE OF HUMAN EXPERIENCE.
The Book of Life
WE'VE ONLY STUDIED A TINY FRACTION OF THAT.
The Cartoon Book of Life

PSYCHOLOGY IS FILLED WITH SO MANY OTHER **INTRIGUING AREAS OF STUDY...**

LIKE **NEUROSCIENCE...**

...ARTIFICIAL INTELLIGENCE...

...LOVE...

...MUSIC...

...ACUTE TRAUMA...

...PARENTHOOD...

...CHILD DEVELOPMENT...

...HYPNOSIS...

...SLEEP & DREAMS...

...AND MUCH MUCH MORE.

...BECAUSE THE **HUMAN MIND** IS SO **ASTONISHINGLY COMPLEX.**

YOU CAN PRETTY MUCH POUR **ANYTHING** INTO IT.
YUP, IT'S **LIKE A SPONGE.**

WE'VE ONLY REALLY **BEGUN** TO LEARN **HOW THE MIND WORKS.**

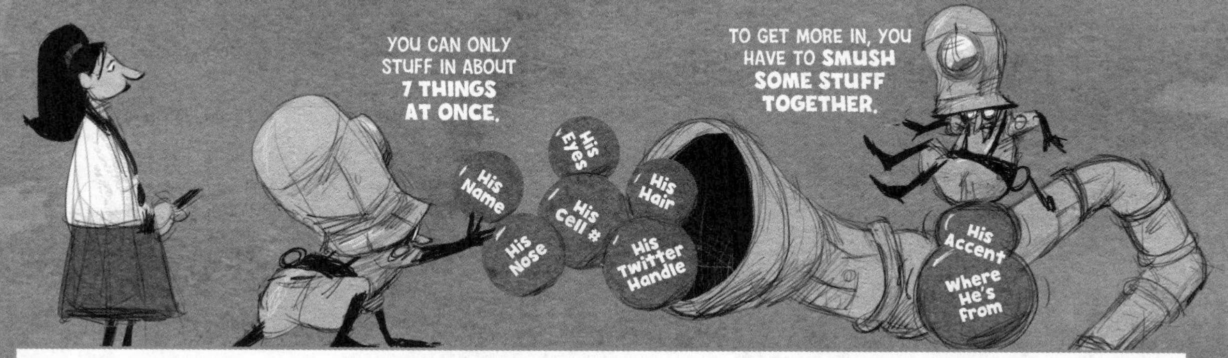
YOU CAN ONLY STUFF IN ABOUT **7 THINGS AT ONCE.**
TO GET MORE IN, YOU HAVE TO **SMUSH SOME STUFF TOGETHER.**
His Name
His Nose
His Eyes
His Cell #
His Hair
His Twitter Handle
His Accent
Where He's from

NEVERTHELESS, WHAT WE'RE LEARNING **ALSO** HELPS US UNDERSTAND WHY THE MIND SOMETIMES **BREAKS DOWN...**

SOMETHING'S **CLOGGED!**
IT'S **ABNORMAL** PSYCHOLOGY!
...SO LET'S FINISH UP BY TALKING ABOUT THAT.

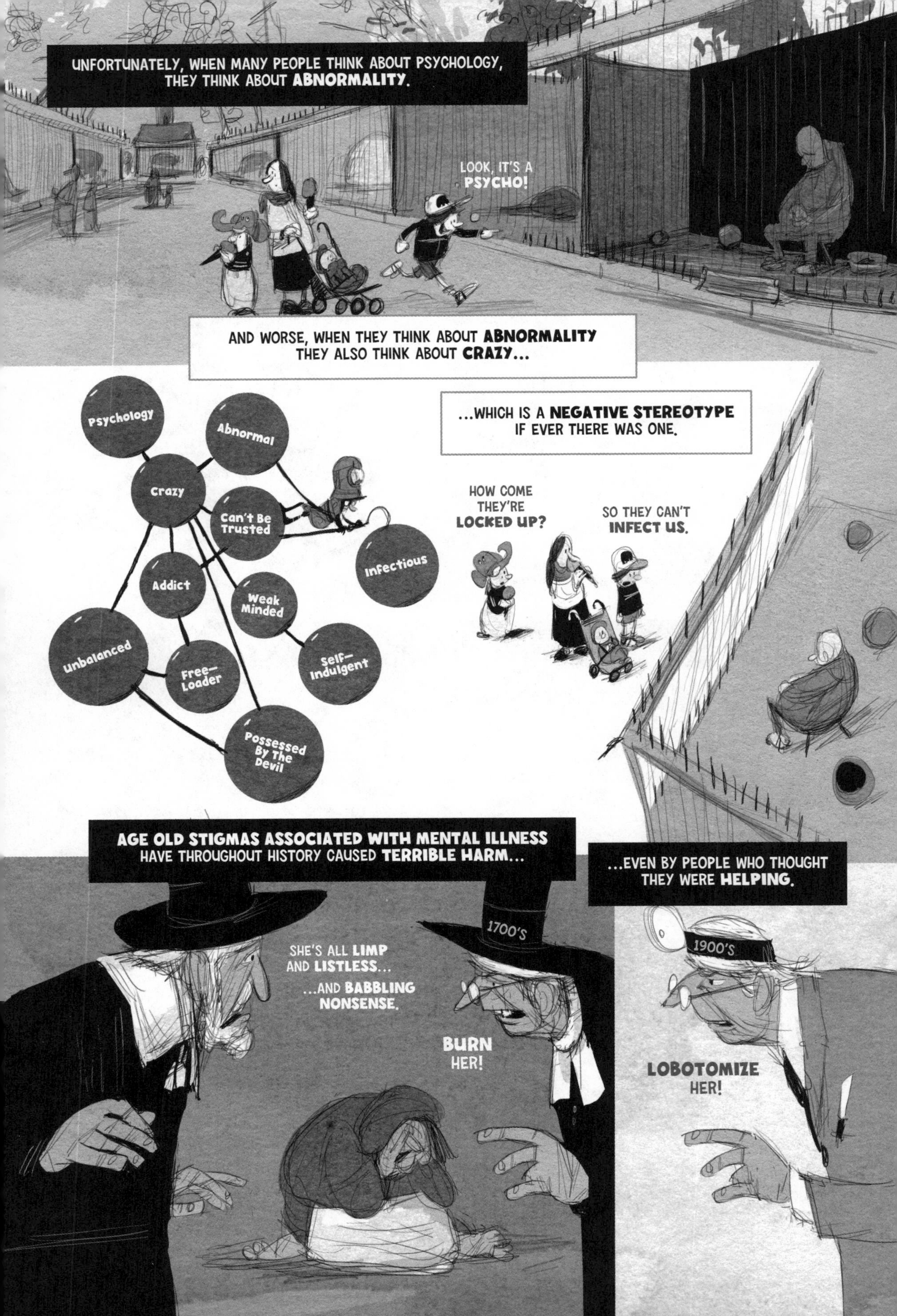
UNFORTUNATELY, WHEN MANY PEOPLE THINK ABOUT PSYCHOLOGY, THEY THINK ABOUT **ABNORMALITY**.
LOOK, IT'S A **PSYCHO!**
AND WORSE, WHEN THEY THINK ABOUT **ABNORMALITY** THEY ALSO THINK ABOUT **CRAZY**...
...WHICH IS A **NEGATIVE STEREOTYPE** IF EVER THERE WAS ONE.
Psychology
Abnormal
Crazy
Can't Be Trusted
Infectious
Addict
Weak Minded
Unbalanced
Free-Loader
Self-Indulgent
Possessed By The Devil
HOW COME THEY'RE **LOCKED UP?**
SO THEY CAN'T **INFECT US.**
AGE OLD STIGMAS ASSOCIATED WITH MENTAL ILLNESS HAVE THROUGHOUT HISTORY CAUSED **TERRIBLE HARM**...
...EVEN BY PEOPLE WHO THOUGHT THEY WERE **HELPING.**
1700'S
SHE'S ALL **LIMP** AND **LISTLESS**...
...AND **BABBLING NONSENSE.**
BURN HER!
1900'S
LOBOTOMIZE HER!

WHILE THESE STIGMAS CONTINUE TO **CAUSE POINTLESS SUFFERING...**

...MODERN CONCEPTIONS OF ABNORMALITY ARE FAR **MORE HUMANE.**

YOU'RE **NOT** **NORMAL!**
WE'RE MORE **ALIKE** THAN **DIFFERENT.**

BECAUSE NOW WE UNDERSTAND THAT ABNORMALITY AND NORMALITY ARE **INTERTWINED.**

AS A RESULT, ANALYZING MENTAL **PROBLEMS...**

...TEACHES US MORE ABOUT **NORMAL MENTAL FUNCTIONING.**

THIS BOY CAN'T REMEMBER ANYTHING ONCE HE **STOPS CONSCIOUSLY FOCUSING ON IT...**

...SO MAYBE WE **ALL** HAVE **SEPARATE MEMORY SYSTEMS** FOR WHAT WE'RE **CONSCIOUSLY** THINKING ABOUT...

...AND WHAT WE'RE **NOT.**

AND CONVERSELY, STUDYING **HOW OUR MENTAL SYSTEMS NORMALLY WORK...**

...TEACHES US MORE ABOUT **WHY THEY SOMETIMES DON'T.**

KNOWING HOW WE **JUGGLE OUR MARBLES...**

...HELPS US UNDERSTAND WHY WE **SOMETIMES LOSE THEM.**

FOR EXAMPLE, AS WE LEARN MORE ABOUT OUR EMOTIONAL SYSTEMS...
EVENT
PHYSICAL AROUSAL
INTERPRETATION
Emotion
...WE GAIN INSIGHTS INTO THE WAYS THEY LET US DOWN.
IN CASES OF DEPRESSION...
...MANIA...
...ANXIETY...
...AND ANGER DISORDERS...
...EMOTIONS ARE EITHER ABSENT OR OVERPOWERING.
LIKEWISE, LEARNING MORE ABOUT COGNITION...
WE ENCODE SOME OF THE STUFF WE ENCOUNTER...
...AND FILL IN GAPS WITH TOP DOWN EXPECTATIONS.
...GIVES US A BETTER HANDLE ON DISORDERS OF THINKING AND LOGIC.
IN CASES OF AMNESIA...
...APHASIA...
...AGNOSIA...
...AND HALLUCINATIONS...
...TOP DOWN INFORMATION IS EITHER OVERWHELMING OR MISSING.

AND AS WE EXPAND OUR UNDERSTANDING OF **SOCIAL AWARENESS**...

OUR BEHAVIOR IS LARGELY MOLDED BY OUR **SOCIAL RELATIONSHIPS.**
...THAT TEACHES US MORE ABOUT THE MANY FORMS OF **SOCIAL BLINDNESS.**

IN CASES OF **AUTISM**...
...**NARCISSISTIC PERSONALITY DISORDER**...
...**REACTIVE ATTACHMENT DISORDER**...
...AND **SOCIOPATHY**...
...SOCIAL BONDS FEEL **TOO WEAK** OR **TOO STRONG.**
ALL THAT SAID, NONE OF THESE CONDITIONS ARE **SIMPLE.**

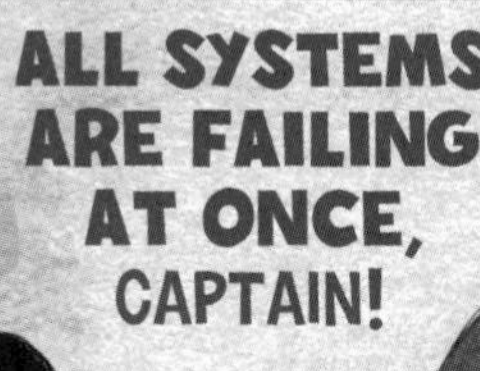
BWAAH! BWAAH!
ALL SYSTEMS ARE FAILING AT ONCE, CAPTAIN!
...CAPTAIN?

IN FACT, THERE ARE SO **MANY DIFFERENT WAYS** OUR **MENTAL WIRES CAN GET CROSSED...**

AFTER HE GOT **STRUCK BY LIGHTNING** HE'S BEEN A **MUCH BETTER PIANIST.**
...THAT THE LINE BETWEEN WHAT'S NORMAL AND WHAT'S ABNORMAL IS OFTEN QUITE **BLURRY.**

CASES OF ABNORMAL PSYCHOLOGY **OCCUR ON A SPECTRUM.**

WE'RE AFRAID OF SQUIRRELS.

THAT'S SCIURO-PHOBIA!

THERE ARE **EXTREME...**

AAHH!

...MODERATE...

DANG, MY DAY IS RUINED!

...AND **MILD** VERSIONS.

I THINK MAYBE I'LL CROSS THE STREET.

AND ALTHOUGH WE MARVEL AT THE **EXTRAORDINARY CASES...**

...AS WE MOVE FARTHER DOWN THE SCALE, WE GET TO **WHAT GETS CALLED NORMAL.**

MY HUSBAND THINKS I'M A HAT-RACK!
THAT'S AGNOSIA!

MY HUSBAND TREATS ME LIKE I'M A HAT-RACK!
THAT'S MARRIAGE.

ALL OF WHICH MEANS THAT THE DIFFERENCE BETWEEN **ABNORMAL PSYCHOLOGY**...

...AND **STANDARD PSYCHOLOGY**...

VOICES IN MY HEAD **TELL ME WHAT TO DO.**
THAT'S **SCHIZOPHRENIA!**
I'M ALWAYS HAVING **CONVERSATIONS WITH MYSELF.**
THAT'S **TOTALLY NORMAL.**

...IS MOSTLY A **MATTER OF DEGREE.**

USE THE **FORCE**, LUKE.
THAT SOUNDS **INSANE**...
...BUT GIVEN THE SITUATION, MAYBE IT'S MY **BEST OPTION.**

WHICH SHOULD HELP ALL OF US IMAGINE WHAT IT'S LIKE TO **SUFFER FROM MENTAL ILLNESS.**

I GET **SCARED** WHEN SQUIRRELS GET CLOSE ENOUGH TO JUMP ON MY FACE.
I FEEL THAT WAY **ALL THE TIME.**

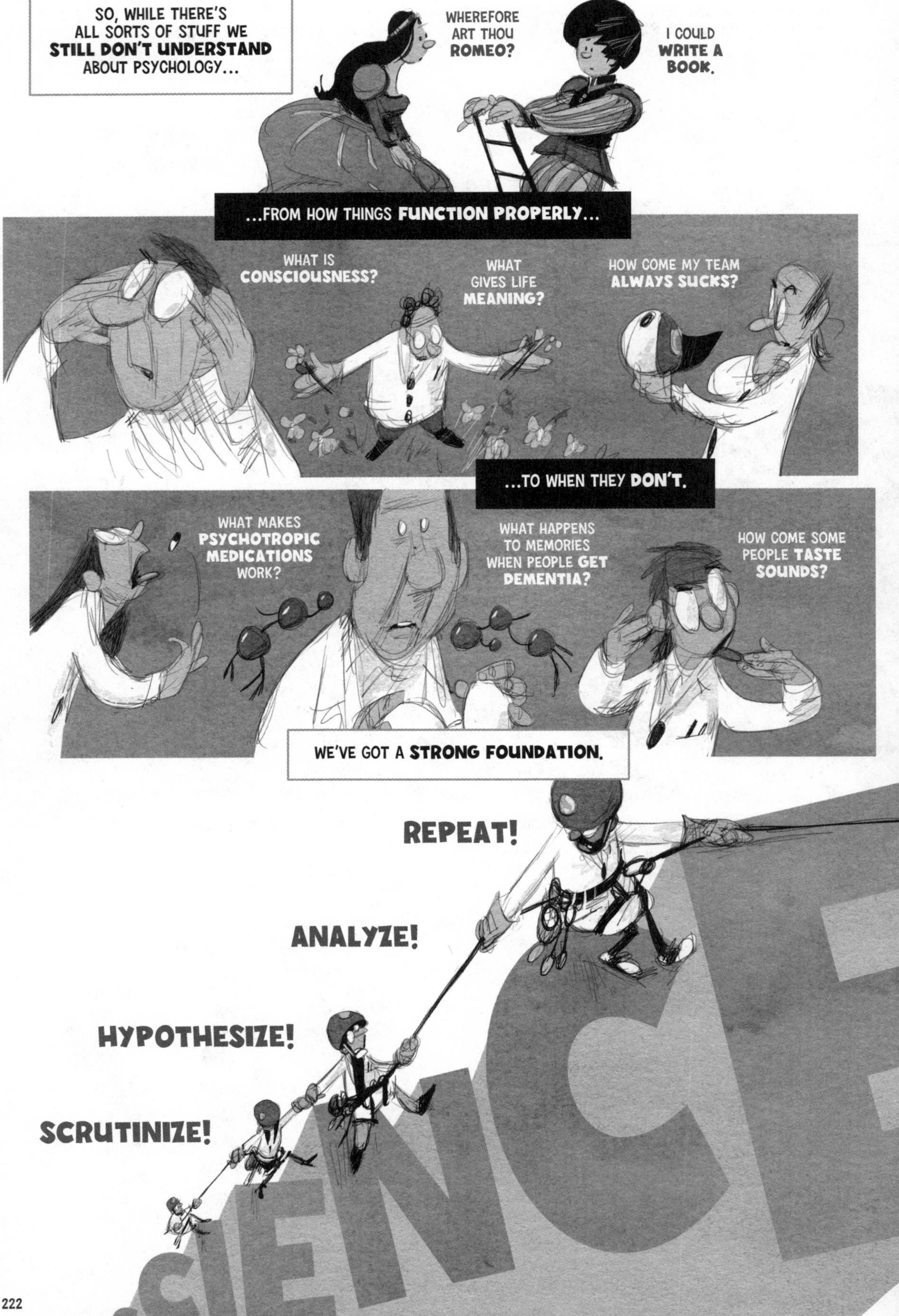
SO, WHILE THERE'S ALL SORTS OF STUFF WE **STILL DON'T UNDERSTAND** ABOUT PSYCHOLOGY...
WHEREFORE ART THOU **ROMEO?**
I COULD **WRITE A BOOK.**
...FROM HOW THINGS **FUNCTION PROPERLY...**
WHAT IS **CONSCIOUSNESS?**
WHAT GIVES LIFE **MEANING?**
HOW COME MY TEAM **ALWAYS SUCKS?**
...TO WHEN THEY **DON'T.**
WHAT MAKES **PSYCHOTROPIC MEDICATIONS** WORK?
WHAT HAPPENS TO MEMORIES WHEN PEOPLE **GET DEMENTIA?**
HOW COME SOME PEOPLE **TASTE SOUNDS?**
WE'VE GOT A **STRONG FOUNDATION.**
REPEAT!
ANALYZE!
HYPOTHESIZE!
SCRUTINIZE!
SCIENCE

WE'RE BEGINNING TO GET A HANDLE ON WHAT MAKES US SO ASTONISHINGLY **PERCEPTIVE...**
I SEE YOU!
...INTELLIGENT...
I UNDERSTAND YOU!
...AND **EMPATHETIC...**
I FEEL YOU!
...WHEN THE WORLD IS SO **INSANE.**
WHAT THE #&*$ ARE WE **DOING HERE?**
BUT THERE ARE MANY MORE **MYSTERIES IN THE HUMAN MIND...**
WHAT'S UP WITH **THIS?**
f(x)

...WAITING TO BE DISCOVERED.